TOTAL HIGH

My Everest Challenge

Grania Willis

Red Rock Press

TOTAL HIGH
My Everest Challenge

GRANIA WILLIS

Red Rock Press
www.redrockpress.ie

Glengyle
Claremont Road
Howth
Dublin 13
Ireland

redrockpress@eircom.net

This edition published 2005

A catalogue record for this book is available from the British Library.

ISBN 0-9548653-3-2

DESIGN AND PRODUCTION
Stephen Ryan
PRINTING
GraphyCems, Spain.
PHOTOGRAPHY
Cover photograph: Peggy Foster. Back cover: Main photograph: Lydia Bradey.
Author portrait: Matt Kavanagh, courtesy *The Irish Times.*
Padraig Harrington portrait: INPHO/Morgan Treacy.
Colour plates: Duncan Chessell, Bill Crouse, David Tait, Grania Willis.

For Joe

Foreword

By Padraig Harrington

We all have ambitions, but not everybody achieves them. Something must set apart those ultimately successful in achieving their goals from those who don't manage to do so. But even for those who do succeed, there is a thin line between success and failure. The higher the goal that you set yourself, the more difficult it is to achieve it. That's just how it is.

This is a compelling story of a regular person in pursuit of her dreams, whilst risking everything. Clearly, raising money for a cause close to her heart was the catalyst to spur on Grania, to push her that little bit harder. But climbing Mount Everest is the ultimate in mountaineering. Many fail and, sadly, many others pay the ultimate price. Effort alone is simply not enough and, to succeed, something else is needed.

In reading this book, one of the images that lingers is that of the climber scaling Mount Everest and passing dead bodies on the way. What state of mind do you require to shut out such reality, that death is such a possibility? To know that, even if you do reach the

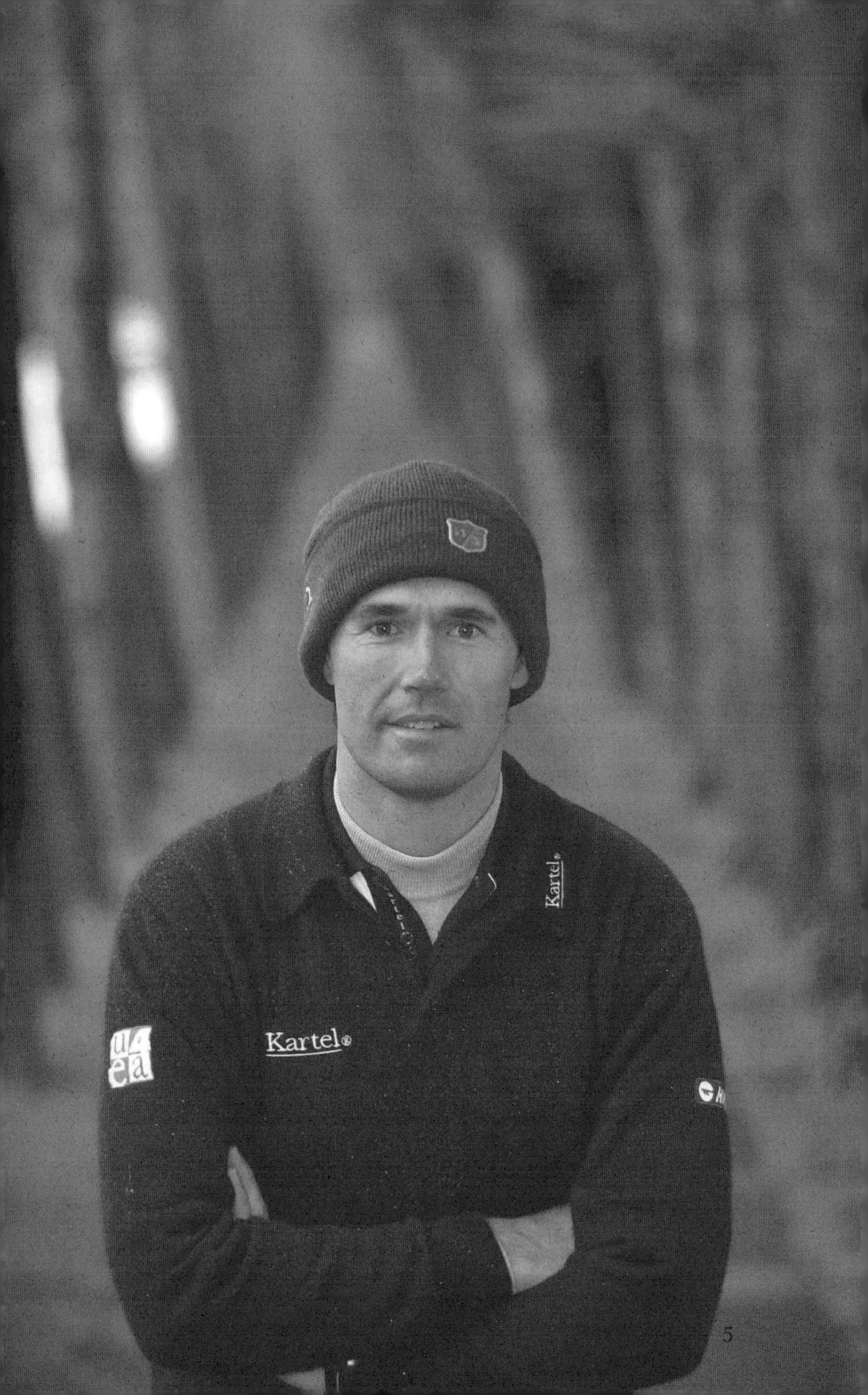
Kartel
Kartel

peak, that you are truly only halfway to achieving your ambition because you still have to retrace your steps in equally treacherous conditions and return to the safety of the base camp?

As in any activity, training and preparation are the key elements. Yet, no matter how thorough you are in your preparations, you need to go beyond that. You need determination. You need the will to succeed. You need to have the drive, the self-absorbed belief that nothing is going to get in your way. These are all key requirements but, even then, they are still no guarantee of success.

To really fulfil your dream, you need to go above and beyond what is normal. To really scale the heights, as Grania has done, you need to be sort of a "nutter"; and I mean that in the nicest possible way.

It's that x-factor that enables you achieve something special and, I believe, this is an opportunity for people to read the story of how and why someone can seek out and conquer their dreams, whilst risking their own life.

I've been a professional golfer for over 10 years. I've followed my own dreams and, in pursuing them, I go through tremendous highs and lows. Sometimes, to me, that pursuit can feel like a matter of "life and death," but my life is never in danger.

The great thing about this book is that it is the story of a regular person achieving great things. It's a story that allows us an intimate insight into what it takes to go in pursuit of your dream, to discover what that extra ingredient is that is required to do so, and how to apply it to fulfilling your dream. I don't, however, have any plans myself to climb Mount Everest. I think I'll stick to chasing my own dreams on the golf course.

Padraig Harrington

October 2005

Padraig Harrington, from Dublin, turned professional in 1995 and is established as one of the world's top golfers. At the time of print, he has won 16 individual tournaments around the globe in his career – including successes in Europe, the United States, South America and Asia – and, representing Ireland, partnered Paul McGinley to victory in the 1997 World Cup. He has played on three Ryder Cup teams for Europe, winning on two occasions (2002 and 2004).

Acknowledgements

The climb, and therefore this book, would never have happened without the help of a huge number of people. I owe an enormous debt of gratitude to my sponsors, The North Face, the Great Outdoors, Hewlett Packard and SORD Data Systems, Peak Centre Ireland and *The Irish Times*, but also to a number of individuals, both within those companies and outside. I have to thank HP's Tom McCabe, SORD's John O'Keeffe and Des O'Connell and particularly my IT guru Brendan O'Brien, Carl Petersen at Peak Centre Ireland, Eadaoin Hutchinson and Alex Beasley at The North Face, Leslie Lawrence and Gerry Collins at the Great Outdoors, David Reilly of Musashi and Malachy Logan, who endlessly championed my cause at *The Irish Times*.

Without my physio Aileen MaGuire, the dream would have remained just that, and without the tuition of Robbie Fenlon and Jane Carney, I would never have garnered the necessary skills to tackle Everest's north side. I also want to thank Shane and Joan Cleary for their unquestioning support and Gavan Cleary for his computer skills, my friends Jenny Bulbulia, P.J. Cunningham and Sean Moran, who I used as sounding boards for this book, Carmel McShea for keeping my feet on the ground and Ger and Sean McKeown for always believing in me. Thank you also to Tom McCormack and Roberta Leahy of ConneXions PR for their tireless work on my behalf.

But finally and most importantly, thank you to my family, for not knowing the worry they should have been experiencing while I was on the mountain.

A detailed glossary of mountaineering terms can be found on page 213

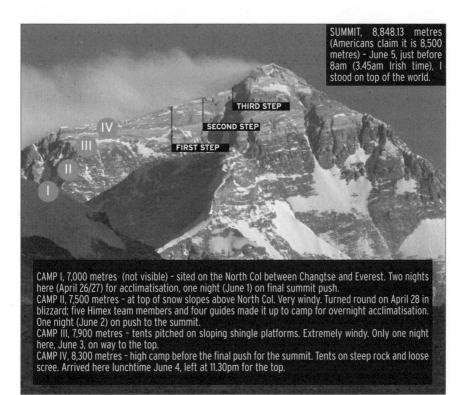

SUMMIT, 8,848.13 metres (Americans claim it is 8,500 metres) – June 5, just before 8am (3.45am Irish time), I stood on top of the world.

THIRD STEP

SECOND STEP

FIRST STEP

IV

III

II

I

CAMP I, 7,000 metres (not visible) – sited on the North Col between Changtse and Everest. Two nights here (April 26/27) for acclimatisation, one night (June 1) on final summit push.
CAMP II, 7,500 metres – at top of snow slopes above North Col. Very windy. Turned round on April 28 in blizzard; five Himex team members and four guides made it up to camp for overnight acclimatisation. One night (June 2) on push to the summit.
CAMP III, 7,900 metres – tents pitched on sloping shingle platforms. Extremely windy. Only one night here, June 3, on way to the top.
CAMP IV, 8,300 metres – high camp before the final push for the summit. Tents on steep rock and loose scree. Arrived here lunchtime June 4, left at 11.30pm for the top.

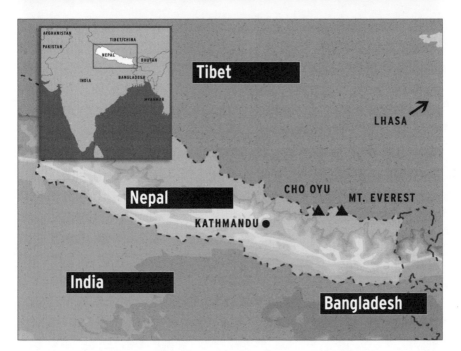

AFGHANISTAN

PAKISTAN

TIBET/CHINA

NEPAL

BHUTAN

INDIA

BANGLADESH

MYANMAR

Tibet

LHASA

Nepal

CHO OYU

MT. EVEREST

KATHMANDU

India

Bangladesh

Himex Everest expedition leader

Russell Brice

Guides

Bill Crouse, Dean Staples, Mark (Woody) Woodward, Duncan Chessell,
Dave (Narly) McKinley, Andy (Frog) Taylor

Expedition doctor

Terry O'Connor

Expedition nurse

Stacey Crowley

Climbers: **Yellow team**

Jeremy (Jez) Benton, Antoine Boulanger, Chuck Dasey, Peggy Foster, Akimoto
Fujibayashi, Charlie Hobbs, Shinichi Ishi, Brett Merrell, Chieko Shimada, Grania Willis

Red team

Kevin Goldstein, Soren Gudmann, Paul Hockey, Mogens Jensen, Jean Pavillard,
Sissel Smaller, Richard Stait, David Tait, Tom Torkelson, Monica Weil Kalozdi, Piers Buck

Base camp manager

Lachhu Bastnet

Sirdar

Phurba Tashi Sherpa

Sherpas

Lakpa, Tashi, Ang Karma, Phurba Temba, Dawa, Nima Wangchu, Son Dorjee,
Karsang, Ngima Dorji, Pasang, Pemba Tshering, Phura Nuru, Ngima Chirri, Phura
Temba, Ngima Nuru, Phuru Galzen, Danuru, Datenji, Phutesi, Lhakpa Tshering, Dorji,
Danuru, Lopsang, Lhakpa Gelu, Mingma Nuru, Pasang Ngima

*"Life is not a journey to the grave with the intention of arriving safely in a pretty
and well preserved body, but rather to skid in broadside, thoroughly used up, totally
worn out, and loudly proclaiming – Wow....what a ride!"*

TOTAL HIGH

1

PART

I

———

Death On The Mountain

A red dot on the distant snow. A vivid speck of colour, out of place so high up on the icy flanks of Mount Everest. My brain struggled with the image. If it was another climber I'd see movement. There was no movement. There never would be. It was a corpse, frozen in time, stretched for eternity on the wintry wastes, his summit of the world's highest mountain uncelebrated.

This was no unknown soldier. No novice cut down for attempting Everest before his time. I was the novice taking on the world's highest mountain, a mountain that has killed almost 200 climbers since man first set his sights on its pinnacle above the clouds. But this was an experienced climber, a member of the Slovenian mountain rescue services. This was Marko Lihteneker. His face so familiar to me from the months at camp.

As I got nearer I could see a backpack lying about five metres downhill from the frozen corpse. Untouched by fellow climbers who had passed since, it lay discarded on the snow. But nothing could have prepared me for the horror of the waxen face and the piteously clawed gloveless hands.

In his dying moments, Marko had ripped open his red down suit as his hypoxic brain told him he was overheating. His fingers, hooked like grotesque talons, looked as though they were still trying to cling to life as he had despairingly tried to gasp the last dregs of oxygen from air too thin to sustain human life.

TOTAL HIGH

It was May 21, 2005 when Marko Lihteneker took that last tortured breath before his spirit departed for the heavens so close above his head. Fifteen days later I stood by his body, halted in my tracks by death laid out before me.

I had climbed through the night, tortured by worries about whether I could make it to the top. But as dawn spread its tentacles across the jagged knife-edge ridge in front of me, here was the one thing I had dreaded most. A dead body. Right in my path.

It was a pivotal moment. If there was any time when I came close to abandoning my bid for the summit, this was it. I could turn round and retreat to safety, fleeing from the mountain's cruelty. Or I could put aside all thoughts of death and go on up the snow slope to the final summit ridge and onto the summit itself.

I went on, ploughing upwards for another two hours, wondering as I struggled towards the grail if I was signing my own death warrant. Wondering if I too was taking myself closer towards the merciless reach of the heavens.

I was battling with terror. I was battling an exhaustion I didn't know the human frame could withstand. And I was battling against the biggest mountain in the world, a mountain that was telling me I wasn't fit to stand on her summit. But I triumphed against them all and, just before eight o'clock on the mist-enshrouded morning of June 5, I stood on the highest point on earth.

Emotions, buried deep during two months of waiting for a window in the worst weather on Everest in almost half a century, bubbled up unbidden and I wept. Tears of triumph. Tears of joy. Tears of sorrow. I'd realised the biggest dream I'd ever allowed my fertile imagination to conjure up. I had become the first Irish woman to climb Mount Everest from the north side.

II

Early Days

I was 48 when I got to the mountain. I was 49 when I came back down. But I had no climbing history. Not like Marko. None of my family had ever had any aspirations towards climbing. I was one of twin girls delivered in the Weir maternity hospital in south-west London on May 14, 1956. Elder sibling Sarah was just 20 months old when two squalling babies burst almost simultaneously into a world that had previously revolved solely around her. I sent Megan out of the womb first to check that this huge new arena was safe for me. Twenty-five minutes later I made my appearance. It was one of the last times I ever let Meg do anything ahead of me. And the very last time that I checked anything was safe before I did it.

Our parents, Dilys and Jerome, were living in London with my father's parents, Robert and Heather Willis. Born in Clonmel, Co Tipperary, Bob Willis had moved to England seeking employment. He found work, and he found a wife, Heather Murphy, whose family was from Kinsale in Co Cork. The couple produced five children – four daughters and a single son. Maeve was the firstborn, followed by Jerome, Deirdre, Nuala and Fiona.

My mother's parentage was more mixed, English with a Celtic twist. Her father Jack Elstone was originally from London, her mother Ella Roberts from Caernarvon in Wales with a long-since forgotten Irish connection. Their three children were Jacqueline and twins, Dilys and John.

Almost eight years after the birth of Meg and Grania – Egg and Banana to our school-friends – Kate was born. She was a constant delight. Sarah, Meg and I would race home from school and the first one through the door would be given the honour of sitting in the giant wooden armchair in the kitchen with Kate on their lap. She would gaze up at whichever big sister was holding her with huge unblinking blue eyes. But our mother would nearly always have to take over feeding her as we only ever concentrated our energies on trying to make the chubby baby gurgle with mirth.

Our parents had met at the Royal Shakespeare Company's home in Stratford-upon-Avon, when my actor father had gone to the wardrobe department for a fitting. One of the seamstresses, red-headed and lively Dilys – she'd been called Spitfire as a child – had totally captivated the young Jerome. But she was wearing an engagement ring. Not long afterwards the ring disappeared from Dilys' hand and a new courtship began with Jerome that was to end in marriage.

During much of our young lives, our father was away on tour, filming or working in theatres. Life wasn't easy for our mother. Money was scarce in those early days and she was kept busy with four children. But she was also a talented costumier and would frequently be up sewing literally through the night to finish off one of her magnificent creations destined for the London stage or the screen. We loved watching her turn a swatch of ordinary fabric into an ethereal, fairytale costume, but her workroom was out of bounds for most of the time. When I was older, I was the only one of the four of us whose stitching was considered neat enough to help her.

Despite my neatness with the needle, I was always the tomboy and always in trouble. At home, misdemeanours were nearly always initiated by me but blamed on Meg, who had a knack for being in the direct path of parental wrath. I managed to avoid retribution most of the time, but things were different at school. I was sometimes studious, but more often rebellious. I wasn't always the ringleader, but I was usually in the thick of things.

The protestations of youthful innocence failed to impress the teacher who one day found me and a group of friends outside the main building with the front of our navy gaberdine skirts hitched up to our waists. A delivery truck driver had mistakenly come into the school quad instead of the kitchens and, in a too rapid manoeuvre to get back out, had shed the pickings of half an orchard onto the tarmac. Thrilled with the prospect of free windfalls, we used our skirts as makeshift sacks and they were bulging with apples when we were caught red-handed. My explanation that the fruit had fallen off the back of a lorry infuriated the rod-backed teacher and I had to duck rapidly to avoid a slap across the ear.

There were times though when the transgression was almost worth the punishment. The school toilets were, in the nature of such things, pretty grim. The vast tiled area between the cubicles and the wash-hand basins was a complete waste of space, but it provided the venue for some serious entertainment in the form of an impromptu skating rink, designed by me. The industrial size blocks of vile smelling carbolic soap were too big to be easily managed by awkward, childish hands. But it was only when the wet soap squirted out of my grasp and went zig-zagging chaotically across the expanse of floor that I realised its potential for fun.

A couple of pieces of string attached the blocks of soap to my feet and, after dousing the floor with liberal doses of water, I tentatively pushed one foot across the now slick tiles. I took off like a rocket and ended up crunched in a heap against the far wall. My two friends were delirious with delight. Gleefully grabbing more soap and more string, they too transformed their footwear into the equivalent of platform skates and the three of us whirled around in a giddy jumble of uniforms and soapsuds until we were brought to a rapid halt by the sound of the head-mistress snorting through disapproving nostrils in the doorway.

Severe reprimands followed, but the incident provided the inspiration for the indoor five-a-side roller hockey club that I formed several years later at college. It attracted a huge following, mostly drawn by the prospect of seeing a corporate sprint for the ball that – in a throwback to the school soap skating days – resulted in us being mashed en masse against the walls of the gym when our primitive braking system failed to work.

There were no reprimands the time Meg and I "borrowed" money from the housekeeping purse to buy sweets. But only because we weren't caught. Having been sent to the corner shop for a loaf of bread, we decided that we needed a reward for our endeavours. Sweets in those days, in our household at least, were restricted solely to weekends. This was a weekday and sugary delights were off the menu, so the chocolate bars had to be temporarily hidden inside our knickers. But supper was already on the table when we got home and there was no time to stash the goodies under our bunk-bed pillows for later.

The chocolate was well beyond edible by the time we escaped to our bedroom. Body heat had melted the chocolate beyond recognition and it had oozed out of its familiar purple Cadbury livery. Our brushed nylon knickers were destroyed. We hid them under the carpet and forgot all about them and it was only when we moved several years later that I thought of the new owner of the apartment lifting the carpet during refurbishments and discovering two pairs of knickers long-since robbed of their baby-blue innocence.

Our paternal grandfather taught us to swim in the freezing waters of the Tooting Bec Lido, an enormous outdoor pool skimmed with ice in the winter months that would leave us scratched and often bleeding, and always purple with cold. We retreated to Granny Heather's kitchen for bowls of porridge, onto which we'd spoon rainbow crystals of coffee sugar that melted into a disappointingly uniform brown. It was in that kitchen that I learned of the assassination of John F. Kennedy. And first heard and grew to love Alistair Cooke's *Letter From America*.

Childhood in London had only one major drawback for me. I was passionate about ponies from an early age and the outlets for riding in the capital were pretty limited. My mother's twin brother, Uncle John, was similarly enamoured of all things equine and encouraged me to learn to ride. I had to clean the family car and polish the family shoes to pay for my lessons. Even though Meg had absolutely no interest in horses she was still disgusted when I was regularly whisked off to Granny Ella's down in Surrey and sent to the local stables, where I would spend hours mucking out, grooming and – occasionally – riding.

When I finally got my first pony, Christopher Robin, a strawberry roan with a name bigger than his tiny physique, I thought I'd die with happiness. He was kept down in Surrey with my friend Lorna's fat black and white cob, Lucky, and the two of us would spend every hour possible galloping round the delightfully named Effingham Common, building jumping courses with traffic cones stolen from all the road-works in the neighbourhood.

I eventually outgrew Robin and he was replaced by a succession of bigger animals that I took to local shows at every opportunity. But it wasn't until I went to college that I got my first taste of international competition. After completing my A-levels at school in London, I went to Lancaster University in the north of England to study English, with archaeology, Greek and Roman drama thrown in as side-lines.

The university riding club was a thriving concern and we organised weekly competitions against other colleges, eventually progressing to the international stage with trips to Germany and France. I also had two horses at the other end of the country down in Sussex with Uncle John, so there were plenty of outlets for my competitive instinct. And I had my first serious boyfriend, tall dark and devastatingly delicious Paul Johnson. Within a year we were engaged.

After completing my degree, I moved back down to London with no idea of a career. What I did know was that married life, even the prospect of married life, wasn't for me. Paul and I went our separate ways and I dreamt of making a life with horses. Purely as a stop-gap I took up the post of secretary to the editor of *Country Life* magazine. I was no sooner in the job than I was poached by *Horse & Hound*, situated next door to Country Life on the 22nd floor of the vast IPC tower-block on the banks of the River Thames. Unintentionally, I had stumbled upon a journalistic career that combined my love of horses with my love of writing.

In the early part of 1980, *Horse & Hound* sent me to Ireland to write a feature on riding holidays. I had a ball and was made welcome everywhere I went in a whirlwind week that covered half the country. Not long afterwards I got a phone-call from the then editor of *The Irish Field*, Valentine Lamb, offering me a job in charge of the sports horse section of the paper. I'd been a journalist for only 10 months and now I was going to be an editor.

I took the job and moved to Dublin later that year. But as I turned my back on London, I didn't feel like I was leaving home, even though all my family and friends were still in England. Life in the British capital had been huge. Too huge and too impersonal. To me Dublin was perfect.

All around me people moaned about the claustrophobic atmosphere, told me they were hemmed in by Dublin's constraints before it became the cosmopolitan city it now is. But to me it was a relief from the enormity of London. It was comforting to be folded in the arms of Dublin theatres like the Gate and the Abbey amongst an audience peopled by familiar faces. The Wexford Opera Festival was a pure delight. I was a willing victim as I was whisked onto a social merry-go-round far more intimate and friendly than any I'd encountered in England.

While my three sisters married and started producing children, I was living the charmed life of a singleton. My new life revolved round the self-contained world of the horsey set. And I loved it. Politics held no interest for me and if I was one of the first of the new breed of female sporting journalists I was unaware of it.

Religion had never really come into the equation. My father had been brought up a Catholic, my mother a Protestant. Elder sister Sarah was baptised into the Catholic church but, when Megan and I arrived and, much later, Kate, no decision was ever reached about our religious affiliations. I never felt the loss until I came to Ireland and only then when staunchly Catholic friends, concerned for my soul, suggested that I should get baptised. I never did, but when I embarked on the journey to Everest I tapped into an, until then, unknown spiritual side of me.

I adored my new life in Dublin and, although they regretted the loss of me, my parents weren't surprised. My father had always told me that I was born lucky. "If you fell out of an aeroplane you'd land on a jelly factory", he'd say to me. I was the Jelly Baby. Life in Ireland in the 1980s was the ultimate jelly factory for me. There was plenty of money in the world of show jumping. And plenty of fun. And I was part of it.

I was writing about childhood heroes like Eddie Macken and Paul Darragh. There were endless junkets on offer. And endless parties thrown by the sport's wealthy backers. It was a gilded existence. But it was a brittle existence too and, when recession hit, sponsors pulled in their horns. Show jumping suddenly lost much of its cache and, simultaneously, its prime time slot on television.

As equestrian correspondent for *The Irish Times* I had to battle hard for space in the paper. In those days, show jumping was included in the news pages, but even when it was moved into sport I still had to fight my corner to get stories in. At the same time I was struggling to increase my input into *The Irish Field,* endlessly biting off more than I could chew and endlessly refusing to give in.

But life in Ireland was still what I wanted. I had a job that I loved and a new man, *Irishman's Diary* writer Kevin Myers. Plus two cats and a dog, Diesel. And my horses, the real love of my life. At a time when most Irish people were uprooting and travelling west to America, I had travelled west to Ireland. And I was going to stay. Coming to Dublin hadn't been a wrench. I didn't feel like I was leaving home. I was going back to the land of my roots. I was coming home.

III

A Big Fall

Climbing Everest had never been a childhood dream for me. Fifteen months before I stood on the summit, I had never climbed a mountain or a rock face. Fifteen years earlier I had been in Navan hospital in Co Meath, my back shattered in a riding accident. I didn't know if I'd be able to walk again unaided. But it was an apparently minor incident that led me to the top of the highest mountain in the world. Walking down the Dublin quays on the way to work on a sunny August morning in 2000, my eye was caught by two indistinct equine shapes on a still-distant bus stop advertisement.

As an equestrian journalist, anything to do with horses has always fascinated me. My own riding career had been brought to an abrupt and painful halt by that back injury, but horses were still my bread and butter, although now only through the written word rather than the competition world. But the bus stop ad turned out to be zebras, not horses. Zebras emerging from the mist, or maybe it was dust, of South Africa, advertising a charity trek for Temple Street Children's Hospital.

Keying the number from the ad into my mobile phone as I walked, I immediately called Temple Street and was put through to the head of the fundraising office. "The South Africa trip is already oversubscribed", Helen Cosgrove told me, "but I can put you on the list for next year if you like." Disappointed, I agreed and then put it out of my mind. Nice idea, but obviously not meant to be. But Helen was as good as her word and, early the following year, I received a detailed information pack about the proposed November 2001 trip, trekking in Nepal. I had no hesitation in signing up, even though I'd never done any hill-walking and would know absolutely no-one on the team. It still sounded perfect to me – walking in a stunningly beautiful part of the world and raising money for a worthy cause at the same time. But it was to prove far more than that. It turned out to be the starting point for a series of expeditions that would take me further and higher than I ever dreamed possible.

Fitness was never going to be a problem. Having ridden competitively to a reasonably high standard on the three-day event circuit, I had always kept myself in pretty good shape, riding sometimes as many as three horses a day, working out in the gym, swimming and running, as well as holding down a very full-time job.

The furthest I had ever run was the approximately six-mile circuit round Dublin's Phoenix Park and I certainly had no ambition towards extending the distance. That was until I was in the gym one Saturday morning in the autumn of 1989, two days before the Dublin City marathon, which traditionally takes place on the Monday of the October Bank Holiday weekend.

"Are you doing the marathon on Monday?", a fellow gymist asked me innocently, as she and I worked ourselves into a lather on some piece of cardio-vascular machinery or other. "Don't be ridiculous", I panted back at her, "I've never run more than six miles. And anyway, I haven't entered." "You're so fit, you really ought to. And you can enter on the day", she told me, simultaneously sowing the seeds of interest and tapping straight into my competitive streak.

I went home with my mind made up. I would run the marathon on Monday, just to see what happened. To see how my body would respond to being pushed way further than it had ever been pushed before. Little did I know at the time, but that was exactly one of the reasons that would trigger the desire to climb Everest over a decade later. I wanted to see what my body would do when it was pushed to the ultimate and beyond.

I had no idea how fast or how slow I should run on marathon day. I'd heard so much about the dreaded "wall" and my hugely competitive instinct refused to allow me to even contemplate failure. I set off conservatively, keeping well back amongst the also-rans and the faster of the also-walks. But a competitive spirit can't be kept in check for long and all too soon I found myself upping the pace as I went into automatic overtaking mode.

I would single out a runner ahead of me and then pick them off with glee. But it slowly began to dawn on me that these people probably knew about pace-setting and were deliberately choosing a speed that they could maintain for the full 26.2 miles. It was a struggle to curtail the urge to try and weave my way through the hordes of runners, but I knew I had to if I was to make it to the finish line. I eventually settled into a pace that was slower than I was really comfortable with, but at least I knew – or rather hoped I knew – that I could keep it up all day.

The constant exhortations of the organisers to keep re-hydrating meant that I picked up a drink at every water station on the way. As I wasn't going fast enough to sweat off the excess, all too soon my bladder let me know that it was rapidly getting towards bursting point. I queued at an official toilet stop, but the delay seemed interminable, so I aborted the mission and ran on again, eventually diverting into what looked like an old railway siding. It was a lengthy pee stop.

Relieved of the bladder burden, I set off again, wondering when the "wall" was going to rear its ugly façade. But it simply never did. As I ticked off the miles my stamina never wavered and, about two miles from the finish, I was furious with myself for going so slowly. I kicked for a sprint finish and, pandering to the competitor within, overtook other finishers straggling towards the line.

My time was officially registered as four hours, one minute and fifteen seconds. I could have come in well under four hours if it hadn't been for what the Americans term a "comfort stop". And who knows what time I could have clocked if I'd gone faster. Or if I had actually trained.

I'd loved the whole experience and determined that, next year, I would train and I'd set myself a serious target time. But, little over three months later, I was lying in a bed in the orthopaedic unit of Navan hospital with a back injury that would eventually call a halt to my riding career. A fall out hunting with the Co Clares had left me with a fracture dislocation at the base of my spine and a disc problem in the lumbar region that required two bouts of surgery to sort out.

I spent endless weeks confined to bed, lying on the flat of my back, miserable and in pain, while my injuries healed. I was in a private room, so there were no other patients to talk to unless they called in to see me. My friends all rallied round, however, and organised a shift system so that I was never on my own for too long. A ground-floor room and French windows also meant that my visitors could come and go whenever they liked. One night, two of them climbed in through the window, way after visiting hours were officially over, giddy after a night out on the town.

We actually had some great evenings in there, although I sometimes felt that my friends were partying without me as they sat on chairs filched from neighbouring rooms, drinking and chatting across my bed while I lay there, feeling as though I was watching some kind of surreal tennis match going on over my head.

I was in the capable hands of Fred Kenny, a huge racing fan and the orthopaedic surgeon of choice for jockeys and broken-up members of the equestrian fraternity, because he could put people back on the road - and therefore back on their horses - quicker than anyone else in the country. Fred had pieced me and numerous other horsey friends back together again after various falls and we all regarded him as both a brilliant surgeon and a kindly father figure. But Fred also had a bite and certainly wouldn't pull his punches. If he thought someone was swinging the lead, he'd tell them so.

If I could have found some lead I would have gladly swung it, if I'd been able to. But, after weeks of lying in bed, I was still in pain, pitifully thin and devoid of all strength. I wasn't improving so, after lengthy discussion, it was decided that surgery on the offending disc was the only solution. I wasn't at all keen to go under the knife, but there seemed to be no other option, so I reluctantly agreed.

I was made fully aware of the potential dangers of spinal surgery, with a risk of permanent paralysis, but by then I was beyond caring. I'd been in hospital so long at that stage and was so worn out by the constant pain and an endless procession of drugs, that I just wanted some sort of finality, one way or the other. Thankfully all went according to plan and, once the disc problem had been sorted out, I was handed over to the physiotherapy department, who got me back on my feet and out of the room that had been my prison for so long. As I shuffled my way down the hospital corridor on my increasingly lengthy daily perambulations, I looked and felt like a 90-year-old, bent over a zimmer-frame. But at least I was mobile.

I was determined to get home as soon as possible after the operation and, although there were plenty of setbacks on the way, finally Fred Kenny gave me the news that I had been waiting so long to hear. My mother, who had been bursting to fly over from London to be with me, came to the hospital to collect me with my then partner Kevin Myers. She was horrified to see that her once fit and agile daughter had become a frail old woman, but she kept her thoughts to herself, pledging to feed me up and get me back as close to full strength as she could before she returned to my father in London.

Once I was back home in Dublin I made what seemed to impatient me to be a desperately slow recovery. At length, Fred Kenny told me that I could get back to work whenever I felt ready, but to ease myself in gently. Shortly afterwards I flew to Sweden to cover the first ever world equestrian games in Stockholm. It would have been a tough two weeks if I'd been in the whole of my health but, still not fully recovered and stubbornly refusing to admit it, I found the whole of the Games horrific. I was exhausted and sore for the entire fortnight and bitterly regretted my decision to throw myself back into full work mode so prematurely.

I suspect that putting myself through so much hardship with my back – both physical and mental – was what began the honing process of the inner strength that I would have to call upon when things began to get tough on Everest. In fact, I'd already undergone part of that toughening process some years before my back injury when, in another horse-related incident, my spleen and liver were ruptured.

As a pupil of Iris Kellett, herself a former European champion and trainer of the legendary Eddie Macken, I spent quite a lot of time show jumping, even though three-day eventing was my true love. I'd ridden a succession of horses, but had formed a pretty good partnership with a home-bred mare belonging to Iris. Muse Light was an attractive steel grey, with a mind of her own. She wasn't the easiest horse in the yard, but I liked her and managed to persuade Valentine Lamb, then editor of *The Irish Field,* that we should lease the mare. Team Irish Field was born, with colleagues Margie McLoone and Marie-Claire Digby drafted in as co-members of the squad.

We had some successes, and a lot of fun. But all that came to an end one

February day when Muse Light, jumping in the second round of an indoor show jumping competition on home ground at Kelletts, fell. As she got to her feet, she planted one of them on my abdomen.

John Hall, Iris Kellett's then husband, raced into the arena and helped lift me, very gingerly, to my feet. I was taken up to Iris and John's apartment above the yard and a doctor was summoned. By the time he arrived a livid red horse-shoe shaped bruise had appeared in the middle of my abdomen. The doctor, concerned that I could be suffering from internal injuries, urged that I be taken straight to hospital. "Don't wait for an ambulance", he said to a stricken Iris Kellett.

Terry Fergus-Browne, who was later to survive breaking her neck in a fall only to succumb to stomach cancer a few years afterwards, rushed me to Dublin's Jervis Street hospital, which had been alerted to expect me by a call from the doctor. I was immediately put on an intravenous drip and – my recollections are somewhat hazy at this point – given some dye so that the damage to my internal organs could be assessed by a scan. Whether the dye was injected or ingested I can't remember, but what is all too vivid is the memory of collapsing as I came back out of the loo. The scans were unnecessary. There was obviously some serious internal damage and emergency surgery was required.

By the time Kevin got to the hospital, nurses were rushing around in all directions. In those days there was an on-call rotation of the hospitals. Jervis Street wasn't on-call that day and Kevin knew that the only reason the nurses were running was because his girlfriend was gravely injured. He arrived just in time to see me being rushed down to theatre on a trolley, with drip attached.

Kevin ran to catch up and, apparently, I extended a limp hand towards him and said, in melodramatic sotto voce tones, "Goodbye". He was convinced he'd never see me again and went back to *The Irish Times* office, unable to bear the lonely wait at the hospital while I was in theatre. He paced up and down in the newsroom, terrified he was going to get a phone-call that would tell him I hadn't come round from the anaesthetic. But the surgeon, Professor Paddy Collins, had done an amazing job on me, managing to stitch back together the ruptured organs, even though that had meant slicing me open from stem to stern in the frantic bid to save my life. When, several days later, I became aware of what had happened to me and the full extent of my injuries, I gingerly peered under my nightie at the new and unfamiliar features of my rearranged abdomen. What had once been smooth, white skin was now a swollen mass with a hideous purple cord of flesh running down the middle, decorated with an array of irregular black stitches stretching from my breast bone to my pubic bone. A thick rubber tube exited from just under my ribcage on the left-hand side, draining into a bucket under the bed. It was not a pretty sight.

The drain was gradually pulled out, about five centimetres a day, and the end snipped off. It felt like the nurses were pulling my insides out with it. But eventually, and much to my relief, the last of it came out and the bucket under the bed was removed along with it.

I've no idea how long I spent in intensive care or in the grim little room next to the nurses' station, where Kevin decided that he'd had enough of human innards and turned the painting of the Sacred Heart to the wall, much to the horror of the nuns still working in the hospital. But, after what seemed like an eternity of endless days rolling into endless night, I was eventually moved to a much brighter room and my spirits, which had remained unusually subdued for me, started to recover along with my battered body.

I was still terrified each night as I went to sleep that I would wake up dead. But each morning I'd wake – alive, thankfully – feeling stronger. I was now able to sit up and read the paper and visitors could actually have a conversation with me, instead of fumbling around for things to say to the pale-faced creature propped up on pillows who seemed to have lost the will to do anything except lie there, slumped forlornly.

There was no possibility of me remaining like that for long though. Once I knew I was out of danger I came back to life. The bounce was still missing, but gradually the old Grania began to return and I looked forward to the day I would get my marching papers from Jervis Street.

The day arrived but, before I was allowed to leave, Professor Collins came and sat down on the end of the bed. "Now Grania", he said in serious tones, and he was very good at doing serious tones. "You've had some pretty severe internal injuries and, because of the damage to your liver, there's going to be no drinking for the next six months." Alcohol was the last thing I wanted, so I acceded to that request without a problem. But I was totally stunned by his next utterance. Fixing me with a steely glare he continued: "And there's to be no riding horses. Or men either."

The three best things in life, gone in one fell swoop. I was devastated. What was I going to do for half a year until the ban was lifted. All work and absolutely no play. It was an unthinkable prospect. But I had to no choice in the matter and, when my six-month sentence was over, I decided not to go back on the drink. It was another 10 years before alcohol was to feature in my life again. I didn't wait that long for the riding.

After the months of deprivation, I finally settled back into a more normal life-style. But the internal injuries had a knock-on effect, resulting in appalling food allergies that would leave me running to the toilet, as well as causing such agonising stomach cramps that I would frequently pass out. On one occasion, the two managed to combine while I was glued to the loo. Putting my head between my knees to try and stop the waves of nausea, I came round to find myself standing in front of the mirror holding my face.

I'd obviously passed out, fallen off the toilet seat and skidded on the side of my face across a nylon carpet, giving myself a huge carpet burn from my temple to my jawbone. It was time to do something about the allergies.

I ended up on an incredibly restricted diet while the specialists in the Black-rock Clinic tried to work out exactly what I was allergic to. I became increasingly thin and increasingly pale, so much so that a work colleague said that her mother always asked after me in hushed tones, expecting her daughter to say that I had passed away the previous week.

I may have looked dreadful, but I just accepted both the look and the feeling that my body was constantly trying to purge itself. That was how my life was now. Gradually, however, I was allowed to increase the range of foods that I could eat without ill-effects and, eventually, the problem was traced to wheat. Unfortunately, wheat is in so many common foodstuffs, not just in the obvious things like bread. I even discovered that Smarties contain wheat.

Thankfully, I wasn't diagnosed as coeliac. The specialists felt that the allergies had been brought on by my injuries and, once my body had fully recovered, I would probably be able to reintroduce wheat into my diet. Incredibly, that's exactly what happened and eventually I was told that the latest batch of blood tests had come back clear. I was no longer allergic to wheat.

But my health problems were far from over. The restricted diet had obviously had an effect on my musculo-skeletal system and, although it was a number of years before I discovered that I had developed osteopoenia and was dangerously close to osteoporosis, I had perpetual tendon and ligament problems. I managed to tear ligaments in my ankles three times in succession, requiring six weeks in plaster each time. The injuries were caused by minor incidents that would have done little or no damage to a more robust person. On one occasion I ripped the ankle ligaments simply by falling off one of my vertiginously high-heeled shoes while playing musical chairs at a friend's wedding.

And back problems continued to haunt me during the early 1990s. I had thought that was all a thing of the past once I'd recovered from the surgery in 1990. But I couldn't have been more wrong.

I had started riding again the following year and was back on the competition circuit. But, in the spring of 1993, a mad night of high jinks during the big international three-day event at Badminton resulted in my back going into spasm the next morning. Another interminable stay in Navan hospital was the result.

Fred Kenny was threatening me with the knife again. I resisted firmly, so Fred decided to try a new tactic. He had me encased from armpit to hip in plaster, a thick white corset that would prevent me from bending my spine. It was hideously uncomfortable, but at least it meant I could have a trial weekend away with my friends, the Connollys, whose home wasn't far from the hospital. I can't honestly remember if I left the orthopaedic unit in an ambulance, but I certainly returned in one, just two days later and in agony.

My natural optimism was sorely tested, but I did manage to find some bright spots that kept my spirits buoyant, even when things looked pretty bleak. Fred had decided that physiotherapy was the way forward, so I was taken by wheelchair to the hospital pool, where I was lowered gently into the soupy warm water. But attempts to do the exercises prescribed resulted in my back locking painfully yet again.

Using the giant hoist, the physio team somehow got me out of the water and I was taken back to my room on a trolley, by now divested of my swimming togs and clad only in a dressing gown. There were quite strict rules in the hospital about dress for the female patients and going commando – in other words knicker-less – was distinctly frowned upon. So I shocked the poor porter rigid when I made a strange request as he was just about to manoeuvre me from the trolley to my bed.

"Can I ask you to do something that I bet no other girl has asked you to do before?", I said, looking at him innocently "Of course", he replied, with a bemused expression on his face. "Well could you put my knickers back on?"

At length, I started to respond to the treatment and I was finally discharged from hospital. But the following year my back seized up in even more dramatic circumstances. I was working in the pressroom at the Punchestown three-day event, 30 miles south of Dublin, when my back locked from the neck down. Since the original injury was at the base of my spine and the surgery had been carried out in the lumbar region, this new development terrified me. I was convinced I was going to be paralysed.

An ambulance was called and I was rushed to nearby Clane hospital, blue lights flashing and sirens blaring. I was in a state of shock, but I vividly remember making a conscious decision to stop breathing. If I wasn't going to be able to walk, I didn't want to live.

I was already on gas and air for the pain, but the ambulance personnel could see that I wasn't breathing. "Stay with us, Grania", I vaguely heard a disembodied voice say. It brought me back to my senses and I decided that perhaps living was the best option.

Conservative treatment achieved nothing and it rapidly became apparent that further surgery would be necessary. I was transferred to Dublin's Beaumont hospital, where neurosurgeon Steven Young agreed to operate on me. But not before one of the hospital priests came visiting prior to my departure for theatre.

Not being affiliated to any religion, I didn't feel the need for the priest's prayers, although I have to admit that I did ask God to look after me on more than one occasion. But the priest went ahead anyway, praying that the Lord would give me the strength to cope with whatever the outcome of the surgery was, even if it meant I'd never walk again. I was not impressed.

Whether the prayers worked or whether God had decided he had plans for me that would require the use of my legs, I don't know. But, as far as I was concerned, Steven Young was a miracle worker. When I came round from the anaesthetic, the pain – apart from the wound site itself – was completely gone.

The next day I was up and walking round my room, the day after I progressed to the corridor and, about a week later, I left the hospital, determined that – this time – it was for good.

The convalescence from this latest bout of surgery was much shorter than in 1990 but, as I slowly began to rebuild my strength, even climbing the stairs was an effort. If someone had told me then that I would be standing on top of the world's highest mountain less than 12 years later I would have said they were completely mad.

Surgeon Steven Young had – much to the disapproval of my mother who wanted to wrap me up in cotton wool forever – said that he was quite happy if I carried on riding because it would mean I was keeping myself fit. But I'd already made the heartbreaking decision to give up horses. I'd been told too many times that another bad fall would probably put me in a wheelchair and I knew my back wasn't strong enough for a return to competition riding with all its inherent risks.

If I wasn't competing, I didn't want to ride, so I had to find something to replace the gaping hole that giving up horses would leave in my life. My competitive instinct, kept dormant for too long while my back problems were being sorted out, needed to be re-galvanised and, ever the thrill-seeker, I also had to find something that would satisfy my lust for an ongoing adrenaline buzz.

IV

Small Steps

Skiing was one adrenaline rush option I considered but, with only one outing a year, I'd never progressed beyond the intermediate stage and was frustrated watching my powder-hound friends disappearing off-piste while I foostered around on the groomed runs. I needed something seriously challenging, something I could really get my teeth into.

After so many months out of the office, I ended up throwing myself back into work on a grand scale. Suddenly, all the time that I'd given to my horses was subsumed by work. My free time literally vanished and I wondered how I'd ever had time to ride at all, let alone compete every weekend.

I knew something had to be done to redress the balance and I did toy with the idea of making a come-back on the competition circuit. But then, in September 1996, I got a phone-call from a friend, Alan Smith, equestrian correspondent of *The Daily Telegraph*. Alan broke the news to me that Sam Moore, an Irish rider from Co Antrim, had been killed in a cross-country fall at the British three-day event in Blenheim.

I was devastated. I knew Sam well and loved his warm and generous personality. Having to write a piece for *The Irish Times* about his death was desperately hard. But worse was to come. Just seven months later, at a one-day event less than three miles from his Co Meath home, former Olympian and European team gold medallist David Foster was killed in a similar fall when his horse somersaulted over on top of him. It was Easter Monday, April 13.

David was a really good friend. Part of the gang. And suddenly he was gone. What made it worse was that his wife Sneezy and virtually all his friends were at the event when the accident happened. Suddenly the sunshine had gone out of the day, out of our lives. We were all totally shattered. His funeral two days later was one of the largest and one of the saddest I've ever been to, with international riders from all over the world coming to pay their last respects.

The two Irish deaths were followed by a succession of fatalities on the international eventing circuit, all caused by horses somersaulting over solid fences and landing on top of their riders. The unrelenting glare of media spotlight was turned on eventing, with statistics revealing it as the most high risk of all sports. Overnight I made the decision that I wasn't going to make a return to the saddle. No matter how much I loved competing, I couldn't put my parents through the worry of going back to a sport that was killing so many of my friends. Which is why, eight years later, I didn't tell any of my family that I was climbing Everest until after I'd reached the summit and was safely back down again.

So it was back to the drawing board. I was still seeking a sport that would be both an outlet for my competitive instincts and provide the adrenaline buzz I so badly needed. But work had expanded to fill all the available gaps in my diary. Something was going to have to change.

That change was a long time coming, however, and it wasn't really until 2001 when I started to get into hill-walking as part of the Temple Street Children's Hospital fundraising efforts that my life took on a new dimension that would lead eventually to bigger and snowier peaks.

The Temple Street trip to Nepal was scheduled for November 2001 and, in a bid to ensure that everyone was fit enough to undertake 100 kilometres of walking in the hot stickiness of post-monsoon Pokhara, Temple Street's fundraising chief Helen Cosgrove organised a series of increasingly strenuous walks in the Wicklow hills in the months beforehand.

I was still working out in Riverside Fitness, an underground gym next door to the Abbey Theatre in Dublin, where I had been a member for many years, so I knew I would be fit enough. But hill-fit and gym-fit are very different. Out on the hill I was adding a new dimension to my cardiovascular workouts and I relished the challenge.

Not everybody I was walking with relished me, however. I found it very difficult to walk slowly and would, in the company of fellow speed merchant, Sean
O'Toole, frequently find myself at the head of the group or – unforgivable sin
– ahead of leader Christopher Stacey.

Together with his wife Teresa, Christopher runs Footfalls, a successful
outdoor pursuits company. He knows the Wicklow hills like the back of his
hand and is part of the Glen of Imaal mountain rescue team. As well as regular
trips over to Snowdon, Ben Nevis and the Lake District, Christopher also runs
mountain skills training courses to try and create safety awareness in the hills.

Christopher was an invaluable guide for the Temple Street training walks,
although Sean and I were constantly in trouble for overtaking him. It wasn't that
Christopher was being excessively authoritarian, it was apparently an insurance
issue. Sean and I said we quite understood, but it didn't stop us and we were
soon marked out as the rebels in the group. So much so that I was even given
a talking-to by the trip co-ordinator, Helen Cosgrove, for being too fit and intimidating the other walkers. I began to wonder if this trip to Nepal was going to
be much fun after all.

But plans had to be put on hold. The combination of the massacre of the
Nepali royal family by the king's nephew in July, the bombing of the Twin Towers
in New York on September 11 that triggered the war in Iraq, and the declaration
of a state of emergency in Nepal after negotiations with the Maoists failed, meant
that the hospital was advised to rethink the trip. Nepal was in a highly volatile
state and we would also be flying into one of the Gulf States en route to
Kathmandu. The trip was postponed until the following March. But when we did
finally get underway, the trip to Nepal was to be the catalyst that would change
my life forever. Not only did I collect a whole new bunch of friends, I fell in love.
Head over heels in love. With a mountain.

After flying into Nepal, we had just one night in Kathmandu before heading
for Pokhara, where we would be doing all our walking. A group of us made the
most of our brief spell in the Nepali capital, partying through the night and getting
on the bus the next day somewhat the worse for wear. It was to set a pattern for
the rest of the trip. Partying till dawn and then walking all day, before repeating
the process over the next 24 hours, and the next, and the next. My stamina levels
were tested, but never to the limit. I was having the time of my life.

Helen had organised helicopter trips to Annapurna base camp for St Patrick's Day. The helicopter could take just three passengers, so Helen, her sister Abby and myself were the first trio to head up the mountain at an hour when I was usually only going to bed. Three Sherpas, guardians of a feature-less concrete block of a building that provided very basic accommodation, invited us in for a cup of tea. They must have wondered if the Martians had landed as Helen and Abby had both dyed their hair bright green in honour of the day.

I was stunned by the beauty, not of my companions' hair colouring, but of the mountain environment we'd been airlifted into. As the noise of the helicopter disappeared into the thin air and silence returned, I knew that this was somewhere I wanted to return to. The seeds of a new addiction had been sown.

The day continued in a similarly thrilling vein. After flying back to the hotel in sedate style, one of the pilots offered us a James Bond style trip, hurling the helicopter down a gorge before heading back, straight towards the high walls of the cliffs and, at the very last minute, shooting up vertically to clear the rocks by inches. I was ecstatic. It was like the scariest funfair ride multiplied off the richter scale.

A St Patrick's Day parade, headed by the Mater private hospital's financial kingpin John Mooney dressed as a leprechaun and the wildly eccentric Sheila Judge as the saint himself, caused some serious head-turning in Pokhara's main street. Even the cows stopped to stare. We featured in the papers the next day and John was interviewed on television, still dressed in his leprechaun suit, green hat, carrot-coloured wig and beard. It was a blast and we wound up the day's celebrations with a pool-side barbecue back at the hotel. I wasn't the only one to end up in the pool fully clad.

I'd adored the whole Annapurna experience. The rest of the day was the icing on an already rich cake. But it was a mountain flight from Kathmandu that really set the Everest plans in train. I had actually got to bed the night before – for all of 25 minutes – as we had an early start. Fog meant a three-hour delay and we sat in the grim lounge at Tribhuvan airport, with the party animals amongst us – including me – fading slightly.

But the trip was so worth the wait. The Buddha Air plane was perfectly designed for mountain spotting, with just one seat on either side of the central aisle so that the peaks were visible to everyone. And, just to make sure, the hostess took us all, one at a time, up to the cockpit so that we could get a full frontal view. By some miraculous piece of good fortune, I happened to be up at the front when the dark summit pyramid of Everest first became visible. The co-pilot pointed it out to me and, from that moment, I was entranced.

The mountain was the most hauntingly beautiful thing I had ever seen. And I knew in that instant that I had to come back. I had to come back and climb it, even though I'd never been near a mountain that didn't have a ski resort on it. I told everyone on the trip about my plans and two of the lads, Gerry Crotty and Martin Doran, both said that they would come with me. I think most people just dismissed it as the fantasy of a sleep-deprived lunatic, but I was the most serious I'd ever been about anything in my life.

The following year Everest was at the forefront of my mind again. Another of my close circle of friends, Jenny Bulbulia, had given me a belated Christmas present, in April. It was Bear Grylls' book *Facing Up*, the story of how he – at the age of 23 – had become the youngest Briton to climb Everest, despite having broken his back in a free-fall parachuting accident two years before. Jenny, who isn't a climber, had been totally inspired by the book. Realising the parallels between Grylls' story and my ambitions, she thought it would at least be a good read.

How right she was. From the very first page, I was totally captivated. I immersed myself in the book and read it in one sitting. Even though I was twice the age Bear Grylls had been when he climbed the mountain, I knew this was my dream. I had to make it a reality.

And, less than a month later, that dream began to come true. I was on my way to Everest. Only to base camp this time, but it was an important step towards the climb itself and it had come about in the most extraordinary way, just as so many things did in the build-up to the 2005 expedition.

As soon as I'd finished the Bear Grylls book, I decided to check up on the Irish Everest 2003 website. The expedition was led by Cork man Pat Falvey, who had summitted Everest from the north side in 1995. Now, eight years later, he was back to try the route from Nepal. The team of six climbers included two women – Dr Clare O'Leary and Hannah Shields – both of whom were aiming to become the first Irish woman to summit the mountain. The group had left Ireland on St Patrick's Day and I decided to track their progress.

It was the first time I'd been on the website and I knew nothing about the support treks that had been organised. But details of the treks virtually jumped out of the page at me and, intrigued, I clicked on the entry. To my surprise there were still spaces on the May trek, which would go to Everest base camp to meet up with Pat and his team.

Two changes in the equestrian fixture list meant that an unexpected gap had opened up in my calendar. Suddenly, I had both the time and the opportunity to go to base camp and it would give me the chance to see the mountain at close quarters. If I got up close and personal and its sheer size terrified me, even from the safety of base camp, then I could save myself a huge investment of both time and money, forget my dreams and go back to a mundane sea-level life.

But, if I got to the foot of the mountain and really could envisage myself climbing it, then this support trek would be an invaluable reconnaissance mission. I could potentially learn a huge amount and return next year or the year after better equipped, at least psychologically, to take on the biggest challenge of my life. I got on the phone immediately and booked myself on the trip.

Once again I knew nobody but, by the time I returned to Dublin, I had forged life-long friendships. And I used the trip as a fundraiser for Temple Street, meaning that while I was moving closer to my ultimate goal I was also securing funds for the children's hospital.

When we'd been in Nepal the previous year we'd only been vaguely aware of the Maoists insurgents. Burning tyres in the middle of one of the main streets of Kathmandu and a curfew in Pokhara, which we unwittingly broke one night, were the only signs of any unrest. There were also soldiers on guard at the gates of our hotel in Pokhara, but we assumed that was normal.

But Maoist attacks, plus the number of deaths amongst the terrorists as they were targeted by the Nepalese Army, had increased during 2002. Tourist numbers had dropped dramatically and, in a bid to tempt the visitors back to Nepal, a cease-fire was declared at the end of January 2003 between the Maoists and the Royal Nepalese Army.

The climbers were always going to be flocking in that year to celebrate the 50th anniversary of the first successful ascent of Everest by Edmund Hillary and Tenzing Norgay, but the trekkers had to be lured back. The cease-fire gave them some reassurance that they would be safe. In fact the Maoists tend not to appear in the Khumbu, operating mostly in the central and western parts of the country although, as I discovered on my way in to climb Mera Peak the following year, they are also to be found to the east of the more traditional tourist route up to Everest base camp.

We certainly saw no sign of the Maoists when we arrived in Lukla, where an unbelievably sloped landing strip is perched on the edge of a heavily forested, steep hillside at an altitude of just under 2,800 metres. The pilots of the 20-seater twin-prop planes have to be some of the bravest in the world. They fly through incredibly turbulent conditions, into the foothills of the Himalaya, all too often shrouded in cloud. And then they have to fling the planes down onto Lukla's unique landing strip, where the precipitous angle helps the braking process for landing and assists in the take-off procedure for departing planes.

As well as passengers – and a steward to hand out bits of cotton wool for earplugs and boiled sweets for choking on – the planes are also filled to overflowing with cargo. Sacks of rice, vast bundles of mattresses and crates of unidentifiable gear all jostled for space with the paying passengers.

I assumed that the weight limits were, to a certain extent, ignored. But I discovered the following year that they are strictly adhered to when I witnessed a stand-off on the tarmac. We'd been stranded in Lukla by bad weather and a group of passengers – thankfully booked on a different flight to me – had been told it was either them or their luggage. The plane couldn't take both.

Desperate to get out of a place that has very little to recommend it other than as the gateway to the Himalaya, the passengers dug in their heels. But so did the pilot. Eventually, after lengthy negotiations, one couple volunteered to stay behind with their luggage. Whether they got back to Kathmandu later that day I never found out.

My first flight into Lukla was, in comparison, trouble-free and we disembarked down incredibly wobbly steps, some of us more grateful than others to be back on terra firma. Marvelling both at our survival and at the unbelievably steep pitch of the runway we'd just landed on, we walked towards the chain-link perimeter fence that surrounds the Lukla airstrip. Soldiers with guns slung over their shoulders patrolled the entrance. Groups of porters were pressed against the fence, hoping to pick up some work, but we could offer them none. Our team was already organised and the porters were swiftly sorting out our gear into unbelievably heavy loads – usually of three kit bags apiece – that they then tied together and carried by means of a thick webbing strap running across the top of their heads.

It has never ceased to amaze me, from that very first sight of the loads they heaved up onto their backs, just how much the porters are able to carry. Most of them use thickset carved sticks with a Y or T-shaped top. These are not just for balance while walking up and down steep inclines, but are also used as either a seat or as something to prop the load on so that the porters can temporarily take the weight off their sweaty and aching backs.

After the heat and stickiness of Kathmandu, the mountain air was welcomingly fresh. But Lukla itself is far from clean. It's a one-horse town, built on a Nepalese version of strip-development all along one street. Open sewers run along the main thoroughfare and, where there is paving, it's laid so haphazardly that ankles are in severe danger of being turned even before the real walking begins.

Cows and chickens mingle with the inhabitants and visitors on the street, adding to the noise and mess. But the tea-houses offer respite and, in some cases, extraordinary fare. On its breakfast menu, the Sunny Garden Restaurant boasted mousley with milk and something called excrembal, which it took me a while to work out was scrambled egg. There were also apple fumbles and grilled fish with waster sauce.

We were simply stopping for a drink, so we didn't indulge in any of these gastronomic delights, heading off instead on the short trek to the village of Phakding, where we would be spending our first night under canvas. The first half of the journey to Phakding is downhill and, when we reached the bridge across the Thadokoshi, a tributary of the Dudh Koshi or milk river, we stopped for lunch beside the tumbling stream. We were already pretty warm and a beautiful turquoise pool looked extremely tempting, but hunger took precedence. And a pee stop was needed too.

The toilet was a small wooden hut, perched high on stilts. Peering through the hole in the floor I could see a mountain of human excrement buzzing with flies below me. An enormous number of mis-hits around the hole meant that even peeing was a delicate operation. But Ann Kelleher, who had followed me down to the "facilities", had a worse tale to tell. On her 2002 trip to Nepal she had stopped at a similar toilet and, unaware of the hut above her head, had squatted to pee under the stilts where others had so obviously answered the call of nature before her. Luckily no-one was using the upstairs loo at the time.

We headed into the Sagarmatha National Park the next day, walking along the banks of the Dudh Koshi, where the grey-green melt-water tumbled and foamed dramatically over enormous boulders, worn smooth over years of immersion. A series of bridges back and forth across the river brought us to the base of a sharp ascent up steep slabby steps that led to the bizarre village of Namche Bazaar.

We fought our way through the huge yak caravans transporting produce up to Namche's weekly market. And we overtook porters with the flimsiest of footwear carrying everything from huge loads of trekkers' duffel bags roped together, to a forest of solid timber planks three times the height of their carrier. The trail is even busier earlier in the season, with the yaks taking up barrel-loads of climbing gear and all the paraphernalia required for siege-style assaults on Everest and the other Himalayan giants.

Namche itself more than compensates for the lengthy ascent. The town is built into a bowl on the hillside and is expanding at a huge rate. Building starts at dawn and continues until well after dusk. The sound of hammers and chisels chipping away at stone is so constant that you only notice it when it stops.

Many of the buildings are painted white with blue roofs. But the apparently regimented colour scheme runs riot in the warren of narrow little streets. Market stalls and basement shops sell literally everything, from toilet paper to climbing equipment, from traditional Nepali clothing to hair dye.

We spent two nights there and used the intervening day for an acclimatisation hike to the Everest View Hotel which, as its name suggests, gave us the first proper sighting of our goal, Sagarmatha, the Sanskrit name for Everest meaning Forehead of the Sky. The mountain looked impossibly distant, but even from this range, impossibly daunting too.

On our way to Pangboche the next day, we stopped at the Tengboche monastery. On either side of a vast archway, rows of prayer wheels have been rubbed bright by pilgrims, trekkers and climbers spinning them in the clockwise direction that is said to send the prayers of the faithful up to the heavens. A flight of shallow stone steps swept up to a doorway from which two dark corridors led to a bright sunny courtyard. The main building sat atop another flight of steps, where a clutter of shoes lay casually abandoned in front of a heavy maroon curtain, waxy and blackened on the edges from the touch of a thousand hands.

It was cool inside, the interior lit only by thin shafts of sunlight coming through windows high up on one side of the room. Monks in maroon robes were seated cross-legged in long rows on a series of low cushioned benches. Those on either side of a central aisle were holding vast curved horns, the ends of which were balanced on the floor, but only a low chanting drone could be heard as we came in.

The room was dominated by a giant Buddha statue, draped with prayer scarves, surveying the proceedings with sloping, kohl-rimmed eyes. Its hands, resting on crossed legs, adopted the pinched thumb and forefinger pose beloved of Buddhas and practitioners of yoga. It was a serene and beautiful presence that was about to be shattered.

A group of trekkers was already sitting on the floor round the edge of the room. In the gloom it was hard to see more than a series of faces floating, apparently disembodied, above a row of stockinged feet and bare legs. Before we'd had a chance to make our way to the empty space beyond them, there was a blast of noise as the monks blew into the horns. The deafening cacophony instantly exacerbated the insistent nagging of an altitude headache.

The ear-blasting horns were finally silenced and the monks, who had been drinking tea whenever they weren't deafening themselves and their audience, filed out of the room like a gaggle of chattering maroon-coloured birds.

The next morning, on the way to Pheriche, I was mesmerised by my first sight of Ama Dablam. At just over 6,800 metres, this ravishingly beautiful mountain is small in comparison to the 8,000 metre giants, but it is still an imposing sight, dominating the valley like a haughty and sensuous sphinx.

Pheriche is home to the Himalayan Rescue Association medical outpost.

TOTAL HIGH

The HRA clinic was literally next door to the tea-house where we'd be spending the next two nights, so we went in to listen to a lecture on altitude sickness. The lecture, given by a Scandinavian female doctor, seemed to be deliberately designed to alarm. It certainly alarmed us. The threat of pulmonary and cerebral oedema hung over our heads like the sword of Damocles.

On the way back to the tea-house we were reminded still further of the dangers of altitude by the jutting triangular steel and stone memorial listing the names of all those who had perished on Everest. We were in sombre mood as we trailed back to our accommodation.

Our mood lightened that evening, however. After dinner we stayed on in the main room. It certainly wouldn't warrant the title dining room, although it was where everybody ate, but it had one major attribute – an ancient, wheezing stove, fed periodically with dried yak dung which was stored in a neighbouring aluminium bucket. The heat was intense, for those who managed to get a ringside seat. Anyone on the periphery was, quite literally, left out in the cold.

Even though we had all abandoned the delights of alcohol, particularly after our sobering lecture at the HRA, we decided a session was in order. If we couldn't drink, at least we could sing. We traded Irish songs for Sherpa songs. And then we danced. The Siege of Ennis met with traditional shuffling Sherpa dancing. And the Buddhist monks sitting cross-legged on the carpet-covered box seats on the far side of the room looked on with confused but amused indulgence.

Sitting reading in one of the window seats in the tea-house dining room late the following afternoon, I glanced up at the towering peak of Ama Dablam. The mountain was blushing gently pink in the dying embers of the sun. Alpenglow had never looked so beautiful.

In the crisp cold of the following morning, we found our laundry frozen on the washing line. We hung it off our backpacks in the hope that it would dry when the warmth got into the sun. By our traditional 10 o'clock lunchtime it was dry but coated in a thick layer of orange dust.

The HRA lecture seemed to have had a negative effect on morale and the sight later that afternoon of the memorial ground to those who had died on Everest did nothing to improve the mood. Surrounded by an incredible mountain panorama, I had eyes only for the plaques to the fallen. It was like a battlefield. A string of prayer flags flapped solemnly in the wind.

Particularly poignant was the memorial to Babu Chirri, a legendary Sherpa who had held the record for the fastest ascent, the greatest number of summits and the longest time spent on the summit – 21 hours without oxygen. His death in 2001 was a tragic waste of a brilliant climber, killed by falling into a crevasse on the very mountain that had made him a demi-god in Nepal.

After a night at Lobuche, where we heard the distressing news that a porter had died on his way up to base camp that day, our next goal was Gorak Shep and, if the weather held, Kala Patthar for our first close-up view of Everest. Below Lobuche, the receding glacier has left a long flat valley floor, where the rocks have been ground down to a gritty sand. It made for easy walking and the gradual increase in height didn't seem to be affecting us at all. It was a glorious day and we were excited as we got nearer to our ultimate destination. But the altitude was lurking in the wings, waiting to strike down another victim.

As we arrived in Gorak Shep, the sun was streaming down and gave a veneer of charm to the grim little cluster of buildings. The Sherpas had spread out a blue tarpaulin for us to sit on and we lay basking, backpacks turned into pillows, while lunch was being prepared. But the food was no sooner put in front of us than Dublin fish merchant Martin McLoughlin, suddenly and dramatically, started to vomit profusely. His deterioration was frighteningly rapid.

Only minutes earlier he'd been showing me a photo album put together by his wife Margo. There were pictures of Martin and Margo before they were married, and lots of their two children, Shane and Clare. "This is my little princess", he'd said with pride, showing me a picture of a gorgeous chubbily naked baby girl gazing up at the camera with enormous eyes. Now Martin was lying groaning next to me, as though home-sickness had brought on a more real and far more dangerous illness. He didn't want sympathy. He just wanted to be left alone.

The Sherpas were happy to look after him so, together with Cork man Gerry Walshe, I headed up the giant slag heap of Kala Patthar. It was already well past midday, but the heavens were still blue and cloudless above us. Aware that we'd made a late start, we didn't stop to take pictures, although I did frequently look back over my shoulder at the unfolding drama of the mountainscape behind me.

I could see the hectic jumble of the Khumbu icefall and, perched at the bottom, the base camp cluster of tents that looked from this distance like piles of discarded rubbish.

Nuptse's needle sharp point drew my eye upwards, but I didn't want to look at Everest. I wanted to save that until I could sit down and savour her beauty. But by the time we reached the final scramble that took us to the top, the weather had changed completely. Typical of the Himalayan weather pattern, the afternoon clouds had rolled in out of nowhere, blotting out the sun and causing a sharp drop in temperature.

As I sat down next to the prayer flags that marked the 5,545 metre summit, the drop to my right had disappeared in the mists. Alas, so too had Everest. The panoramic view of the giants that should have allowed me to scan across from Changtse to Everest, Lhotse and Nuptse was gone.

Martin hadn't improved while we'd been gone. It was agreed that he'd be better off in the tea-house rather than a tent, so Donegal born Mary Casey and I went to find him a room. It was pitch dark outside and the next morning we discovered that our head-torches hadn't revealed a fraction of the horrors we were about to see.

We were taken into a building so dilapidated and stinking that I wouldn't have housed an animal in it, let alone a sick human. The owner shouldered open a thin, lop-sided door into a large, musty room. Every available space was taken up by slumbering Sherpas and porters, so he led us down a dank corridor to a small narrow cell with a low wooden platform on one side. I could hear the scuttle of rodents in the dark corners. We asked if there was anywhere else, but the man shook his head.

We went to get Martin and he followed us back meekly, too weak to resist. As we settled him down on the unyielding bed, my head-torch flickered briefly onto his face. He looked as though he firmly believed death was a preferable option.

Four of our team had headed off to climb neighbouring Island Peak and we had been left with a basic first-aid kit. But it was only when I opened it up that I discovered just how basic it was. Aspirins and a roll of bandage made up the bulk of it. Neither were much help to Martin. I gave him Diamox, Motilium and headache pills from my own medical bag, leaving the bottles on the floor in case he needed them during the night. I hoped the rats wouldn't eat them.

Miraculously, Martin was hugely improved the next morning and we set off on the final leg of our journey to base camp. We were on the edge of the glacier itself now and the terrain had changed totally. We were walking on rocky, icy paths and, worse, scree on top of ice.

There was no sign of any activity when we arrived. There were tents everywhere, pitched on any patch of rock or ice that offered something approaching a flat surface. There were even tents teetering on the edge of ice-skimmed pools of water, pools that would freeze every night and thaw out during the day, dragging the tents ever closer to the lip.

We wandered through the tented city, but it was a while before we spotted the Irish camp, strangely silent. Carol O'Leary, whose sister Clare was climbing the mountain, went into the mess tent first. None of us expected to see Clare, but there she was, looking pale and fragile after being forced to abandon her bid for the summit on the way to camp III after days of vomiting and diarrhoea. There was some kind of warped irony in a gastroenterologist having to give up her dream of Everest because of a stomach bug.

Much later that day I asked Clare if she would consider coming back for another attempt. "No", she said emphatically. "The team has been fantastic and I don't think we'd have the same dynamics again." Her answer surprised me. It was less of a surprise when she came back a year later and achieved her goal of being the first Irish woman to summit Everest.

As soon as the sun went down behind the mountains, the temperature plummeted. I'd left my head-torch in my backpack and had to feel my way back to my tent in the pitch dark without any real sense of where I was going. I was wary of the icy melt-pools. I knew that a Sherpa had fallen into one of them during the day and had to be fished out rapidly. If I tumbled in at night there would be no rescue. No-one would even know I'd fallen. I'd freeze to death in an instant.

I did fall, but thankfully not into a pool. Skidding on some icy scree, I shot down a sharp incline, my fall arrested by a large rock. I got up cautiously, not wanting to precipitate another plunge into darkness.

By the time I got to the tent I was shivering with cold. Washing was definitely out of the question. I managed a cursory scrub of my chattering teeth before snuggling into the depths of my sleeping bag.

I fell asleep instantly, but was woken some time later by the insistent aching of my bladder. I grabbed my boots and thrust my feet into their frigid depths. Not bothering to tie the laces I crawled out of the tent. I was just lifting my hand towards my face to switch on my head-torch when something stopped me. The sight that met my gaze was so staggeringly beautiful that I completely forgot why I'd come out in the first place.

A brilliant moon, close to full, suffused the inky black of the mountains with an eerie glow. Each dark peak had a silvered, luminous edge to it, the silver lining that I was always looking for in clouds. The snowy reaches of the slopes seemed to be lit from within. It was the first time since our arrival that I'd had a chance to take in the majesty of my surroundings. It was intoxicating.

A photograph would never have done it justice, but I didn't need a picture. It's stored forever in my head. And I knew in that instant, even though Everest herself was hidden behind the dark massif of Nuptse, that I would come back.

V

Times Change

I left Kathmandu in love. In love with Everest. I certainly didn't have any
fond memories of base camp, one of the most godforsaken hell-holes in
the entire world, but I was totally in thrall to the soaring beauty and
indefinable power of Sagarmatha herself. My plan to get up close and
personal with the mountain hadn't deterred me. It had had the opposite effect.
I was more determined than ever to come back with a climbing expedition.

Suddenly mountaineering books were vying for space on my bookshelves
with all the equestrian tomes. Climbing magazines cluttered up my coffee table
and my desk, where previously only horses had reigned. Friends were buying
me books on Everest rather than glossy works on all things equine. Looking
back, my new-found passion had obviously been preordained 20 years earlier
by the prophetic naming of my two cats – Hillary and Tenzing – after I'd seen
them as tiny kittens shinning up bales of straw in a friend's stables.

The only problem now was finding the time, not just for the climb, but for
the huge amount of training I was going to need as well. A surprise gap in my
work schedule had allowed me to get to base camp, but how would I ever get
the 10 weeks that I was going to need for an assault on the world's highest
mountain? The solution presented itself to me in a most unexpected form.

An optimist to the last, I had been struggling to find a silver lining to the
storm cloud that had been hanging over the office for the best part of two years.

After buying new state-of-the-art presses, *The Irish Times* had reported projected losses of close to €30 million late in 2001. An unspecified number of redundancies had been sought and were achieved by the spring of 2002 under a voluntary severance and early retirement package. Included in the swingeing cuts were 40% of the editorial staff. It was a devastating restructuring. Now there were rumours that management was planning to sell off the paper I also worked for, the weekly racing bible, *The Irish Field*.

I remembered ringing a friend the previous August and telling him there was talk of the paper being sold. He bet me a case of wine that nothing would come of it. I never got the wine, but the paper got sold.

The Irish Times was duty-bound to re-deploy us if we wanted to stay on. I was offered a job in the newsroom. But if we wanted to remain with *The Irish Field*, the new owners told us we would have to reapply for our jobs, even though most of us had been with the paper for years. I was approached by the new editor Leo Powell, who offered me the chance to stay in my job with a better salary than the one I was already on. I could take him up on his offer and take the redundancy package from *The Irish Times* as well. It was tempting, but I had much bigger plans and a colleague, Ann McLoone, encouraged me to take the plunge.

"You've got to take the package", she said to me. "You're the only one of all of us with a plan. Go climb that mountain."

The decision about Everest wasn't difficult. Walking away from a guaranteed salary was. But, after weeks of heart-searching and with Ann's words giving me the final impetus, I turned down both *The Irish Times* and *Irish Field* offers. I collected my redundancy cheque in mid-September 2003 and turned my face towards Everest.

A couple of weeks before my departure from *The Irish Times* I had been invited to a dinner party in Co Wicklow by a couple who were to become wonderful friends, Shane and Joan Cleary. I'd known Shane throughout his 12-year tenure as chief executive of the Royal Dublin Society, but had only discovered his love of climbing earlier that year. Having decided to do the trek to Everest base camp as another fundraiser for Temple Street Children's Hospital, I'd written to Shane at the RDS looking for sponsorship.

As venue for the annual Dublin Horse Show, the RDS is the holy grail for many of the equestrian community but, although it is considered one of the social highlights of the year, it is a week of sheer hard slog for the journalists covering the fixture. Despite the horrendously long hours, I always enjoyed the show and had developed a good working relationship with Shane.

I'd written to him in the hope that the RDS would cough up some money, but it was Shane himself who pledged a donation. It turned out that Shane had been an avid climber in his youth, but then family and work commitments had curtailed his outdoor activities. He'd spent some time in the French and Italian Alps the previous summer with Dublin mountaineer Robbie Fenlon, now based out in Chamonix. My letter apparently sparked an increased interest in the sport and, the following May, Shane took early retirement from the RDS so that he could return to the hills and crags. The result of my begging letter was a new-found friendship with Shane and his wife Joan, plus a much valued climbing buddy.

I'd told Shane during the 2003 Dublin Horse Show in August that I was now planning an attempt on Everest myself. Keen to help me, Shane suggested that I should meet Robbie Fenlon, who was going to be back in Dublin briefly later in the month with his French Canadian girlfriend Genevieve. The dinner party was arranged so that I could tell Robbie of my plans.

I was quite intimidated at the thought of meeting Robbie. He is a renowned and brilliant climber, who had been a member of the 1993 Irish Everest expedition on the north side of the mountain and had only missed out on bagging the summit because there wasn't enough oxygen on the final push for anyone other than team leader Dawson Stelfox to go to the top.

Far from being intimidating, Robbie turned out to be disarmingly charming, but I still felt diffident about discussing my plans with someone so proficient, a virtuoso of his trade. I thought Robbie would be totally dismissive of me, putting me down as an airhead, a wannabe who had just decided on a whim that it would be fun to climb the highest mountain in the world without any previous experience.

We did discuss my plans, but I'm sure Robbie thought he'd never hear any more about it. If he did have any negative thoughts about me that night, I know I changed his mind the following June, when Shane and I spent a fortnight climbing with him in the Alps.

I think he was genuinely impressed by both my determination and my levels of fitness and reasonable proficiency after such a brief introduction to the world of climbing.

By the time I flew out to Chamonix in June 2004 to meet up with Shane and Joan and, a week later, with Robbie, I'd added two very important people to my climbing arsenal. The first was Aileen MaGuire, a physiotherapist in Dublin who Shane had recommended to me. My knees, after years of being bashed off horses, off fence posts and off the ground, had initially responded well to my new pastime. But they had recently started to give me increasing trouble on descents and, if it hadn't been for Aileen, even hill-walking would have been off the agenda. She not only sorted out my knees, but subsequently treated me for various injuries, including a torn hamstring in February of 2005 that threatened to wipe out the entire Everest project.

The other woman who was to have a profound influence on my climbing career was Jane Carney. A seriously talented climber in her own right, Jane is also a skilled and patient teacher. Hearing about Jane was another in a long line of coincidences that seemed to be conspiring, in the best possible way, to put me on the path towards my goal.

Even though I had left work, I knew that I still had a lot of work to do. I had to learn how to climb for a start. Hill-walking had become a regular pastime and, after getting lost with a friend, David Curran, on a soaking Co Wicklow walk that was meant to end back in Glendalough and wound up in Glenmalure in the neighbouring valley, I realised I had to do something about my mountain skills. Or rather, the lack of them.

After descending in the gathering dusk into the valley, David and I were sitting up at the bar in the pub in Glenmalure, steaming gently in our sodden clothes. We got talking to a couple, Ben and Fionnuala, who eventually gave us a lift back to Glendalough. It was Ben who suggested that I should join the Irish Mountaineering Club and, the following Thursday I went along to the Church Inn, then the regular haunt of the IMC.

Moira Creedon, who has since become president of the IMC, introduced herself and told me that a group of newcomers to the club would be going to the UCD climbing wall the following Tuesday night, if I wanted to come along. I agreed immediately and put the date in my diary. But I had a rather more al fresco date before that as I had booked in for the first part of a two weekend mountain skills course with my Footfalls friend, Christopher Stacey.

The mountain skills weekend turned out to be a huge amount of fun. Despite being at a dinner party on the Friday and a friend's 60th birthday on the Saturday, which meant short rations of sleep on both nights, I managed to stay awake enough to take in a huge amount of information – and a huge amount of walking – over the weekend.

There was a lot of laughing too. The intricacies of map reading, compass use, Naismith's rule, aiming off and the art of triangulation were all a foreign language to me, but I was beginning to interpret some of it by the end of the first two days.

Liz Murray, who was working towards her mountain leader qualification, joined us on the Sunday. She had already heard about my Everest hopes from Christopher and we fell easily into conversation. I explained to her that I hadn't even started climbing yet, but that I did have grand ambitions.

Liz suggested I should get in touch with Jane Carney who, she told me, would be the ideal person to school me in the rudiments of rock climbing. I called Jane the very next day and we agreed to meet in Dalkey Quarry, overlooking Dublin Bay, on the following Friday. It was only when I put the phone down that I realised the day we had picked was Friday the 13th.

Possibly because of my thespian upbringing, I am hugely superstitious. Friday the 13th seemed an ominous day to be making my entry into the climbing world. Little did I realise that Dalkey Quarry is also thronged with magpies that would swoop in a flash of black and white behind me – always singly – mid-climb, daring me to take a hand off the rock to salute them.

Noel Burke, a friend from the gym, had always told me it was bad luck to be superstitious, so I decided that day that I would fly in the face of superstition. To hell with Friday the 13th. And to hell with the magpies. If I was going to climb I needed to depend on skill, not superstition.

I survived the dreaded date. And the dreaded magpies. In fact I not only survived, I positively relished the challenge.

I knew instantly as I followed Jane up the route known as Paradise Lost that this, for me, was paradise. Not paradise regained, as I'd never been there before, but paradise found in all its glory. This was what I wanted to do. I wanted to climb. The combination of supposed ill-omens and the climbing itself had created an adrenaline rush that I found seriously addictive. I was already on the road to becoming an adrenaline junkie again.

Jane and I met the following day in Dublin's best known outdoor adventure store, The Great Outdoors, and Jane introduced me to the store's managing director, Leslie Lawrence, base camp manager for the 1993 Irish expedition and who was to be so generous in his support of me on my Everest venture. Having borrowed Jane's gear for my climbing debut, I was ready to buy my own. Fully kitted out, I arranged to meet Jane again on the Monday for another session in the quarry, but the weather had other ideas. After tackling just one route, Jane and I were cold and wet, so we decided to adjourn to the friendlier climes of the indoor climbing wall in UCD.

I'd gone there the previous Tuesday to meet Moira Creedon but, much as I'd enjoyed the experience, climbing in runners wasn't much fun. Now I had rock shoes and suddenly I wasn't slipping off the holds. I felt I was making great progress until I saw Dermot Somers, another veteran of the 1993 Everest expedition, swarming up the toughest routes with sublime ease and grace.

Two days later I was back at the climbing wall and passed my belay assessment, demonstrating that I could feed out rope for a fellow climber as they ascended, lower them safely back down again and hold them in the event of a fall. Passing the assessment meant that I no longer had to climb with an instructor. It was a minor step on the way to Everest, but it was definitely a step in the right direction.

I'd gone early to the climbing wall that evening, as I had planned to head over to the Arts Block afterwards for Pat Falvey's lecture, Against the Sky, about his 2003 expedition on Everest. At the same time as I had been down in the relative safety of base camp, Pat and his team were pinned up high on the mountain, sheltering from a storm in tents that seemed too flimsy to withstand such a battering. They went for the summit the following night, but Pat had been lucky to survive, ending up snow-blind and dangerously hypoxic. While Mick Murphy and Ger McDonnell forged their way to the top, Pat had to turn his back on the summit. Only the assistance of his team mate Ger on the descent saved him.

Derry dentist Hannah Shields had also been forced to turn around, suffering from frostnip and the agonising pain of three ribs broken during a bout of coughing. It made me realise just how fragile even the strongest climber's body can be, destroyed by something as simple as a stomach upset, the repercussions of a cough or, as I discovered two years later, even a toothache.

The lecture theatre was packed and Pat spoke to an enthralled audience. I stayed on afterwards to talk to him, but he was thronged by well-wishers all wanting to offer messages of good luck for him and Clare O'Leary, who were leaving for another crack at Everest in a month's time.

Eventually I managed to get Pat to myself, but not for long. When I told him that I was heading back to Nepal at the end of March to climb Mera Peak, he suggested I should come to Everest base camp afterwards and stay on at the Irish camp for the summit bid so that I could write about the expedition for the paper. I was thrilled to be invited, but told Pat that I very much doubted I'd be able to extend my trip.

As it turned out I did extend it, but not for as long as I would have needed if I was going to stay on for the summit push on Everest. I wished Pat good luck, went and found Clare to wish her luck as well and then headed home. My mind was already on other things. I had arranged to go on a two-day winter camp with Liz Murray and was getting ridiculously excited about it. I felt like a child waiting for Christmas, giddy and bubbling with enthusiasm. The only adult feeling I could compare it to was falling in love. I had that delicious hollow feeling in the pit of my stomach, but it wasn't solely excitement about spending a night under canvas in Wicklow, it was because I knew this was another tiny piece in the jigsaw – a jigsaw that had a picture of Mount Everest on the box.

I had borrowed a one-man tent from Jane's partner Conor and re-borrowed a sleeping bag from my former work colleague Lorna Siggins, which she had taken to advanced base camp on the north side of Everest when she went as official reporter for the 1993 expedition. I had used the sleeping bag on my trek to the south side base camp the previous year. I thought it would be too warm for a February night out on the Wicklow hills but, as it turned out, I needed every ounce of down it contained.

I met up with Liz and our two fellow campers in the car-park in Laragh on the Saturday morning. The four of us crammed ourselves and all our gear into a taxi, stopping after about eight kilometres, in the shadow of Carrigshouk.

Having paid off the taxi driver, we hauled on our packs and it was only then that I realised just how heavy mine was. A tent, an enormous sleeping bag and mat, waterproof gear, plus food and water for two days and a night amounted to a hefty load for someone unused to carrying so much. And I didn't even have a stove or a saucepan as Liz had said she would bring those.

We embarked on a pretty steep ascent almost immediately and conversation ceased.

Having reached the top of Mullaghcleevaun – at just 849 metres, ridiculously tiny compared to my ultimate goal – we descended steeply to Cleevaun Lough, setting up camp on the shores of the lake. Despite a sharp north-easterly wind, we managed to stay very sheltered, but as soon as the sun went down it became bitterly cold.

We ate early and retired to our individual tents before dark, but were back out again at 7.15 for some night navigation practice. We didn't stay out long. The grass was frozen into ankle-breaking tussocks and the icy peat made for treacherous underfoot conditions on descents.

The steep side of Mullaghcleevaun reared away into the darkness on our right and the lake cut off another aspect, so we did a triangular walk on a bearing that brought us back to camp. We ventured east after that, scrambling through the frigid peat hags. At the top of a short ascent we stopped to take in a stunning view of Dublin at its most beautiful, twinkling diamonds of light on the black velvet blanket of darkness. We considered that reward enough and returned to the warmth of our tents. We were snuggled up in our sleeping bags by just after eight o'clock, a night-time routine that I was to get very used to on future expeditions.

Not surprisingly, I woke early, but it gave me plenty of time to pack up my gear and tape my knees as I'd been instructed by my physio. Over the years, my kneecaps had become misaligned because of outer thigh muscles strengthened by years of riding. The tape pulled my kneecaps back into place and meant that I could now tackle the steepest descents without pain. It was a huge breakthrough.

Knorr quick-cook all-in-one Pasta Formaggio wouldn't be my first choice for breakfast, especially as we'd eaten it the night before too, but it tasted delicious and I knew it would provide the energy we were going to need for five and a half hours of walking with heavy packs back to Laragh.

We broke camp early, dragging on our backpacks and strapping them on firmly for the long haul back up the side of Mullaghcleevaun. It was wickedly cold in the shadow of the hill and the ground was frozen iron-hard. There was plenty of ice too and we had to watch where we put our feet to prevent ourselves skidding back down to the camp site we'd just left. We were greeted by a lethargic winter sun at the top, but its watery rays had very little effect on the temperature. The only way to stay warm was to keep walking.

We descended gradually to Barnacullian, before following the ridge towards the unimaginatively named Stoney Top. But before we reached its summit, the weather deteriorated dramatically. The sun disappeared behind yellowish clouds. A biting wind lashed snow into our faces like handfuls of stinging gravel, but the beauty of our surroundings almost made it worthwhile. It was a lunar landscape, although very different to the images of Everest base camp that were still vivid in my mind. Low floating mists swirled around the frozen peat hags, turned white by a rime of frost. Tufts of grass decorated with a frozen lace of ice looked like shredded fresh coconut with lush white on one side edged with brown on the other.

My hood, drawn tightly to keep out the elements, also kept out my companions, but even the self-imposed isolation was a part of the experience. I remembered Dermot Somers' advice to enjoy the hill or mountain of the moment and not view it simply as a rehearsal for a bigger test.

Our route took us on to Tonelagee and Brockagh mountain, but the weather had cleared to reveal the Wicklow hills in all their winter glory as we made our descent back down to Laragh. It had been a weekend like no other I had experienced, but I felt I had passed yet another initiation test on the way to my ultimate goal.

Three days later I was back out in the Wicklow hills for the second of my mountain skills weekends. I somehow managed to wrap my brain around the complexities of route cards, working out timings for each section of a day in the hills based on Naismith's rule and bringing ascents and descents into the complex calculations. I felt like a child released from a difficult maths lesson when we finally headed off up the hills.

My second stint of night navigation was much more successful than the previous weekend's aborted attempt at Cleevaun Lough. Under a stunningly beautiful moonlit night, the clear star-studded sky made head-torches virtually unnecessary. It was glorious and I felt as though I could have stayed out till dawn.

VI

Ice Cold In Scotland

My next trip to Nepal in early 2004 was a much bigger stepping stone on the path to Everest. The previous November, Sylviane Hickey, a friend from the Temple Street walking group who had been on the first excursion to Nepal and knew all about my Everest ambitions, had phoned me. "Do you want to go climbing in Nepal next year?", she'd asked me in her wonderful mix of a deliciously sexy French accent and Dublinese. "Yes", I'd said enthusiastically. "Tell me more."

Sylviane said she'd heard about a proposed trip to Nepal to climb Mera Peak the following spring. She wasn't interested, but thought that I might be and gave me the contact details of Alan Sharp, who was co-ordinating the whole trip. He told me he was hoping to put together a small group to tackle the 6,400 metre peak and the plan was to leave Dublin at the end of March. It sounded perfect. I could get some experience at altitude, but on a climb that was officially designated a trekking peak.

Now, four and a half months later, I had at least started rock climbing, but I had absolutely no knowledge of mountaineering. I had never even put on a pair of crampons and was very aware of the fact that I needed to experience as many of the conditions that I was likely to meet on Everest as I could. Mera would obviously enhance my climbing CV, but I needed more.

I had arranged to go to Scotland with Christopher Stacey to climb Ben

Nevis the weekend before I was leaving for Nepal. And I had booked in for an ice-climbing lesson at the Ice Factor in Kinlochleven, close to Ben Nevis and home to the largest indoor ice wall in the world and Europe's biggest climbing wall. Now I needed proper ice boots and crampons.

Scotsman Neil Smyth, boot-specialist in the Great Outdoors, had rung to tell me that the boots that I'd ordered had arrived into the shop. I went into town to collect them and Neil showed me how to adjust the crampons so that they would fit snugly on the sole of the boot. He then offered to put on the extreme gaiters that I'd bought to protect both the boots and the lower part of my leg. As Neil struggled to haul them over the boots, I could tell by the grimace on his face that, once on, these gaiters were never going to come off.

Both the boots and crampons came up Ben Nevis with me a week later, but not on my feet. I had decided to take them in my backpack, not because I thought I would need them, but to make my pack heavier in a bid to increase my mountain fitness. It was a filthy day and my waterproof gear was put to a severe test, a severe test that my jacket failed miserably.

Once we got above the snowline, conditions deteriorated even further. We met several groups descending who said they had turned round because it was a total whiteout further up the mountain. By that stage I was climbing with just one other person, Kate Payne, who I'd met on many of the Temple Street training walks and who'd also been on the Nepal trip. Kate was a strong, fit walker, but her brand new boots were far from waterproof and her feet were getting dangerously cold. We were encountering horrendous conditions and I wasn't surprised when I heard Kate's voice from behind. "I'm going to go back", she said, "but you go on."

I turned to see a miserable-looking Kate. She was obviously desperately cold. I knew how quickly hypothermia could set in and I had no intention of leaving her and going for the summit on my own. "No, I'll come back with you", I said to her and I could see the relief on her face.

We weren't that far from the top, but it was the right decision to turn around. Conditions worsened as we made our way back down, with visibility reducing dramatically. I could understand why there were florescent-jacketed members of the mountain rescue team out on patrol on the hill. They'd warned us earlier that the fresh snow had created treacherous conditions higher up.

Half an hour later we almost bumped straight into a group still going up the mountain. It was only when they got right up to us that I realised the group was the rest of our team being led by Christopher. The quintet looked nearly as wretched as poor Kate. Their hoods almost concealed their faces and their shoulders were hunched against the driving snow. They obviously weren't enjoying themselves.

"Did you make it to the top?", Christopher asked. "No", I replied, "it's dreadful up there." "Ah, you should have stayed with the group instead of racing on ahead", Christopher said. I felt like a child being rebuked. Christopher was only half-joking. Well aware of how dangerous Ben Nevis can be in such conditions and how many people have been killed on the mountain, he'd been seriously concerned for Kate's and my safety. As a mountain rescue team member at home, he was well qualified to take his team on up the hill and he did, leaving Kate and me to descend in silence. My crampons and ice boots were still in my backpack, unworn.

Well below the snowline, we came across a person sitting dejectedly on a rock, huddled inside a blue waterproof. It was Jean Stacey-O'Toole, another member of our group. "I'm so cold and so tired", she said, looking up at us from under her hood. She looked tiny and vulnerable and was even more whey-faced than Kate, so we scooped her up and brought her down with us.

We eventually arrived back down at the Ben Nevis Inn where three others from our group were sitting at the far end of the bar around a wood-burning stove. The heat was so intense it was like a furnace. We sat and steamed and gradually Kate and Jean thawed out.

Much later, when I was getting concerned about Christopher and his party, I called him on his mobile and he told me they were just coming off the summit. The news of the others' success depressed me. If they could make it why hadn't I? Maybe I'd been too hasty in turning round. Or maybe I shouldn't have been so impatient. If I'd waited for the rest of the team I could have got to the top with them. I was seriously concerned. If I couldn't make it up the Ben, how on earth was I going to even start on Everest, let alone reach the summit.

It wasn't until one of my welcome home parties after I had summitted Everest that I discovered that Christopher and the team never did get to the top of Ben Nevis that day. It was Christopher's joke and one in which the rest of the gang were complicit. But, I was assured, they did make it when they went back for another shot the following October.

The downpours continued on into the night, but the next day dawned sunny and clear. I was going to be climbing indoors on the ice wall, while the others went for a gentle amble along the West Highland Way after the rigours of the Ben. Christopher had helped me organise the ice-climbing and arranged for the walking group to go from Kinlochleven so that he could drop me off at the Ice Factor.

We drove out of Fort William heading south along the coastline before branching off the main road towards Kinlochleven. Dressed in its early spring colours, nature was at its most sensational. The glorious natural beauty of the lochs and their surrounding hills contrasted starkly with the dreary drabness of Kinlochleven itself. But, I consoled myself, if I had to be indoors on such a glorious day, at least I would be adding a new skill to my armoury for Everest.

The Ice Factor's chief instructor, Simon Powell, introduced himself before talking through what he had planned for me in the giant freezer that housed the 18-metre high ice wall. There were three main climbing areas, all with ropes dangling down from steel chains at the top so that novice climbers could always be safely belayed from below. There was also an ice cave, where Simon introduced me to the art of swinging my axes so that they would bite solidly into the ice with minimal effort from me. It wasn't easy to master, with the point of the axe frequently bouncing straight off the ice and sending showers or even chunks of ice straight into my face. But there was something deeply satisfying about the dull thunk the axe made when my aim was true.

Simon then showed me how to use the front points of my crampons in conjunction with the axes, always keeping three points of contact with the ice. And then it was up to me. I climbed almost non-stop for three hours. It felt like three minutes. I just adored it and, if I could have extended the session, I would have, but other clients were already donning their crampons outside and I had no option but to call it a day.

VII

Peaks Of Perfection

Failing on Ben Nevis was a huge disappointment, but it reaffirmed my belief that I had to redouble my efforts and fast-track both my climbing skills and my experience at altitude if I was to keep Everest within my sights. The Scottish ice climbing had been an important step towards honing my technical skills and I added another valuable string to my altitude bow in the following month when I returned to Nepal to tackle my first 6,000 metre peak and ended up bagging two.

Mera, to the east of the Lukla, stands at 6,400 metres but, despite its height, it is officially designated a trekking peak. Of the five-strong expedition led by Alan Sharp, none of us had any real climbing experience and I was keenly aware that we might find the new exposure to altitude tough. I knew that Mera was not technically demanding, but it would still be enough of a challenge to form part of the ever-steepening learning curve towards Everest.

My crampons, which had only seen action on the ice wall in Scotland, finally made their debut on real Himalayan ice on the Mera glacier. But there was another new experience too. The mind-numbing cold, combined with the altitude, weakened my body far more than I had expected. The long slog on summit day sapped my energy dramatically, but it gave me the chance to push my body out of my comfort zone and beyond.

Tired though I was, I discovered that my strength returned surprisingly rapidly. So when the opportunity arose to extend my trip and take in the 6,200 metre Island Peak, I jumped at the chance. Island Peak, just south of Everest and almost in the shadow of Lhotse, is also relatively straightforward, but tackling two 6,000ers within 10 days would provide a good test of my stamina.

A bout of vomiting and diarrhoea the night before our summit bid left me drained, but I knew the psychological value of success on this second peak would outweigh any physical distress. I was seriously struggling on the final ascent, but my determination pushed me on through the pain barrier and, suddenly, there was no more climbing to do. I was there. Another summit.

I was elated and felt like I'd climbed Everest already, but my real objective was obscured by the huge face of Lhotse behind us. It was a sobering sight. Island Peak felt pretty high to me, but Lhotse was more than 2,300 metres higher and Everest another 350 metres higher again. I still had a lot more work to do before I was ready.

I may have been worn out by my first real experience of altitude, but it had given me a base level of fitness that was to stand me in good stead for my climbing trip to Chamonix six weeks later. Shane and Joan Cleary were already in France and I flew out to join them so that Shane and I could get a week's hill-work done before we met up with our guide, Robbie Fenlon.

Steve Adkins, a close friend of my twin sister Megan, had generously given us the use of his apartment in Les Bois, just outside Chamonix. The apartment was within walking distance of the Flégère cable car and was perfect for almost instant access to the mountains. By the time we met up with Robbie a week later, Shane and I had topped up our fitness with a series of long days spent in the hills. We hit the rock as soon as we had Robbie on board, driving to Vallorcine for a day on the crag. That day we re-christened Robbie Spiderman in deference to his supreme style as he swarmed up a rock-face. And I became Catwoman.

It was the start of two weeks of intensive climbing, taking in mountains and glaciers as well as rock. We climbed in France and Italy and even drove down to the Med for a spot of sea-cliff climbing when the weather turned bad in the Alps.

We learned lots, we laughed lots and we ate lots. Overcrowded huts meant we had to abandon an attempt on Mont Blanc, but we raced up Gran Paradiso in Italy just for fun. It was a perfect fortnight and I felt that my climbing had improved hugely by the end.

But the trip had an even more perfect finish as it added another all-important step on the road to Everest. I was toying with the idea of climbing Cho Oyu, the 8,201 metre peak that straddles the Nepalese and Tibetan borders and thought it particularly appropriate that I should tackle it in 2004, the golden jubilee of the mountain first being climbed. On October 19, 1954, two members of an Austrian expedition, team leader Herbert Tichy and Joseph Joechle with a Nepalese Sherpa, Pasang Dawa Lama, became the first to reach the summit of a peak that New Zealander Edmund Hillary had attempted in 1952, the year before he entered the history books for his success on Everest. Thankfully I was unaware that the world's most famous bee-keeper had failed on his Cho Oyu bid, otherwise I might have re-thought my plans.

I asked Robbie's advice and he was unhesitating in his agreement that I should definitely consider Cho Oyu as my next peak. "You should talk to Russell Brice", he said, telling me that this other New Zealander, legendary for his commercial expeditions to Everest, also did annual trips to Cho Oyu.

The Les Bois apartment wasn't available for our final week, so we relocated to a tiny flat in Argentiere, literally a few hundreds yards away from Russell's Chamonix Experience office and shop, another in the string of coincidences that paved my way towards Everest.

Meeting Russell for the first time was like a two-way job interview. He was sizing me up as a potential client and I was checking him out as a potential guide. My journalistic traits to the fore, I quizzed him about the logistics of putting together a major expedition. His CV more than stood up to scrutiny. As well as his own personal successes, including being the first to tackle the fearsome pinnacles route on Everest, he had also established one of the best if not the best success record on both Everest and Cho Oyu in his 10 years of running commercial expeditions.

I was already picturing myself making successful ascents of both when Russell brought me down to earth by telling me that he only did expeditions to the north side of Everest. "I specialise in the north side", he said in a Kiwi accent untouched by living for well over a decade in France. I knew that the north side was much tougher than the south and suddenly felt the handicap of my inexperience weighing me down. This was never going to work.

"Why don't you come to Cho Oyu", Russ suggested, "and then you can make up your mind about Everest afterwards. I always keep places for clients who've already done Cho Oyu with me."

We discussed dates, but even those didn't seem to fit. Suddenly the route to Everest seemed not quite so smooth. The Cho Oyu expedition started on August 26. I would still be in Athens reporting on the Olympics and wouldn't be back in Dublin until August 29. "No worries", said Russ, drawing up a new itinerary that would allow me to arrive in Kathmandu on September 2 and then go overland to catch up with the rest of the team at advanced base camp by September 12.

The hurdles were evaporating already. I agreed to think about it and Russ, salesman to the last, advised me not to think too long, the places were filling up fast. I left the office on a cloud of excitement. Shane was equally enthusiastic when I got back to the apartment and, when I met up with Robbie later that evening, he couldn't understand why I hadn't said yes immediately.

"But would I be capable of doing the north side of Everest?", I asked Robbie. "No doubt", he replied. "Go for it. Ring him now." I didn't have Russell's number with me and, by the time we left the restaurant it was too late to call him, but I already had a text written on my mobile saying that I was a definite yes for Cho Oyu and that I'd finalise Everest plans after that. As soon as I got through the door into the apartment I raced to the kitchen, punched Russ's number into my phone and sent the text. The "message sent" screen was enough confirmation for me. I was in.

I had very little time for climbing over the next five weeks, but I crammed in as much as I could – including a trip to Carrauntouhill with Shane – because I knew that the whole of August would be pretty sedentary. A week at Dublin Horse Show, followed by almost three weeks in Athens, all at sea level and the Olympic stint in horrendously hot temperatures. It wasn't the ideal build-up to my first major expedition.

My confidence took two sizeable knocks before I even left Dublin for the Games. Pat Falvey, who had just succeeded in his bid to become the first Irishman to climb Everest from both the north and south sides, met Shane and me for a drink when we were down in Kerry to do Carrauntouhill. "Don't do the north side", Pat warned me after I told him I was considering tackling Everest from Tibet now that Clare O'Leary and Samantha O'Carroll had succeeded from Nepal. "You're compromising your chances of success. The Second Step is very intimidating and summit day is very tough." It was as though he'd poured a bucket of ice down the back of my tee-shirt.

But worse was to come. The night before my departure for Athens, Dermot Somers rang me. He'd said when I met him at the UCD climbing wall that I could call him if I needed any advice. I'd phoned and left a message. This was him returning my call, but his reaction to my news that I would be climbing Cho Oyu in preparation for Everest certainly wasn't what I was expecting.

"Everest is becoming less Everest every day", he said to me. "There are too many commercial expeditions with inexperienced climbers relying totally on the expedition leaders and staff. The greater the altitude, the greater the risk. You need to be independent, self-reliant and that only comes with years of experience."

I said I was working towards that and, knowing he was very friendly with Robbie Fenlon, told him that I'd been training with Robbie so that, if the worst happened and I found myself alone on the mountain, I might have a chance of being able to get myself down.

"Well you won't", Dermot said bluntly. "Way more experienced mountaineers have been bounced off that mountain and many of them have died." I thought it prudent to steer him away from that train of thought and asked him if he had ever thought about going back. "No", he said emphatically, "partly because it's the toughest thing I've ever done, but also because the mountain is being overrun by commercial expeditions and inexperienced climbers. You may feel that there's a barb in that remark."

I don't believe Dermot intended wounding me with his comments. He was simply expressing his own views strenuously. What I didn't know at the time was that commercial expeditions are anathema to Dermot. I heard afterwards that he'd said in a radio interview that he views climbers using commercial outfits as "high-altitude tourists".

Most purists would agree with Dermot's sentiments, but it's too sweeping a statement to dismiss all members of commercial expeditions as high-altitude tourists. Of course there are many inexperienced climbers that sign up with the commercial operators, but the screening process involves more than just proof of the ability to pay. And the mountain itself will usually weed out the weakest before they become a danger either to themselves or to others.

At the opposite end of the spectrum, there are many vastly experienced climbers who simply don't have the time to get involved in the logistics of organising their own expedition, so hand over the task – and a considerable amount of money – to commercial operators so that they can concentrate solely on the climb. It doesn't make them any less deserving of a place on the mountain.

An email from Robbie several weeks later, timed to arrive just before I left for Tibet, cheered me up enormously. It was like an antidote to Dermot's remarks.

"I'm sure you'll stand a very good chance if you get the right conditions", the email ran. "You definitely showed yourself to be tough, determined and capable when you were here in June. I also think you have a very positive attitude and a lot of endurance. These qualities are what seem to get results on the type of mountain you are going to. But go easy on the other members of your expedition. I'm sure they'll get burnt out if they try to keep up with you."

It was just the affirmation I needed.

I returned from the Olympic Games in Athens totally drained. Show jumper Cian O'Connor had won Ireland's first ever equestrian medal at Olympic level. Not only was it Ireland's only medal of the 2004 Games, it was gold. The media frenzy was instantaneous and massive. The workload, always heavy at any Olympics, intensified proportionately. The Irish public couldn't get enough of the golden boy and, as an equestrian correspondent, I was constantly being called on for expert opinion.

In the midst of the celebrations I was trying to get myself into mountain-mode, but external forces seemed to be conspiring against me. The killing of 12 Nepalis in Iraq had sparked riots in Kathmandu. A curfew had been imposed and the airport was closed. The Arab airlines had all cancelled their flights for the foreseeable future and I was booked with Qatar Airways. My Cho Oyu expedition was in serious doubt.

Re-routing through Beijing and Lhasa seemed to be a possibility, but I needed a permit to get into Tibet and that was sitting in Kathmandu awaiting my arrival in a city that had been closed to the outside world. I called in favours from everyone I knew and several that I didn't, including the Minister for Foreign Affairs. Two days of intense negotiations ensued, during which phone-calls were being made on my behalf throughout the night between Dublin and Beijing. But to no avail. I had a visa to enter China, but still no permit for Tibet.

Things didn't sound too good in Kathmandu. A newspaper report revealed that police had shot dead a man who broke the curfew in the Nepalese capital. The city's main mosque had been ransacked and a copy of the Koran torn up. The Saudi Arabian Airlines and Qatar Airways offices had also been targeted. Despite the violence, I still thought I'd be better taking my chance in Kathmandu than going to Beijing and getting stuck there.

The curfew was ongoing, but the airport was re-opened and I was re-booked onto a Thai Airways flight. It turned out to be the perfect solution. Fellow expedition member, Valerio Massimo, had always intended catching the September 3 flight out of Heathrow. If my original flight hadn't been cancelled I would have had to wait for him in Kathmandu anyway. At least now we would be arriving together.

When I'd first spoken to Valerio during the flight changing panic, I'd told him that I was trying to get a permit for entry into Tibet from Beijing and perhaps it would be a good idea to put his name onto it too. "What's your full name?", I asked him. "Valerio Massimo", he replied, his very English tones belying his obviously Italian roots. There was a brief silence. "Would they need my name as it appears on my passport?" "Probably", I said.

There was a longer silence before he said, with a degree of diffidence, "It's Prince Valerio Massimo". Assuming it was a joke, I inhaled sharply for a witty riposte. "It's actually His Serene Highness Prince Valerio Massimo", he added before I had a chance to respond. I was too dumbfounded to speak.

His languid arrival at the Terminal Three departure gate the next day, long after our 12.30 flight was due to depart, suggested that he was well used to being waited for. And waited on, I suspected.

Everyone else had long since boarded and the Thai Airways staff were doing their best to get me onto the plane. I'd told them I was waiting for the final passenger, expecting Valerio to arrive in a breathless whirl of bags at any moment. But far from rushing, he strolled in, tall and unruffled, as though it was his private jet waiting out on the tarmac.

I had been up at four that morning and the combination of sleep depriva- tion and shredded nerves from the endless visa and travel negotiations had left me on a fairly short fuse. Hearing that the reason for Valerio's late arrival was that he'd spent the morning enlisting the help of a personal shopper to pick out a selection of gourmet foods which he felt were vital for a trip to Tibet did nothing to improve my humour.

I couldn't decide if I was relieved or annoyed when Valerio swanned straight upstairs to first class when we finally got on the plane, leaving me to my fate in steerage. At least it meant I could regain my composure rather than sit seething, but before I had a chance to do either, Valerio was standing over me with two glasses of champagne. He handed one to me, chinked glasses and then, mercu- rially, he was gone. I forgave him immediately.

We were met in Kathmandu by Tamding from Mountain Experi- ence, the Nepalese arm of Russell's company Himalayan Experi- ence. He took my trolley and started to wheel it towards a ramshackle mini-bus while Valerio struggled with a wayward trolley groaning under the weight of two huge and obviously brand new North Face duffel bags. As he attempted a left-hand turn through the glass doors out of the baggage hall, there was an avalanche of red bags and a small child just missed being crushed beneath 66 kilograms of climbing gear, best Italian Parmigiana, olive oil and gourmet risottos.

As we drove out of the airport, with the luggage crammed into the back of the mini-bus, I asked Tamding about the curfew. "It's on now", he said, "but tourists can go through."

The streets of the capital were eerily quiet. The mayhem of blaring horns, roaring engines and the toot-toot of bicycle rickshaws had been replaced by groups of gun-wielding soldiers, the odd sacred cow and a scattering of mangy dogs. Even the birds had been silenced. It was very different to the crazily bustling city I had left only four months earlier.

Soldiers stopped us at every junction demanding to see Tamding's pass, but we still made incredibly quick passage through the streets to the Hotel Tibet in the Lazimpat area of the city. Owner/manager Tsering greeted us in the lobby in perfect English learnt, she told me later, from Irish nuns at the Catholic school in Kathmandu.

The warmth of Tsering's hospitality was in stark contrast to the scene at Friendship Bridge two days later when we crossed the border into Tibet. Huge gold lettering welcomed us to China, but the treatment I witnessed being meted out to a local woman was far from welcoming as she was given a stinging slap across the face by one of the armed and acne-ridden soldiers when she didn't move fast enough.

It was a chilling reminder that Tibet, despite its official "autonomous" status, is still an occupied country and the Chinese border guards are a constant and not always pleasant presence. Individuals are not granted permits for Tibet and journalists certainly aren't welcomed, so I was listed on the expedition's group permit as a housewife and wasn't about to reveal my true calling.

With our passports stamped, we drove on up through the sensational Kola Kosi gorge towards our base for the next two nights, Nyalam. It was a considerable jump in altitude from the 1,800 metres of Kodari, our last stop in Nepal, to 3,700 metres in Nyalam, so we took it easy the next day, drifting down the main street and checking out the sights. Government-sponsored shops were stocked with everything from cleavers to bananas, but the non-Government shops offered very little.

We left town two days later without regret, but with a pillow. Valerio had tried to buy his pillow from the Snowland Hotel where we'd been staying. "No, you buy new one in Xi Feng shop", he was told and directed to a shop a couple of doors down from the hotel. It was opposite the "Department Store", possibly the tiniest but certainly the least well stocked establishment in town. In contrast, the Xi Feng shop had everything, including pillows, and Valerio came out clutching a hideous blue nylon creation, complete with frilly edges and the embroidered legend "Happy Life" across its centre. I could picture the words branded, along with the creases of sleep, onto Valerio's face.

We swept out of Nyalam on the Friendship Highway, which rapidly deteriorated from a road into a dusty trail across the brown, undulating Tibetan plateau. And finally, as we approached Tingri, the last bastion of anything resembling civilisation before we headed for the mountains, we could see our goal, the massive lumbering shoulders of Cho Oyu. We climbed stiffly out of the jeep outside our billet for the night, which the narrow vertical sign declared to be the

Hi Ma La Ya Ho Tel. The grimly filthy courtyard, surrounded on three sides by single-storey dilapidated dwellings, made me think it must have been used, many years earlier, as the set for a Tibetan version of Psycho, except there were no showers.

As we turned onto the new road to Cho Oyu base camp the following day, the mountain directly ahead of us appeared monstrously large, considerably bigger than the distant triangle of Everest. It seemed odd to have my two goals laid out in front of me, but before I had a chance to reflect on the enormity of the task I'd set myself, the mountains disappeared from view in a sandstorm kicked up by the jeep in front of us.

Having been told it would take us four hours to get to base camp, we were surprised when our driver stopped beside a sprawl of tents after only 45 minutes. But we could see the Himalayan Experience logo on the tents nearest us and two men were coming towards the jeep, their hands already outstretched in welcome. The first, who introduced himself as Kul Burdhu, grasped my hand with both of his and shook it warmly, displaying a dazzling array of gold teeth as his face creased into an enormous grin. Chhuldim, a tall and sparse Tibetan with his long black hair entwined with red fabric plaited across the top of his head, also proffered the double handshake of welcome.

We were now at 4,900 metres. Far from my appetite diminishing, I was already hungry and looking forward to lunch. But, with a high percentage of Nepalese staff, Russell Brice runs all his expeditions on Nepali, not Chinese time. Although my watch said it was midday and my stomach said it was lunchtime, the clock in the large mess tent said it was only 9.45. It was going to be a long wait.

Food took on a ridiculous importance over the next few days as Valerio and I waited for Russell, known as Big Boss to his Nepalese and Tibetan staff, to give us the go-ahead to join the rest of the expedition at advanced base camp. Knowing that an army marches on its stomach, Russ feeds his troops with the best food available and Valerio and I certainly didn't want for anything at base camp, or at ABC when we finally got there.

A row of large blue barrels lined the walls of the mess tent. Each was stuffed to the gunwales with a vast array of snacks and comfort food. And three large meals were cooked for us each day. But Valerio preferred his own food and would frequently rustle up a risotto or pasta for the two of us in place of cook boy Kul Burdhu's offerings.

The local Tibetans were rather more enthusiastic about the Himex food and the women would stand at the open door of our mess tent, smiling straight at us as they lifted a packet of crisps or a chocolate bar. I watched as one of them, carrying a small child piggy-back with its naked cheeks gleaming through the rear-end opening in its tiny dungarees, vanished into the store tent, where a row of dark red carcasses hung. Her childless companion, who I hadn't even noticed going in, dashed out of the tent with a very noticeable bulge under her blue fleece jacket. Shrieking with mirth she disappeared with her spoils.

Speaking to Russ at ABC on the radio later in the day, I was disappointed to discover that the expedition had already held a puja, the religious blessing ceremony that always precedes any climbing expedition in the Himalaya and without which the Sherpas won't set foot on the mountain. I was inclined to agree with the Sherpas and wanted to ensure I'd appeased all the mountain deities before I trespassed on their territory.

With nothing else to fill the time, we watched other teams haggling with the yak men over the price of getting their gear up to ABC. Everything had to be weighed and, once a price had been agreed, the yaks had to be herded in and loaded up. It was a noisy and lengthy business, with the yakpas shouting vociferously at each other, their yaks and the climbers that were trying to hire them. But at least it was entertainment.

Valerio and I were keen to get away from the unremitting dreariness of base camp, but Russ was insistent that we spent three nights down there before we moved up to ABC. New Zealander Lydia Bradey, one of the Himex guides, backed Russ's view. "Take your time", she said over the radio, "it's pretty high up here and I've been getting my share of headaches."

I'd been hit by a stomach upset and, as on Island Peak, didn't know whether it was something I'd eaten or the altitude, but I was happy enough to postpone our departure for 24 hours.

Kul Burdhu had organised a tractor to take us up to interim camp and we would then walk the rest of the way up to ABC. We loaded our gear into the small trailer and the three of us – Valerio, Kul Burdhu and me – squeezed ourselves in on top of everything. I was perched on top of a huge sack of toilet rolls. Valerio and I were delighted with our chariot. Complete with prayer flags fluttering above its tiny engine, the ancient three-wheeled tuk-tuk looked like a cross between Easy Rider and a giant roller-skate. But it wasn't so impressive when it started moving. For all its size, the engine was unbelievably noisy and belched out clouds of dense, oily black fumes that threatened to suffocate us as we trundled at a desperately slow pace out of base camp. We would have been quicker – and cleaner – walking.

It took us an hour and a half to get to interim camp. We probably could have walked it in half the time. Queasy from the journey, we went into a drooping tent, where huge yak carcasses hung from the roof and a stove smoked gently in the centre. We were gestured over to the carpeted seats at the far end of the tent and weaved our way through the roughly painted red boxes that served as tables. I drank boiled water, Kul Burdhu slurped Pot Noodle and Valerio stalked in and out of the tent trying to organise porters.

Two had come down from ABC and were now Pot Noodling with Kul Burdhu, but they obviously weren't going to manage all the gear. There was a great picking up of bags and a great shaking of heads but no progress. Eventually it was decided that we'd be better with two yaks. But the yaks had to be caught first and then fed, by hand, with tsampa patties made out of barley flour.

Two long hours later we left interim camp in the company of Karsang, a Tibetan with a delightfully warm and expressive face. He and I walked together, but conversation was restricted by the language barrier. As we scrambled up the rocky trail he picked up an enormous wing feather, presumably from one of the huge black goraks that were constantly circling overhead like vultures. "You fly to top", he said as he handed me the feather.

We didn't fly to ABC. It was a tortuously slow journey along an endless moraine. A young yak carrying the heaviest of Valerio's North Face bags, presumably the one containing the food, eventually collapsed under the load. The yakpas sat down and waited until it had recovered. But finally, as we were trudging our way up a sharp ascent, I looked ahead and saw what looked like a figure sitting on a rock.

"Who's that up there?", I asked Valerio as I pointed uphill. "It's a cairn", he said dismissively. But five minutes later the cairn stood up and waved. It was Mark Inglis, a New Zealander who was bidding to become the first double amputee to climb Cho Oyu. He had lost both his legs to frostbite from the knee down after being stranded in a two-week storm on Mount Cook 22 years earlier. He'd eventually got back into climbing and had made an emotional ascent of Mount Cook before deciding to head for the Himalaya. But his athletic prowess wasn't confined solely to climbing. He had also won silver in the paralympic cycling in Sydney 2000.

Mark was a delight. Hugely warm and entertaining, with a wicked sense of humour, he had come down to welcome Valerio and me and had brought tea and chocolate. And the warmth of the welcomes continued when we arrived at ABC. The rest of the Himex team were as anxious to meet us as we were to meet them. We'd all been consumed with curiosity about each other and now, finally, we were a full team.

I was woken the following morning by an enormous splodge of condensation plopping onto my face. I had slept right through the night at an altitude of 5,800 metres, the same height as high camp on Mera where sleep had eluded me.

The rest of the expedition members had been at the boulder field that calls itself ABC for eight days now and the waiting was driving them stir-crazy. But, after the boredom of base camp, I was delighted to be with the Himex team and the other 38 expeditions bidding to summit in the 50th anniversary year of the mountain first being climbed. And the prince and I even managed to gate-crash a neighbouring team's puja.

Three days after my arrival at ABC, Russ told us that the weather had cleared higher up the hill and we would be heading for a two-night stay at camp I the following day.

I set off with American-born Chuck Dasey. He was the perfect climbing companion. Easy going, with a wonderfully dry sense of humour, he would sit in the mess tent, saying little but missing nothing. Then he'd suddenly unleash a verbal sidewinder missile that would catch everybody amidships. I adored his company. But the combined effects of altitude and a sedentary August were beginning to tell on me and I struggled on the long and unforgiving slog up the scree slope to camp I. I wasn't sorry when I finally saw the Himex tents perched at the bottom of a rearing snow slope.

The next day gave us the chance of a dry run up the ice cliff, a 50-metre wall of sheer ice between camps I and II and one of only two bits of technical climbing on the mountain. Close to the back of the group, I didn't realise that the others had all bypassed the direct route up the face and had taken on an airy traverse on fixed ropes, so I ploughed straight up the ice, collapsing in an exhausted heap at the top. I hoped I'd be stronger on the summit push.

Mark Inglis, known simply as Inglis, developed problems with one of his prosthetic legs on the descent of the snow slopes on the way back to camp I. Some emergency repair work was carried out, but word spread on the mountain telegraph that one of the Himex clients had broken their leg on the hill. "Yeah", Russ said, when questioned by climbers from another team, "Inglis broke his ankle, but I went back up with a few nuts and bolts and it's okay now."

When we descended back to ABC for a rest and some calorie cramming before the summit push, Inglis opted to stay up at camp I for what turned into a prolonged and lonely vigil. The moraine and the scree slope were tough on his stumps and he wanted to make sure they were well healed before the summit push.

After all the talk about his broken leg, Inglis's ears must have been burning at breakfast time the next day too. We'd had no radio contact since we'd left him at camp I the day before, but someone suggested that he'd probably used parts from his radio to mend his leg and would have to lie with his limbs in the air to get reception.

That same day we heard the welcome news that three Singaporeans and three Sherpas had reached the summit. At last a trail had been broken, but the forecast of four days of high winds on the upper reaches of the mountain didn't bode too well for an early summit for anyone else. We'd already heard of other teams being blown back off the mountain, so our planned September 22 departure was postponed for 24 hours.

I went and lay in my tent for the afternoon, listening lazily to the sounds of Layla and Shine On You Crazy Diamond drifting up from the mess tent. Naturally gregarious, I was surprised that I found the hours alone in my tent not solitary but restorative. I was building up to the biggest challenge of my life so far and, although physically I wasn't at my peak after my stint in Athens, I knew my mind would be right. I no longer sought the camaraderie of the mess tent card games, fun though they were. I was enjoying a more contemplative state and, after the puja, felt that I was nearing readiness.

The delights of Mountain Monopoly and cards were beginning to wear thin for the others too, particularly for the early birds who'd already spent 11 days at ABC. But tensions were temporarily relieved by a monster snowball fight, with the Sherpas displaying an enviable ability to pound their enemies – us – with deadly accuracy and at a speed that would put a machine-gun to shame.

Karsang, the feather-giver, employed a barrel lid alternately as a tray for ammunition provided by his cook-boy son Xangbu or as a shield. We were losing the battle already, but when a posse of eight Sherpas appeared over the crest of the moraine like Indians at the top of the pass, we were outnumbered and outgunned. Even with reinforcements from a neighbouring Aussie expedition, we westerners had to admit defeat.

But, finally, on September 23, we were given the green light and took off up the dreaded scree slope for one last time en route to the top. Camp I meant a reunion with Inglis, who looked wide-eyed and distinctly thinner than when we'd last seen him. The following morning we moved on up to the ice cliff where, in deference to summit day, we opted for the traverse before moving on up the energy-sapping steep snow-fields to camp II. At 7,000 metres, this was a new height record for me and for most of my team-mates.

From the plateau of camp II we could see our next day's goal. It looked a relatively short distance and didn't seem too steep. But appearances, in this instance, were incredibly deceptive. It turned out to be a seriously laborious slog. Even the Sherpas, who climbed in short, sharp bursts of activity, had to stop frequently and stood, bent almost double with their hands on their thighs, their sides heaving.

But the weather was perfect. Sunny, warm days were followed by bitterly cold nights, heralded by some of the most beautiful sunsets I have ever seen as the dying rays tinged the peaks around us flamingo pink. The mountain above us looked magnificent as thin streels of candy-floss cloud scudded across its shining upper flanks.

As we settled ourselves in at camp III that night, I took a final lingering look out of the tent at our first challenge on summit day, the rock band, a sheer face of rock and ice only a few hundred metres away from us. We'd be tackling it in the dark as we were scheduled to be out on the mountain at 2.30am.

The prince and I were, as predicted by Russ, delayed and it was closer to 3.30 by the time we left. Sadly, Mark Inglis was already on his way back by then, forced into abandoning his summit attempt only 100 metres away from camp after a succession of problems. He was having trouble with his stumps but, much worse, his oxygen mask obscured his feet. We were all afflicted with a similar problem, but we could at least feel where we were putting our feet. Inglis, quite literally, had to be able to see his feet to be able to climb. He spent the whole of the next day, at 7,400 metres, taking the padding out of his mask and remodelling it so that he could see and breathe at the same time.

Cocooned in our down suits and with our oxygen masks strapped to our faces, the rest of us were in a silent, narrow world lit only by our head torches. But I'd barely got started when I had to stop. Trying to clip into the fixed line at the bottom of the rock band was proving a nightmare. My down mitts just didn't allow me the dexterity required even for this simplest of tasks. I had to take them off and find a replacement pair of gloves in my backpack before I could start the ascent up the rock face ahead of me.

The delay at least meant that I didn't have to queue and it was a joy to get onto something technical. My crampons scraped on the rock or bit into patches of ice as I climbed. Without the handicap of my mitts, I was able to use my jumar on the fixed rope and, as I hauled myself up, a mental image of me on the Second Step on Everest summit day flashed into my head.

As I scrambled over the lip at the top of the rock band, I looked ahead at the line of head torches straggling up the mountain. In the dark it was impossible to tell where the head torches ended and the stars began, but I knew I had some catching up to do.

I managed to tag onto the tail-enders of our team at the top of a steep snow slope as the sun came up almost unnoticed. One minute I was climbing in the dark, the next the peaks around me had turned from black silhouettes to pearl grey and suddenly to a dazzling white as the sun's rays hit them.

The day was already becoming uncomfortably warm and I had managed to spill almost the entire contents of my water bottle. As I plodded on upwards, my throat began to feel as though someone had scoured it with a wire brush. Swallowing was becoming increasingly difficult. I was getting seriously dehydrated and losing touch with the rest of the team. My stamina, never tested to this extent before, had finally drained away with the last of my water.

It was a battle of wills to keep going and my resolve took a further dive when I saw some of my fellow team members on their way back down. This wasn't the way I had pictured summit day. I stopped and scooped snow into my mouth, trying to soothe my parched throat.

But my determination not to be beaten was still strong and, finally, I could see the prayer flags that marked the true summit and there, behind them, was the magical view of Everest's north face. I had done it. I'd summitted my first 8,000 metre mountain and there, right in front of me, was my goal for next year. It was terrifying and thrilling all in an instant.

Kiwi guide Lydia Bradey and Lopsang Sherpa took summit photos for me as I held my miniature tricolour aloft, or as aloft as my shattered body would allow. And then we turned our backs on Everest to make the long descent to camp II. Close to exhaustion, I could see how easy it would be just to flop down in the snow and give up. I had to push myself harder than I'd ever pushed myself before, coming face to face with the wall I'd only heard others talk about. I finally fell back into camp and, after attempting to eat, slept fitfully, woken constantly by the fear that I would never wake again which I remembered so vividly from my first major riding accident. But I did wake and found that my strength had returned.

By the time we got back to ABC, news had come through that the two Marks – Inglis and his guide Mark Whetu – had summitted that morning with Lopsang, the Sherpa who had climbed, oxygenless, to the summit with me the day before. It was Lopsang's 10th summit and his second in two days. And it was Inglis' 45th birthday. We sang Happy Birthday over the radio to him that night.

While others were blown off the mountain or simply failed to make it, the entire Himex team had – in the words of another great Kiwi climber, Edmund Hillary - "knocked the bastard off". It was time to celebrate. And celebrate we did, from base camp to the seediness of Xangmu and all the way to Kathmandu.

Flushed with our success, some of us now had much bigger ambitions, but I was depressed by my failing energy levels. If I had flagged so badly on an 8,200 metre peak, how would I cope on the north side of Everest where top camp was another 100 metres higher, with the most demanding part of the climb still to come on summit day.

Russ put it still further into perspective. "Everest is a major expedition. Cho Oyu is just a game in comparison", he told me. "Everest is about half as tough again and twice as painful."

Mark Whetu was even more blunt. "Everest is 10 times tougher", he said. The Maori climber still bares the scars, both physical and mental, to prove exactly how tough Everest is. A three-time summiteer, Whetu had been forced to bivouac overnight close to the summit after reaching the top with a client desperately late on a May evening in 1994. Whetu lost his toes to frostbite. The client lost his life.

But for all his realism, Whetu was still convinced I stood a good chance of making it to the top of Everest. "You just have to go with the right attitude", he told me. "If you don't think you can make it you won't. You've got to believe in yourself. It's a mental challenge just as much as a physical one."

Russell put the gun to my head the night before my departure at an ungodly hour the next morning. "If you're coming to Everest, make up your mind now and leave your boots here in Kathmandu. I can put them in store for you so you won't have to take them home and they'll be here for you when you come back next year."

My decision made, I left my boots in Kathmandu. I never saw them again.

VIII

Family Tragedy

As I flew home to Dublin my mind was a whirl of excitement. A text message from my climbing buddy Shane Cleary told me that I was the first Irish woman to summit Cho Oyu. And now I was committed to Everest for next season. I couldn't believe how much my life had changed. I reflected on six wonderful weeks spent in one of the harshest environments on earth, but one in which the strongest of friendships were forged.

How was I going to get back to normal life after such an experience, I wondered. But I didn't have a chance to get back to even a semblance of normal life. No sooner was I back in Dublin than the biggest equestrian story I'd ever had to cover broke. Cian O'Connor, the show jumper who had saved Ireland's sporting morale by claiming Olympic gold in Athens just before I left for Tibet, announced that his horse Waterford Crystal had tested positive for prohibited substances. All hell broke loose. The media frenzy that had surrounded the winning was as nothing compared to that which surrounded the possible losing of the medal.

I was thrown straight into the thick of it and, at one stage, could even claim squatters' rights on the front page of *The Irish Times*. As one of only a handful of specialist equestrian journalists, I was also constantly being asked to do television and radio interviews about the controversy. Suddenly the mountains seemed to belong to a different life.

The drama surrounding O'Connor and the medal ran and ran. The rider requested confirmatory analysis of the B sample of his horse's urine. On its way from the laboratory in Paris that had declared the original positive result the sample was intercepted in the grounds of the top testing lab in England. It was never seen again. A headline emblazoned across the entire front page of one of the tabloids the following day ran: "Who's taken the piss?" The British police were called in.

That night the offices of the Irish Equestrian Federation were broken into and files relating to another horse of O'Connor's that had tested positive to one of the same drugs were taken. The information contained in those files was then leaked to RTE and topped the news bulletins on both television and radio that day. The Gardai were called in.

The story had taken on the pace of a Hollywood movie. Allegations and innuendo were aired in the media and in pubs all over Ireland. Accusations and counter-accusations flew. And I was flat to the boards writing about it all.

Training for Everest was put on the back burner. I didn't get near a hill or a crag or even the gym during October. But then October ran into November and on into December and still the story wouldn't stop. I flew to London for Christmas and was doing radio interviews on my mobile phone outside a pub in Sussex while my family was inside celebrating the festive season.

Christmas dinner itself was at my elder sister Sarah's house in London. All the immediate family were there and, as everyone squeezed into their seats round the long dining table, the usual Christmas day reminiscences started. Always favourite was one about how, several years earlier, I had bought a fart cushion for my only nephew Joe and the mayhem and mirth it had caused when he'd put it under Grandpa's bottom just as he lowered himself onto his seat.

Joe was now 19. He'd just finished his first term studying geography at Leeds University and he'd grown up. But the playful, life-loving character was still there, inside a now tall and lanky frame. Joe's bright blue eyes would sparkle with merriment at the slightest provocation, his mop of flaming red hair joining the rest of his body in shaking with laughter. Joe and I had very similar senses of humour. The fart cushion was just one ridiculous present in a long line of ridiculous presents. He was always easy to buy for.

I had got him a book this time. 1,000 Places To See Before You Die. When we all met again at my aunt Jackie's the next day for further feasting I didn't know that that was the last time I'd see him. I went home to Dublin. He went back to college.

Nine weeks later, just as I was leaving the gym after an early Saturday morning workout, I got a phone-call from my twin sister Megan. She was crying so hard I could barely understand her. "It's Joe", she said, sobbing. "What? What's happened?", I pleaded, knowing it was something catastrophic. "He's had a heart attack. He's dead."

I felt as though I'd been punched in the solar plexus. I couldn't breathe. I couldn't comprehend what I'd just been told. Joe wasn't even 20. How could he possibly have had a heart attack? How could he possibly be dead?

"Get over quickly", my sister was saying. "We need you here."

In response to a desperate phone-call from me, my friend and neighbour Carmel McShea drove into town, scooped me up and took me back to her house. Jenny, the friend who'd bought me the Bear Grylls book that had re-ignited the Everest plan less than two years earlier, came as soon as Carmel told her the news. And then Yasmin Lowe, a wonderfully warm friend of Carmel's who I'd met only a couple of times, rushed over too. I sat on the sofa and wept until I thought there were no tears left. The girls sat and wept with me.

My cousin Chris, over in Dublin for the Ireland-England rugby match at Lansdowne Road, was in a pub when he got the news. He abandoned his pint and the rugby match and came straight to Carmel's house. And there were more tears.

I flew to London that night. Meg and my younger sister Kate met me at the airport and we drove to my parents' house. The three of us could barely speak, but they managed, between bouts of sobbing, to tell me that Joe had been out running that morning with one of his house mates, Stu. They'd sprinted the last couple of hundred metres back to the car-park in front of their apartment block.

"I feel really tired", Joe said as they pulled up. And then crumpled and fell, face first onto the pavement. He was dead before he hit the ground. Mouth-to-mouth and heart massage from his frantic flat-mates could do nothing. The ambulance was there inside two minutes. But it was too late.

My sister Sarah got the terrible phone-call from Leeds Infirmary shortly afterwards to say that her son had been brought in and was in a bad way. The nurse didn't tell her immediately. She said she'd phone back. She gently told Sarah later that day that she couldn't bring herself to break the news all in one go. She'd rung back 20 minutes after the first call to tell Sarah that her son, her only son, was dead.

Sarah's husband Fred was away at a conference in Boston. Sarah rang him in the middle of the night to tell him the worst possible news. Their oldest daughter, Harriet, had just embarked on a post-university round the world tour. It was two days before they managed to get in touch with her in Vietnam, shattering her young life with those dreadful words.

Sarah and her youngest daughter Eleanor went straight up to Leeds on the first train they could catch. My mother went with them. They were too devastated to drive. Fred was with them by shortly after midnight in a hotel booked for them by the university. They went back to the hospital so that Fred could kiss Joe goodbye, stroking his poor battered face where it had hit the pavement, chipping a front tooth.

Sixteen-year-old Eleanor refused to be parted from her parents for a moment. Nobody slept for those first dreadful 48 hours while they were waiting to hear from Harriet. The second night, Sarah sat up in bed and saw Eleanor, cross-legged on the floor and rocking gently as she brushed her long hair, the same glorious red as Joe's. She was eating digestive biscuits, her first meal since her brother's death.

My poor father was distraught. He sobbed on my shoulder, inconsolable in his grief. "My lovely grandson, my lovely grandson", he kept repeating. He was heartbroken. Joe had been the light of his life. His only grandson in a family that had produced no boys since his own birth 76 years earlier. A boy with four sisters, a man with four daughters. And now his only grandson, a grandson who shared his love of cricket and rugby, had been so cruelly snatched away from him.

The initial post mortem was inconclusive. The coroner wouldn't release Joe's body and the family had to wait almost a fortnight before the funeral arrangements could be made. Totally non-religious, Sarah and Fred wanted a humanist service. Joe, in a hideously prescient conversation about burial with his parents several months before, had said he wanted a green woodland funeral. Joe was an eco-warrior to beat all eco-warriors and a staunch supporter of the charity Make Poverty History.

I flew back to Dublin briefly to do a lecture at the Outdoor Adventure Show in the RDS, but returned to London the following week to help organise Joe's memorial. Sarah and Fred had asked me to be – for want of a better expression – master of ceremonies. I was deeply touched but also dreading it.

We spent hours in front of the PC putting together the programme, crying and laughing in equal measures. We knew the memorial was going to be tough on everyone, but especially for Sarah and Harriet, who were both going to be speaking. My father had said to Sarah that if she felt herself overcome with emotion, she should take a deep breath and exhale slowly before continuing. Both our opera singing aunt and uncle were going to be singing and it was Nuala who gave us the real clue to preventing emotional outbursts. A singing teacher in New York had told Nuala during a lesson that she wasn't breathing properly.

"I want you to breath more deeply", the teacher had said to her, "right down to your pubic bone. Think hairline to hairline."

It cracked us up and we used it on more than one occasion, both during the service and in the build-up to it. But, incredibly, I don't think Sarah needed it when she delivered her wonderfully touching and brilliantly funny eulogy of her only son to a packed assembly hall in Joe's old school. Her resilience and dignity was truly amazing and, actor's daughter to the last, even her timing was perfect. It was an astounding performance.

Leeds University had organised a coach for the huge number of students who wanted to say their final farewells to Joe. It was heartbreaking to see small clusters of them weeping quietly, their arms around each other as they looked at the pictures of Joe as a child and a young adult.

We gave Joe a more private send-off two days later. Honouring his request, he was given a truly green burial in a quiet corner of a vast multi-denominational cemetery in Surrey. The hearse had arrived on time, but then went to the opposite end of the cemetery. It turned out there were two green burial sites and the funeral directors had chosen the wrong one. When he realised his mistake, the driver reversed the vehicle onto the grass to turn round and the hearse got stuck in the rain-sodden ground.

The first we knew about it was when we saw the owner of the cemetery, an eccentric Turkish Cypriot, rushing off with his jeep and two burly assistants. The hearse appeared shortly afterwards, decorated with thick spatters of mud above the wheel arches. A joker to the last, Joe was - quite literally - late for his own funeral.

I'd already decided that I wasn't going to tell my family I was going to Everest. Several friends had said they thought it was unfair not to share it with them but now, in the aftermath of Joe's death, I knew I'd made the right decision. They'd been through so much already. The last thing I wanted to do was put them through 10 weeks of worry about me.

If I'd had any family left living in Ireland it would have been difficult to keep them in the dark about my Everest plans. I had pledged to do the climb for charity and my PR man Tom McCormack – introduced to me in a stroke of genius by work colleague John O'Sullivan – had done a great job publicising my fundraising efforts. I was on television, on the radio and my story was splashed across the newspapers.

My choice of charities hadn't been difficult. Around the same time as *The Irish Times* had announced its financial crisis towards the end of 2001, my father was diagnosed with prostate cancer. The whole family was devastated, but treatment was swift and successful. The following September two of his sisters, Maeve and Deirdre, died within 10 days of each other, both from cancer. I had no doubt in my mind that St Luke's cancer hospital in Dublin would be one of the recipients of my fundraising work. The Irish Hospice Foundation seemed an obvious partner. The Grania Willis Everest Challenge 2005 fundraising effort was launched and money started rolling in even before I'd left for Tibet.

With so much publicity, I was beginning to feel pressurised and was getting increasingly concerned about my fitness levels in the build-up to what was undoubtedly going to put my efforts on Cho Oyu into the shade. But I had two secret weapons in my armoury. The first was Kiwi Carl Petersen, a sports physiologist and manager at Peak Centre Ireland, which had offered me sponsorship in the shape of a scientific fitness analysis and a personalised training programme. The second was also Antipodean, an Australian-manufactured machine, Go2 Altitude, which simulated the effects of altitude by providing reduced oxygen levels. Like Carl, the Go2 Altitude machine was housed in the Peak Centre Ireland base in Dublin's Sandyford industrial estate.

The weapons didn't stay secret for long as I wrote about them in *The Irish Times* health supplement, where I purged my conscience by admitting that my January fitness analysis at Peak Centre hadn't gone quite according to plan. I'd done two similar tests with Bernard Donne in the Trinity human performance laboratory the previous year, one before I went to Mera and Island Peak and the other post climb. In the run-to-failure test, my VO2 max – the amount of oxygen consumed per kilo of body mass per minute – had increased impressively from 55.4 to 64.5 in the intervening two months.

But I'd had a bad January in 2005. During a marathon run of late-night sessions that threatened to cause repetitive strain injury to my right arm and gave a serious workout only to my liver, I tried convincing myself that going to the gym with the mother of all hangovers was a good way of mimicking conditions on the mountain. Altitude sickness in its less acute forms is remarkably similar to a serious dose of the morning-after the night-before, so I reckoned if I could subject myself to a super-tough workout while feeling like death not very successfully warmed-up, my body would be ready for the big challenge at the end of March.

It didn't work. My VO2 max had plummeted to a depressing 53 and my haematocrit levels, the percentage of red blood cells in whole blood, had dropped from a May 2004 post-climb 0.441 to just 0.374. Carl would have got a better reading if he'd gone for alcohol levels.

It was a serious wake-up call. Even though the Chinese had declared their belief that Everest had shrunk by just over a metre, I swore off drink and knuckled down to some serious training, plotted by Carl and designed specifically to improve my endurance. The workouts were tough, but I could feel the benefits almost immediately. The path to Everest seemed to be smoothing out again.

Then, on February 1, Nepal's King Gyanendra dismissed his government and put the politicians under house arrest. He declared a state of emergency and closed the international border. Memories of my abortive attempts to reroute on the way to Cho Oyu swam into my head. A week later I tore my hamstring. Suddenly the path to Everest seemed strewn with rockfall.

Having survived a car crash and an exhilarating week of ice climbing in France at the beginning of January, I managed to tear my hamstring while winter climbing in Scotland a month later. To this day, I still don't know how I did it. There was no fall, not even a slip. The only possible cause was when we were practising ice axe arrests in deep snow.

A visit to a physio in Fort William confirmed my worst fears and I spent the rest of the week miserable, unable to climb and too impoverished, or maybe just too mean, to pay the extortionate fees to change my flight home.

The very day that Ireland's rugby captain Brian O'Driscoll and centre Gordon D'Arcy flew out to a plush cryotherapy centre in Poland for treatment on their injured hamstrings, I was hobbling to the Ballsbridge Physiotherapy Clinic to see Aileen MaGuire. Her face – and her fingers – said it all. As she probed the back of my right thigh with gimlet fingers, I let out a yelp of pain.

"It's right where your hamstring attaches at the back of your knee", she said, her features creased in a frown of genuine concern. "I'm worried there might be some cartilage involvement too. We'll need to get it scanned." The significance of her pronouncement escaped me until she told me that if there was cartilage damage I'd probably need surgery. She didn't need to say anything more. That would be the end of Everest for this year.

Aileen rang consultant Conor O'Brien in the Blackrock Clinic. A former rugby player, O'Brien specialises in sports injuries and agreed to see me the following Friday. He too was concerned that there might be a cartilage tear and arranged an MRI scan for February 24, less than five weeks before my flight to Kathmandu.

A vet friend, Warren Schofield, who specialises in limb injuries in horses, suggested I should look into extracorporeal shock wave therapy. I didn't even know what it was, but I was prepared to try anything. Aileen preferred more conventional methods of treatment, however, so I stuck with daily and agonising physio sessions. Thankfully the scan came back clear and I was given the go-ahead to start training twice daily in the pool at the Markiewicz Leisure Centre close to *The Irish Times* offices. I still wasn't able to do weight-bearing exercise and, in total, missed five weeks of training, but running in the pool with a huge and cumbersome resistance belt gave me a pretty good workout and entertained the more conventional swimmers as they ploughed up and down the lanes next to me.

The injury had been hard to cope with, but Joe's death weakened my resolve still further. I came incredibly close to calling off the whole expedition. As I'd struggled to compose my emotions before making the opening address at the memorial service, I'd told myself I was being selfish even contemplating Everest. I couldn't risk putting my family through another tragedy. I'd call off the climb. But, in the next instant, I decided no, I would go ahead with the expedition. I'd pledged to raise funds for the two charities and I was going to go through with it. And I resolved then and there that I'd dedicate my summit, if I made it, to Joe.

Now, with just a month to go before departure, my hamstring was healed and I was ready to get back into my city centre gym, Riverside Fitness. Carl re-wrote my training programme and I re-wrote my diary.

I was up at five every morning, in the gym by just after six and at Peak Centre by some time after nine for my altitude training. The daily sessions on the Go2 Altitude machine were actually the only part of my day when I could switch off both my body and my mind. Intermittent hypoxic training sounded strenuous, but all it involved was sitting watching DVDs for an hour while I alternated five minutes breathing through a mask on reduced levels of oxygen with five minutes breathing normally. The most taxing part was trying to remember where I'd got to in the movie the previous day.

Having trained my body I still had to train my mind. Once I was finished in Peak Centre, I raced round the corner to SORD Data Systems where IT whizz-kid Brendan O'Brien was trying to school me in the art of communication. Brendan, in league with SORD's managing director John O'Keeffe and sales director Des O'Connell, had put together a state-of-the-art technology package that was going to provide a link between me on the mountain and the people of Ireland, via the pages of *The Irish Times*. Hewlett Packard's Tom McCabe came up with the hardware and I was kitted out with an HP iPAQ, a foldable bluetooth keyboard and an HP digital camera.

But learning how to use it all so that I could get words and pictures back to Dublin was a mammoth task. And we didn't even know if my brain was going to work at such altitude and in such cold conditions, let alone whether the HP gear would function.

TOTAL HIGH

It was like being back at school again. I was a grumpy student, not because I didn't enjoy the lessons, but because I was frustrated by my own ineptitude. But Brendan was unbelievably patient with me and eventually his teachings began to sink in.

When it came to the rBgan unit though, it was a case of the blind leading the blind. I had never heard of an rBgan, let alone used one. But then neither had Brendan. The satellite transmitter looked like the result of a breeding programme between a laptop and a briefcase. It had the outward appearance of a laptop, but no innards. But what it did have was radiation so powerful it could fry gonads at 30 paces.

Once the rBgan unit was aligned with the Thuraya satellite 22,000 miles away, technically I could connect with the rest of the world, whether I was in Kathmandu, on K2 or Everest. Brendan and I tried it out in the SORD car-park. Not only did we manage to send emails, I also talked to Lisa Crowley, researcher on RTE radio's Gerry Ryan Show using Skype on my iPAQ. I was getting into territory – and acronyms – I didn't even know existed.

But Brendan and I had an even more unusual venue for one of our sessions. I wanted to be sure that the HP gear was going to work in the cold, so my endlessly obliging PR Tom McCormack organised for Brendan and me to spend the afternoon in the freezer at the Merrion Centre Tesco in Dublin. Kitted out in some of the down gear from another of my major sponsors, The North Face, Brendan and I braved the cold and survived. So did the iPAQ. The keyboard and the camera were less happy, but I felt they would acclimatise.

The down gear that Brendan and I donned for our frigid afternoon in the freezer was the result of some casual chat in the Great Outdoors. Director Gerry Collins had said to me that he'd try and get me some other sponsorship to back up the input from the Dublin store. After a few phone-calls, he put me in touch with Alex Beasley of The North Face. I met up with Alex and his colleague Andy in the Westin Hotel next door to *The Irish Times* in mid-January to discuss sponsorship. A friend from work, Ian O'Riordan, came with me for moral support. The result was an agreement for North Face to kit me out completely for the expedition. And a horrendous hangover after negotiations turned seamessly into a musical session that continued beyond four in the morning.

Sports editor Malachy Logan had by now brokered a deal for support from *The Irish Times* in return for twice weekly coverage of the expedition. My sponsors were in place, my communications training was complete and my fitness was almost back on track as my March 30 flight to Kathmandu drew near. But I still had one major task to complete. The judicial hearing to decide whether or not show jumper Cian O'Connor would get to keep his Olympic gold was set for Easter Sunday. The airport conference centre in Zurich was the venue and, once again, the case was generating massive media interest.

After a 13-hour hearing before the International Equestrian Federation's judicial committee, a whey-faced O'Connor came out to face the press pack. He had been cleared of a deliberate attempt to enhance his horse's performance, he told the news hungry hacks, but Ireland's only medal from Athens was gone.

Amazingly, after such a traumatic day, he turned to me as he was being swept away by his PR guru Wally Young and solicitor Andrew Coonan. Touching me lightly on the arm, he said simply: "Enjoy Everest, Grania."

My farewell party in Dublin pub Scruffy Murphys was a whirl of signing autographs and posing for photos – and these were my friends, not the press. Everyone wanted a piece of me and I never got a chance to sit down and talk for more than two minutes to anyone. I felt like a bride without a groom.

Good luck charms, guardian angels and hand warmers were stacking up in a pile next to all the cards. But there was a serious undercurrent beneath the jollity. Friends did their best to conceal their concerns, but I could see it in their eyes as they wished me luck. Even Erica, who had sent me a text when I left for Cho Oyu which read, "Don't die, I'd miss you", wasn't being flippant this time. And Ger, who'd arrived with her husband Sean and a whole gang of supporters, spent most of the latter half of the evening in tears.

Last-minute preparations included a dash into town, at the suggestion of Cork climber Samantha O'Carroll, to buy adult nappies. I headed for O'Hara's Pharmacy on Dublin's Aungier Street. But I didn't buy the nappies, which were priced at an extortionate €17.85. I told the shop assistant, Rose, that I'd only be using one and wasn't prepared to shell out almost €18 for a single nappy.

Rose obviously though I was totally mad as well as incontinent when I explained to her that I needed the nappy for just one day. I was going climbing in Tibet, I told her. Then, seeing a look of boredom cross her face, added in that I was tackling Everest. It was like a magical password. Within minutes she had two sample nappies wrapped in a paper bag. I hadn't spent a penny, I reflected to myself as I left the shop.

The nappies were at least squashable and didn't take up too much space in my North Face duffel bags. Everything else, especially my climbing gear, was bulky and uncooperative. I called in reinforcements. Jenny came to the rescue and, while I frantically pushed down gear into stuff sacks, she was trying to measure and fit my new backpack onto my moving torso.

With so much down gear in so many different stuff sacks, I was blindly cramming whatever I could find into the duffels, without first checking its identity. It was only after I'd carefully put my magnetic Nikken knee supports at the opposite end of a bag from my Polar altimeter watch that I discovered an extra stuff sack still sitting on the bed. I'd packed three sleeping bags and no summit suit. I vetoed the idea of a sack-race style ascent in my sleeping bag and decided the summit suit was a better option.

Meanwhile Jenny was working out precise numbers of a huge variety of vitamin pills using the calculator on my mobile phone. The resulting pharmacopoeia was incredibly heavy and was partially responsible for a debate about excess baggage at the airport the following day. At least half the pills came home with me at the end of the expedition.

Finally, two duffels and a backpack were filled. It was just short of two o'clock in the morning. My alarm was set for five. In-keeping with the frenetic pace of my life in the final weeks before my departure, I squeezed in a final workout in the gym, a Go2 Altitude session and a last visit to SORD before heading to the airport in real style in Carmel's new Mercedes coupe.

I didn't want a huge send-off, but Roberta Leahy from Tom McCormack's PR firm ConneXions arrived with a whole posse of press photographers. I'd courted publicity since the launch of the project and, for the sake of the two charities, I needed to maintain a high profile. But it was tough keeping up the smiling exterior. I was beginning to wonder if I'd set myself too big a target this time.

TOTAL HIGH

PART **2**

I

The Assault Begins

I t was late when we arrived in Kathmandu the following evening. The city was back to its bustling best when Danish climber Soren Gudmann, Briton Richard Stait and I crammed ourselves and all our bags into one of the Lilliputian minibuses I'd become so familiar with on my last visit to the Nepalese capital.

We went straight to the Hotel Tibet and met up with the rest of the expedition members on the roof of the hotel. It was a joy to see familiar faces from Cho Oyu amongst the group – Jez, Chuck, Dean, Chieko and Fujibayashi, Monica, Jean and Tom and of course Russ himself. But there were plenty of new faces and, with two expedition groups of 10 climbers plus the guides, it was going to take a while to get to know everyone.

Incredibly, there was a face I recognised amongst the newcomers. There, standing in front of me and introducing herself as my room-mate Peggy Foster, was a Canadian climber I had met briefly at Everest base camp two years ago just after she'd been forced to abandon her summit bid because of oxygen mask problems. We talked into the small hours in our room that night.

I had a busy morning ahead of me the following day as I was committed to writing my first Everest Diary for the paper, so the shops in Thamel were out of bounds for me. But American guide Bill Crouse had other ideas. "We're going shopping", he said to me at breakfast. "We've got to buy you some boots."

"I have boots already", I told him. "No, you don't", he replied enigmatically, cutting me off as I started to explain that my boots were in Russ' store. "They're not there any more. We think a Sherpa must have taken them by mistake."

As well as our north side expedition, Russ' Sherpas were also being used for a private expedition, led by Mark Whetu, on the south side of the mountain and the team had left the previous day. My boots had apparently gone with them. I wasn't amused at the time, but much later when we were settled at base camp, I did think it would be quite a coup if I could become not only the first Irish woman to summit Everest from the north side, but also the first whose boots summitted simultaneously from the south side. Sadly the boots never made it.

While Peggy, who volunteered to act as my foot model, went into town with Bill to buy my replacement boots, I sat in the sunshine on the roof of the hotel, writing my story for the paper. It was a eulogy to the iPAQ and the guys at HP HQ loved it apparently. But in truth I really was in love with the diminutive hand-held computer, especially when it agreed so readily to communicate with the rBgan and sent my copy whizzing into the ether and onto the pages of the newspaper for the following morning.

Alas things didn't go quite so smoothly when we reached Lhasa. Despite the best efforts of my Mera mate Chuck, who has a quasi-military background in the US, and Los Angeles Fire Department chief Brett Merrell, I failed to get a signal up on the roof of the Chinese Tibetan Mountaineering Association hotel. We were lucky not to be arrested as spies and I ended up sending my story from a vast and incredibly sleazy internet café thronged with youthful Chinese indulging their Playstation fantasies.

Dean, one of the guides from Cho Oyu, thought I was mad, not for trying to communicate with a satellite from the roof of the hotel, but for trying to climb Everest and send columns back to the paper as well. "You can't possibly write and climb", he said to me. "At some stage you're going to have to make a choice. It's either writing or climbing. You can't do both." "Well it'll have to be the climbing", I said, "because if there's no climbing there's no writing." But I knew deep down that I would be able to do both. The mountain would inspire me.

With the latest despatch out of the way, I had a chance to explore the Forbidden City. Lhasa is a confusing series of contradictions where glorious ancient Tibetan monasteries sit cheek by jowl with hideous Chinese modernity. The city is dominated by the magnificent Potala Palace, visible from miles around and seen on walls in homes all over Tibet and in our mess tents on the mountain. The original Potala was built in the seventh century, but its present white and ochre edifice was erected in the 17th century for the fifth Dalai Lama, although it is believed he died 12 years before its completion.

We decided to save the Potala for our second day in Lhasa, opting instead to spend the morning wandering around the 15th century Drepung monastery up in the hills overlooking the city. After lunch a group of us joined the Barkhor kora, the pilgrimage circuit round the Jokhang, the most sacred and one of the oldest monasteries in Tibet.

As we waited for a bus to go to the Potala the next morning, I was talking to one of the Kiwis, Mary Hobbs. A fellow journalist, also masquerading as a "housewife" on the permit, Mary was on the expedition as support for her husband Charlie, a mountain guide who runs a restaurant at the foot of Mount Cook in the New Zealand Alps. The pair are Scientologists and rumours circulated amongst the group that the Hobbs had come to Everest to do a recce for fellow Scientologist Tom Cruise.

Without intending to confide in anyone, I found myself telling Mary about Joe's death and could feel my heart being wrung out as I spoke. Mary could see the hurt in my face. "He's with you, Grania", she said quietly, her hand on my arm. The sceptic in me wanted to dismiss it as whimsy but, as she uttered the words, a slender pale brown bird alighted on a window-sill opposite.

"Do you think that's Joe?", I asked Mary and, as I pointed to the bird, it lifted its crest in a flash of brilliant ginger feathers, the colour of Joe's hair. From then on, Joe was with me always, in the wind scudding over rippled sand at a river's edge, in the swirl of dust from the vehicle ahead, in a wisp of cloud in an otherwise cloudless sky high up on the mountain. He was a constant and reassuring presence. And I was comforted.

We got to the Potala later that morning. Its white and red façade was staggering in its vastness. But before we even started the long climb up to the entrance, we stood and watched in amazement as hundreds of the Buddhist faithful prostrated themselves on the kora round the Palace. Wooden blocks tied to their hands protected them from injury as they flung themselves headlong. The clack as the blocks hit the pavement mingled with monotone chanting and the quieter sounds of prayer beads being rubbed by fervent fingers and the whirl of miniature prayer wheels.

As at Drepung and the Jokhang, there was an all-pervading smell of yak butter inside as pilgrims spooned gobs of the pale straw-coloured fat into the giant butter lamps in every chapel. Soren and I bought a bag of butter and a prayer scarf apiece and joined in the ritual. And we followed the devout crawling under enormous bookcases that disappeared into the gloom of the ceiling, in the hope that some of the wisdom contained within the philosophical tomes above our crouched creeping bodies would be imparted to us.

We saw statues depicting the Buddha of Boundless Life, the Buddhas of the Past, the Present and the Future and the Buddha of Infinite Light. And the Dalai Lama, in all his incarnations except the banished current incumbent, was omnipresent. I could have been swept into Buddhism in an instant.

But, despite the glories of the Potala Palace, it was Tashilhunpo that had the greatest effect on me. Shigatse's 15th century monastery, with its narrow cobbled laneways and gold-roofed buildings, houses the world's largest gilded statue. The 26-metre high image of the Future Buddha in the Chapel of Jampa could so easily have been vulgarity at its tawdry worst. But the serenity in the Buddha's expression and the curve of the delicately pinched golden fingers are breath-takingly beautiful. I didn't want to leave the chapel, but I was caught up in a tidal wave of pilgrims and carried back out through the impossibly heavy maroon curtain into the glare of sunlight.

Spirituality and serenity drained away with equal rapidity as we dropped down from the 5,220 metre high Gyatsola pass into the ghastliness of Dingri, on the outskirts of Shegar which is also, confusingly, known as New Tingri.

The reception of the Qomolangma Hotel seemed promising, but once through the curtain-draped doorway in the right-hand corner of the lobby, the true nature of the beast was revealed. A cheerless, draughty corridor led to the bedrooms. Peggy and I were put into four different rooms before we found one that was habitable. In one room the light switch lay on the bedside table. A hole in the wall with naked wires sticking out of it marked its original home. In another the door handle was on top of the chest of drawers.

A sign on the roadside proudly advertised facilities including 24.00 showers, whatever they were, but the only hot water we ever found was in the thermos flask left on the chest of drawers, next to the door handles and light switches.

And we had to endure not one but two nights here. However grim base camp was going to be it couldn't be as grim as this.

But at least the stopover meant we had a chance to get in some exercise, the only exertion for most of us since we'd left home. It wasn't exactly taxing, but the 4,600-metre peak above the Choide Ganden Lekshe Ling monastery finally provided us with the first view of our goal. As we clambered through the spaghetti tangle of prayer flags at the top, there was Everest, straight in front of us. And over to the right was my 2004 summit, Cho Oyu. Cameras and videos went into overdrive.

It was no great wrench to leave Dingri the following morning and we sailed past the "Friembshit Resturant" without a twinge of regret. It was an important day. We were on our way, finally on our way to Everest base camp. But we'd been driving for only a short while when were stopped at a checkpoint. We were apparently crossing an invisible internal border, but the bridge across the river ahead of us looked hideously narrow and our driver wasn't at all convinced that the minibus – built on rather more substantial lines than its Kathmandu brethren – would fit across.

The Chinese guards were trying to send us on a four-hour detour, but Dean intervened as mediator and the mention of Russell Brice's name worked like WD40 on a rusty padlock. It was a trick Valerio and I had perfected en route to Cho Oyu the previous year. The words "Russell member" worked like a charm almost everywhere.

As negotiations on the bridge crossing continued, we were all told to get out, although whether the driver thought that would make the bus thinner or whether he thought the bridge wasn't strong enough to hold a bus full of westerners was unclear. We chatted to the soldiers while we waited for the driver to pluck up enough courage to drive across.

The bus did fit across the bridge. Just.

Once on the far side, we drove along the riverbank for some distance before the road started to wind upwards. The bus wheezed up a series of steeper and steeper switchbacks that finally brought us to Pang La, the 5,150 metre pass where George Mallory was photographed lying down with his telescope trained on Everest before he embarked on his ill-fated 1920s expedition on the very route we would be tackling. A large plaque on a Tibetan version of a lay-by named some of the giant peaks spread out like jewels on a vast frieze before us – Makalu, Everest, Lhotse and Cho Oyu. It was a spectacular panorama.

As we dropped down into the next valley, the peaks started to vanish one by one until only the dark spectre of Everest's summit triangle remained. Then that too disappeared behind the brown undulations of the hills. Caves and grottoes were hollowed out of crags on the far side of the river and the multicoloured layers in the rock looked like an expensive terrine in a Michelen starred restaurant. Scruffy Tibetan children, delighted to be momentarily relieved of the boredom of tending goats and their bleating kids, waved cheerily at us as we drove past.

The road surface alternated between the smoothness of a crisply ironed bed sheet and a rocky, ploughed field. A red tassel dangling from the rear view mirror reflected the terrain we were crossing, swaying gently or executing a frantic, frenetic jig. It was hypnotic. But, as we came round a bend, there she was, unexpectedly in front of us. Qomolangma, Goddess Mother of the Universe, in all her awe-inspiring, gut-clenching majesty, enthroned at the top of the valley.

It was a backdrop that I never tired of. Even after weeks at base camp, the sight of Everest, imperious above us, could still move me. But she wasn't always there. The worst weather in 45 years sat on the Himalaya, all too frequently robbing us of our view as it shrouded the mountain in cloud.

Everest base camp on the north side of the mountain bore very little relation to the south side equivalent I had seen and hated two years earlier. On the south side the icy scree and frozen pools, the tumbling icefall and the shallow horseshoe of mountains create a landscape exclusive to Nepalese base camp. Only the very tip of Everest, the crown of Sagarmatha herself, is visible, a tiny black triangle dwarfed by her neighbouring giants.

South side climbers are denied the chance to study their full route in the flesh from the comfort of their starting point. They know the task ahead of them, but from base camp are unable to see anything except the chaotic jumble of giant seracs and web of crevasses that make up the icefall as it snakes its way up towards the Western Cwm. From there the long haul up the Lhotse face is right in front of them, but even after the South Col and the traverse across the gully before the ridge, it is the south summit that dominates the skyline, not the true summit.

In base camp Tibet, where tents sit on the rocky, dust-blown valley floor,

Everest fills the eye, dominating the scenery. Yellowish brown peaks soar on either side of the valley, occasionally topped with a snowy cap, but it is Qomolangma that catches the attention and refuses to let go. Even Russ' base camp manager Lachhu, working on Himex expeditions for over a decade, is still in thrall to her. "Come see mountain, she is red", he would say in almost reverential tones, urging us all to rush outside and pay homage to Everest as the last rays of the sun tinted her slopes a delicate rosy hue.

North side base camp provides a stunning view of the entire north face, including the north ridge on the classic Chinese 1960 route. And from ABC, the whole route up to the North Col and on up the north ridge to the north-east ridge, complete with its imposing steps, is laid out in all its terrifying enormity. Daily exposure to that view did nothing to diminish its ability to send my stomach into an acrobatic frenzy.

Our first few days at base camp were spent not just acclimatising to our new altitude of 5,200 metres, but getting accustomed to the icy wind that came howling down the Rongbuk glacier. Bad during daylight hours, it would save its true force for the night, hitting our one-man tents with the force of a freight train just when we were feeling at our most vulnerable.

Sleep, a precious commodity at a new altitude, proved even more elusive as I lay, alone and anxious, waiting for the wind to send my tent bowling down towards the shanty town of tented bars and souvenir shops that had mushroomed overnight further down the valley. If it was this bad at base camp, I wondered what it would be like further up the hill where the camps were even more exposed to the elements.

Although the lake in front of the Himex camp was a vast immovable expanse of corrugated ice, the wind would create whirling dust storms on the valley floor that would sandblast our faces, sending grit into eyes, nostrils and lungs. The pernicious dust got into everything and tent zips were particularly badly affected. Russ had told us that two and a half kilometres of zips had been used on the brand new tenting. "If it breaks it can't be fixed till we get back to Kathmandu", he said. Zips clogged with the harsh gritty dust refused to function. Only the vigorous use of toothbrushes and soapy water could cajole them back into action.

Base camp survived, but our interim camp was flattened and work on putting up advanced base camp had to be postponed, even though three caravans of 82 yaks had already carried the bulk of the expedition gear up to the 6,400 metre site.

When the winds finally abated and Everest returned to her throne at the top of the valley, we set about another acclimatisation process, getting to know our neighbours. The Koreans in the camp closest to ours were unsmilingly private, but they had come for the grim business of trying to bring back their three dead from the previous year's expedition. And the Chinese on the far side of us were also ostentatiously self-contained. They drove around base camp in smart new jeeps and had huge flags fluttering above their main tent, which housed the team of surveyors that had taken on the onerous task of re-measuring the mountain.

But the Jagged Globe, the Norwegian and the combined Russian/Seven-Summits camps became the object of regular visitations from those of us who became known as the social butterflies of the Himex team.

I was keen to meet renowned explorer Sir Ranulph Fiennes. Despite his fear of heights and his very recent marriage, he had decided to temporarily swap his legendary flatland exploration for mountaineering. But when Peggy and I went visiting there was no sign of either Ran or his friend Sibusiso Vilane, who had become the first black African to summit Everest two years earlier, when part of the same team as Peg.

The publicity surrounding Ran's climb and his bid to raise £1.5 million for the British Heart Foundation had nearly undone all my plans to keep my family in the dark about the purpose of my 10-week sojourn to Tibet. My twin sister had phoned the day before I'd left Dublin. "Are you climbing Everest with Ranulph Fiennes?", she had asked, without preamble. "No", I'd said, emphatically and truthfully. Fiennes was climbing with a different team, not with me, I thought but didn't say.

Apart from Fiennes in the Jagged Globe camp, we had plenty of home-grown characters in the Himex expedition and there were two in particular that my journalistic nose wanted to sniff out. They were both in a different team to me. With such a large group, Russ had split us into two teams, each with our own separate mess tent, plus shower and toilet facilities. There was huge but friendly rivalry between the yellow and red teams, but there was also plenty of mingling between the two groups, with the card school especially well able to cross the colour divide.

I'd already got to know one of my "victims" for interrogation for *The Irish Times* column, Australian Paul Hockey, on the way from Kathmandu to base camp, but the other had arrived by a different mode of transport – a very different mode of transport. Dane Mogens Jensen had an athletic background that suggested he would have little trouble summitting, provided the weather gods were willing. The 32-year-old had started climbing only three years before his Everest attempt, but with 11 Iron Man triathlons under his belt and as a member of Denmark's triathlon team for three years, his endurance was beyond question.

As if his stamina still wasn't sufficiently proven, Mogens had cycled and run the 10,764 kilometres from his home in Denmark to Kathmandu. After a five-day acclimatisation trek in the Khumbu valley on the trail to Everest base camp south side, he then set off with his bike and his runners to complete the journey across the Nepalese/Tibetan border to Everest base camp north side. But there were two further details that made Mogens' story even more remarkable. He'd been diagnosed as a chronic asthmatic seven years earlier and, determined to prove that asthma is no restriction on athletic endeavour, was aiming to climb Everest without oxygen.

Another person tackling the mountain without something that the majority of climbers would consider a necessity was Paul Hockey. The 42-year-old Japanese speaking tour guide had lost his entire right arm to cancer as a three-week-old baby, but his 2005 Everest attempt surprised even him. Having turned round at 8,550 metres, just below the First Step, 12 months earlier, he had sworn he would never come back for a second attempt.

"But I went home and my mum was dying of ovarian cancer and she asked me, very pointedly, was I going to try again. I opened my mouth to say no and yes came out", he told me. So he came back, determined this time not only to make it to the summit, but also to raise even more money for the Children's Cancer Institute of Australia.

Also raising funds for a children's charity and another refugee from a previous Himex expedition was David Tait, who had been forced to abandon his 2004 climb when his wife Vanessa been taken ill at home in England. David had brought Vanessa with him this time, but only as far as base camp. Once she'd seen David safely settled into his new home, Vanessa returned to Kathmandu.

David was on the same road himself very shortly afterwards. But it wasn't separation anxiety that prompted his rushed departure. Despite a thorough dental check-up on March 1, including x-rays, David had developed a raging toothache. Russ organised a jeep for David and he was driven in a mad dash back to the Nepali capital for emergency treatment on an old root canal.

David, who had raised £200,000 for the British charity, the National Society for the Prevention of Cruelty to Children, in 2004 and was on the fundraising trail again, was back at base camp 72 hours later. He paid out $25 for the gold filling and $2,000 for his travelling expenses. But the toothache returned and David spent the rest of the expedition, when he wasn't climbing, plugged into his iPod and his painkillers.

The puja, designed to ward off evil spirits, had failed with David's aching tooth. But the Everest 2005 puja was, in every other sense, such a spiritually uplifting occasion that I wondered if the one that Valerio and I had gate-crashed on Cho Oyu had been any relation at all.

The Tibetan prayer book had been consulted to find the most appropriate date. "The puja will be tomorrow", Russ told us on April 11th. But it turned out that the lama at the Rongbuk monastery had misread the prayer book, or more precisely, had misread a wrinkle in the prayer book. The puja would be delayed 24 hours to April 13th, the eighth anniversary of my friend David Foster's death.

Lachhu was busy from early morning, baking cakes and biscuits for the ceremony. Uncooked rice and barley flour had to be found from the store tent. And the top of the flagpole had to be decorated with cream and white prayer scarves. It was a busy morning. A fire was lit on the side of the chorten only metres away from my tent and the pungent smell of burning juniper floated into the still morning air. The fire had burned down to glowing embers by the time everyone was seated round the chorten. A replica of the mountain and her acolytes, baked by Lachhu out of barley flour, took pride of place.

The two lamas from the Rongbuk monastery, clad in their familiar maroon robes, sat cross-legged on a mat, surrounded by trays and jugs filled with offerings to the gods. Gobs of butter were smeared on everything to ensure a smooth passage to the intended deities. And the chanting began. The lamas read from long, narrow prayer books, whose tattered and faded pages looked as though they pre-dated the birth of the religion enshrined within them.

Mugs of tea, sweetened with condensed milk, were handed out and we drank, in between trying to emulate the method of throwing rice into the air adopted by the lamas and Sherpas. They seemed to be able to make a small handful last infinitely longer than we could, holding it in the palm of their left hand and scooping up a small amount with the pinched fingers of their right before casting it heavenwards in magnificently sweeping gestures.

After over an hour of chanting, the flagpole, now topped with long strings of prayer flags, was hauled into place on top of the chorten. The other ends of the prayer flags were taken to the far reaches of our Himex camp, strung across the tents so that our prayers could catch on the winds and be carried upwards to the heavens. As the last of the strings was attached to the monument to Marco Siffredi, the 23-year-old snowboarder who had been killed on his second snowboard ascent of the mountain in 2002, a black gorak landed on the top of the flagpole. It was the best of good omens apparently, but it was Joe to me.

It was an emotionally charged moment for others too. Expedition doctor Terry O'Connor had put a picture of his father out for blessing amongst all the other expedition gear. His father had died the previous December. And Shinichi Ishi, the Japanese newcomer who had joined forces with Cho Oyu veterans Fujibayashi and Chieko, was mourning the loss of his friend Shoto Ota, who had died in a fall at the Second Step when descending from her 2004 summit success. Ishi had turned round on his way to the summit then and was hoping to succeed in memory of his friend this time. And Australian guide Duncan Chessell was reflecting on the loss of his friend Mark Auricht, who died after turning round 150 metres from the top when Duncan had nailed his first summit four years earlier.

But as the final climactic burst of rice-throwing brought the puja to a close, our spirits soared again and we all rushed around hugging and kissing, wishing each other luck and a safe passage up and back down the mountain. The cook boys came round with trays of cakes and weird biscuits made with tsampa that tasted like sand mixed with sugar. The whoosh of cans of beer and minerals being opened punctuated the air. And Lachhu appeared with a bottle of whiskey, pouring it into our cupped left hands in a tradition we seemed to know only by osmosis. We drank it quickly before the amber liquid seeped away between our fingers.

Acclimatisation was our main objective during the first week at base camp. The weather had improved and, even though the mountain still wore her characteristic summit plume like a prayer scarf, winds in the valley had died down. It gave us a chance to scramble up some of the larger scree slopes that reared up from the valley floor, aiming to get as close to 6,000 metres as we could in our bid to avoid an excessive reaction to our move up to advanced base camp.

A 1,200-metre ascent to ABC was going to be punishing on our systems and the early acclimatisation hikes were a vital part of preparing our bodies for the onslaught. But we accelerated the process on our final night at base camp with an impromptu party. The Sherpas decided to introduce us to some of their culture, embarking on the shuffling dance I remembered so vividly from the night in Pheriche two years earlier..

But I'd never come across the long-necked, three-stringed instrument that one of the Tibetans began to strum vigorously as an accompaniment. The discordant noise it produced suggested it was an instrument of torture rather than a musical instrument, but the Sherpas danced enthusiastically to it, so we joined in. With arms draped round each other's shoulders in a huge circle, we tried to get the hang of the foot shuffling, heel tapping dance, and failed dismally. There obviously was a set pattern, but we couldn't follow it.

The neighbouring Norwegians came to our rescue and the sounds of Bob Marley's throbbing music lured us into the red mess tent, where the dancing took on an even more frenetic pace. I was dancing with Vidar, whose red hair and beard needed only a Viking helmet to complete the Norse god look. But it was only as we collapsed in an exhausted heap at the end of the song that someone helpfully pronounced that No Woman No Cry lasted a full seven minutes. At 5,200 metres, seven minutes felt like 70. But it was all part of the acclimatisation process.

Whether it made the 22-kilometre trek up to ABC any easier is hard to say. Even with an overnight at interim camp, the trudge up the endless moraine

103

certainly took the edge off most of us, apart from Russ, who strode up with his arms folded as though he was out for a walk on the beach.

The scenery had changed dramatically on the way up. Pumori, which had graced the skyline as we made our way up to the plateau where the Chinese surveying team had another camp, disappeared. And Everest had vanished even before we turned left up the steep ascent towards interim. Further on the monotony of the moraine was broken up by gloriously towering penitentes, vast ice sculptures that had taken on the shape of anything from ships in full sail to wedding cakes and an enormous crysalis. And Everest returned to her place in the firmament above interim camp, although her summit was temporarily dwarfed by the huge icy flanks of Changtse as we headed up towards the camp that would be our home for the next couple of weeks.

The Himex camp was right on the top of the moraine, overlooking the rest of ABC, with the glacier and fabulous views of the 7,000 metre Lhakpa Ri laid out before us. But it was Everest that drew my focus. Looking up to the North Col and on up to the north-east ridge, I could see our entire route to the summit. The mountain no longer had the haughty look of the north face from base camp, but its enormity seemed more real.

The acclimatisation process began anew as we accustomed ourselves to the new height. Treks further up the moraine, past the sprawling Chinese camp and on up to Crampon Point, just below the snowline, were a regular feature. But so were card games. And washing clothes which froze almost immediately, regardless of whether they were hung inside or outside our tents. Long stalactites hung from every item of clothing as the drips froze before they reached the ground. I wondered, as I had when a child, whether I'd be able to snap the arm clean off a shirt or the leg off my long johns.

By the third week in April, a fortnight after our arrival, the Sherpas had chopped the platforms for the tents at camp II and III and had fixed the ropes up to high camp at 8,300 metres. The rope was part of a delivery of 10 kilometres of seven-millimetre thick rope that had arrived while we were still at base camp. It put into perspective just how big the mountain was, but also how huge an undertaking an Everest expedition is. The logistics were mind-boggling. Russ had told me that the store tent had enough food in it to last one person 19 years. And two of the cook boys were on almost permanent ice-chopping duty, hauling sack-loads back to camp for melting to create the 160 gallons of water needed on a daily basis.

By day the heavens were a glorious blue, but temperatures rarely strayed above −20°C and would plummet with the descent of the sun behind the mountains. Down jackets and trousers came out. The Norwegians had already resorted to their summit suits.

The combination of the cold and an apparently never-ending series of sleepless nights had weakened fireman Brett Merrell's spirit. He'd had trouble acclimatising and announced at breakfast one morning that he was leaving. We were all stunned. The LA-based firefighter had started out so strong and focused and looked the ideal candidate for summitting. But he'd had enough and was heading to Thailand for some diving.

Six days after our arrival at ABC, we pushed on up to the North Col. Chuck, who was beginning to show the early signs of altitude related respiratory problems, decided to stay at ABC in the hope that a couple more days acclimatisation would get him back on track. Fujibayashi also stayed put, still nursing a knee injury, and one-armed Paul, who needed someone behind him on the fixed lines so that they could hold the rope taut for him, opted out too.

We'd already stowed our climbing hardware in barrels at Crampon Point and we stopped on the way up to pull out our harnesses and crampons. As we scrunched across the glacier towards the bottom of the snow slopes, I looked up at the vast mountain amphitheatre that surrounded me. It was hauntingly beautiful on a still calm day, but I knew its characteristics would change drastically in bad weather.

We clipped into the first of the fixed lines to start up the slope. I could see the dark scars of crevasses, stark and dangerous against the white of the snow. We were on unfamiliar territory now, but I soon came to know every undulation on the route. What I also came to know well, but could never get used to, was the way the Sherpas would come galloping past on the descents, literally running down even the steepest slopes with one hand resting lightly on the fixed line.

Anything, even the easy slopes, seemed tough on that first day as our bodies got used to the unfamiliar sensation of exertion at a new altitude. But there was still the ice wall to come, the only bit of vertical climbing we would meet before summit day, when we would have to face into the First and Second Steps in the dark. The ice wall is relatively short, but sheer. Looking up it I could see a line of blue rope snaking its way up the face. There was already a series of shallow steps kicked into the ice where earlier climbers had ascended, but the effort was still sufficient to leave me breathless by the time I got to the top.

As I traversed across towards the ladder that spanned the first of the crevasses on the route, a descending climber greeted me in familiar Irish tones. Only the tones were familiar though, the face was unknown. He introduced himself as Humphrey Murphy. Too modest to tell me himself, I found out afterwards that the Donegal father of two was aiming to climb solo and without oxygen. Humphrey was wonderfully friendly and I regretted not being able to spend more time with him, but he was on his way down and I was on the way up.

My first trip across the ladder felt distinctly insecure. My feet weren't long enough to straddle two rungs, so I had to make sure the rung was right in the middle of my crampons before I shifted my weight. But at least I could see my feet, which I wouldn't be able to going up the vertical ladder at the Second Step on summit day when my oxygen mask would obscure my view. I couldn't begin to imagine how I would feel on the multiple ladders used to cross the Khumbu icefall on the south side.

The ground flattened out immediately after the ladder and the snow was strewn with icy debris. Obviously an avalanche path, it made me feel like I was going through a bowling alley. I didn't waste time going through it, but my pace slowed considerably as I started on the next ascent. Yellow team leader Dean was just ahead of me and I could see red team leader Bill and Norwegian climber Sissel Smaller taking a break at the top. I flopped down on the snow next to them.

Chuck didn't seem to have improved when we got back to camp and he was joined on the sick list that night by Charlie, who went from rude good health to dangerously ill within a matter of minutes. His decline was frighteningly rapid. One moment he was sitting talking to Russ' friend Kari Kobler, the next he was blue-lipped and grey in the face.

Terry was summoned and, after hearing the familiar Rice Krispie crackle in Charlie's chest, immediately diagnosed pulmonary oedema. A night on oxygen improved Charlie's condition, but not enough and the following day the decision was made that both he and Chuck, who had now developed pneumonia, would have to return to base camp to recuperate. Drained of all energy, they only got as far as interim camp that first day and had to stay there for the night before continuing the next morning.

Monica, Jean and Tom, the trio known as Team Monica, had also decided on an early return to base camp. Everyone else planned a return to the North Col for a two-night stay and a push on up to camp II before heading back down to base camp to wait for the window in the weather that would allow us to make our bid for the summit.

I still felt surprisingly well. I'd had no headaches, but both Sissel and I had been affected by peripheral oedema. Our faces, particularly around the eyes, would swell up overnight, and my lips quite often looked as though I'd had an overdose of botox injected into them. Terry told us that it was nothing to worry about, just another in the long line of side-effects caused by living at altitude.

I'd been asked to do an interview with TV3 and was glad that it would only be a phone interview. I certainly wouldn't have liked images of my swollen face being beamed back to Ireland. I didn't think the altitude had affected my vocal chords, but the girl I spoke to in the studio said she was having trouble hearing me. "Probably because I'm on Everest", I said to her. "Are you lost on your way to the studio?", she asked. "No", I yelled down the line in exasperation, "I'm on Everest and I'm supposed to be on air in a couple of minutes." The television interview never happened. Radio was a much easier medium and I had regular slots on RTE's Gerry Ryan Show throughout the expedition.

Three days after our initial trip to camp I at the North Col, we headed back up. Peg and I were sharing a tent, but spent most of the afternoon of our arrival squeezed into the next-door tent with Jez and Soren, playing cards from inside layers of down gear. Temperatures had already dropped dramatically, but the weather deteriorated even more drastically the following day as we were going up to camp II.

We had set off up the early snow slopes in reasonably good conditions, but the wind returned with a vengeance, threatening to blow us off the mountain as the day wore on. Every step was an effort. But then the snow started. Dean, my self-proclaimed "best friend and guide" suggested we should turn round. I had no intention of turning round, but Frenchman Antoine Boulanger had already headed back down and Dean told me we were going with him. In decreasing visibility I couldn't see the rest of the team up ahead so, reluctantly, I turned back.

It was a wise decision. Shortly after we got back to the North Col, Paul was on the radio to say that he too was turning round. Caught in the worst of the blizzard alone and on the steepest part of the climb, Paul began to fear for his safety and radioed down to Russ. "Where's Woody?", Russ asked about the Kiwi guide who had started the day in Paul's company. "I told him to go on without me", Paul said, "but now I'm stuck." Without someone to keep tension on the rope, Paul couldn't use his jumar and the wind was making climbing impossible for him.

Within minutes Russ had dispatched a Sherpa back down from camp II to rescue the stranded Australian. The Sherpa took one look at Paul and reached up to his face. "He grabbed my face and ripped a huge chunk of ice off it", Paul told me afterwards. A large disc of frost-bitten skin on his cheek gave testimony to the tale. "It hurt like hell. It was a bit like the Turin shroud. I could see the shape of my face in it."

In 80-100kph winds and blizzard conditions, just five clients and four guides made it up to camp II that day on what turned into a seven-hour journey to hell. "It was total survival mode", Peg said to me the next day when the weary crew staggered back into ABC.

"That was a mild day on Everest", Russ told us later. But the mild day had ripped the North Col store tent from its moorings and hurled it, complete with contents worth $6,000, into a crevasse. It took five Sherpas half a day to rescue it.

While pulmonary and cerebral oedema are the two most serious, and potentially fatal, manifestations of altitude, there were plenty of other minor complaints that made living at altitude uncomfortable. Coughs that had started with the dust at base camp had worsened when we went up to ABC. But there was no respite from them when we returned to base camp for recuperation before the summit push. The coughs had become entrenched. I would cough so uncontrollably sometimes that I would start retching. It was amazing that I managed to keep any food down.

The bouts of coughing had got so bad that I sometimes felt as though I was going to cough myself inside out. I discovered to my horror one morning that the process had already begun. I had developed a haemorrhoid. It wasn't a subject I felt comfortable discussing, least of all with a doctor as gorgeous as Terry, but I certainly didn't want the condition to worsen. Of course it didn't faze Terry at all, even though I was squirming with embarrassment trying to tell him about my complaint as an endless trail of people came in and out of the comms tent, venue for his morning surgery.

Split cuticles were another irritant and they refused to heal. Pulling gloves on and off made them worse, but it wasn't just our cuticles that split. Cracks appeared in our fingers and on our tongues. Superglue was the perfect antidote for the cuticles and fingers, but I drew the line at applying it to my tongue.

Russ had never employed an expedition doctor before, but Terry was kept busy looking after not just the climbers, but with a succession of complaints presented by the Sherpas and local Tibetan yakpas. He was called upon to stitch a gashed head after a fight broke out between two yakpas down in base camp shanty town, but it wasn't the only suturing he had to do.

Kiwi guide Dave McKinley, whose nickname Denali – Mount McKinley's other name – had been reduced to Narly, had brought a pair of possum-skin trousers with him. A rich tawny suede, the fur-lined possum pants looked good and felt good and Narly got great wear out of them at base camp. But he pulled at a loose thread one day and the seam round the entire crotch simply unravelled. The Doc was called for emergency suturing and decided to use it as a teaching opportunity. Nurse Stacey Crowley and Narly proved apt pupils in the art of stitching skin back together.

But there were serious sides to Terry's work too. He was called down to the ruins of the old Rongbuk monastery, where the lama's elderly mother was dying. Pneumonia wracked her wraith-like body. Arrythmia and congestive heart failure added to her problems. She was not expected to live, but Terry brought her back from the brink. The lama's gratitude was boundless and Terry returned to camp with enough blessings to last him at least five years.

There were plenty of other doctors at base camp. Fred Ziel, a Californian medic who specialised in endocrinology and diabetes, had summitted Everest from the south side with the same Jagged Globe team that Peg had been on in

2003. He was back with Jagged Globe, this time aiming for the north/south double, along with black South African Sibusiso Vilane.

The Norwegian team had a different sort of medic with them. Chiropractor Eirik Bjargo, together with British doctor Julian Thompson, was conducting a medical study as well as bidding for the summit. The pair were taking saliva samples from 100 volunteers to test for the Angiotensin II enzyme. A similar sample group was being tested on the south side. Those with the enzyme seemed to be more predisposed to success on high-altitude mountains than those without, he told us.

Several of the Himex group volunteered, including me, but we will never know the results of the anonymous study. I was simply listed as sample number 29. But presumably Eirik, along with several other members of the Norwegian team, were missing the gene as they left early after succumbing to a succession of altitude related complaints.

The Russian doctor, Andre Selivanov was another medic that seemed to be constantly on call. But it didn't stop him enjoying the delights of vodka. He and the Russian team leader, Alex Abramov, brought a bottle of Stolichnya to the Himex party in early May. Russ had invited everyone at base camp and the Norwegians and the Russians became the stars of the show, with Andre and Alex displaying a Russian drinking technique that was a health risk in more ways than one.

A shot glass full of vodka was placed on the bent elbow of the victim and, with the arm at right-angles to the body, the would-be drinker was supposed to launch both the glass and its contents towards his mouth with a deft flick of the elbow. The result was much spilt alcohol and innocent bystanders felled by shot glasses.

The Italians, peripherally attached to the Himex team, also added a cosmopolitan flair to the proceedings. Obviously of the same school of thought as my Cho Oyu prince, Valerio, they had brought 600 kilos of food and God knows how many litres of wine with them to base camp and on up to ABC. A substantial number of bottles were emptied that night.

And there were quite a few people in need of doctors the next day.

Russian Alex had already been treated in hospital for shrapnel wounds after being caught in a bomb blast, part of the ongoing unrest in Nepal, on his way to base camp. Two members of his team, Irish couple Lynne Stark and Noel Hanna, just missed the bomb, ironically since they both come from northern Ireland. But there was a bigger bombshell waiting for Noel when he got to the mountain.

As adventure racers, Noel and Lynne were two of the fittest people at base camp. Noel had added an extra twist to his bid for the seven summits, planning to record the fastest return to sea level from each of the seven continents' highest peaks. But he started to suffer eye problems as soon as he got to ABC. Blurred vision was causing him some concern so he took time out from the mountain and went back down to Xangmu for treatment in the new hospital. He found the hospital, but there were no doctors and no medical facilities.

A phone-call home resulted in a follow-up call to a specialist at the Royal Victoria Hospital in Belfast. With no other symptoms evident, the specialist thought that the problem could be temporary short-sightedness brought on by exposure to altitude. There was no change during three days in Xangmu, so Noel returned to base camp and went up from there to interim, ABC and the North Col. His vision was still blurred.

Four days relaxation back down in Xashigum with Lynne and their guide, Harry Kikstra, who runs the Seven Summits website, also had no beneficial effect, so Noel got second, third and fourth opinions from British, Canadian and Indian medics back at base camp. His eyes were examined with an ophthalmoscope and bilateral haemorrhages in the macula area of both eyes were diagnosed. He was told unequivocally, go home or go blind.

So Noel and Lynne packed their bags and went back to Co Down, but not before bringing me goodwill and masses of presents – including the DVD of Seven Years In Tibet – for my mid-May birthday. The pair were desperately disappointed, but a check-up in Belfast a month after their return put it all into perspective when Noel was told that the bleeds were symptoms of a much more serious malaise. He had had cerebral oedema. If he'd gone up the mountain he wouldn't have gone blind, he would have died.

The mountain had already claimed two lives on the south side, even before Noel and Lynne left for home. At the end of April, Canadian doctor Sean Egan had collapsed and died of a heart attack, despite a descent to Pheriche after feeling unwell at base camp. Peg was devastated to hear of the death of her friend and fellow Canadian.

Four days later, American guide Mike O'Brien fell into a crevasse in the Khumbu icefall after descending from camp II with his brother Chris. He broke his leg in the fall but, while a rescue attempt was being mounted, his condition deteriorated and within half an hour he was dead. He and his brother had been climbing the mountain to raise funds for the Hereditary Disease Foundation after losing their mother, sister, grandmother, aunt and uncle to Huntington's disease. O'Brien's death was a second tragedy for team leader Dan Mazur as Panamanian client Alex Chen and Phurba Tamang Sherpa had been killed in a fall on his SummitClub expedition to Pumori earlier in the season.

The upper reaches of the mountain continued to be battered by jet stream winds. And even the lower flanks of Everest were suffering, with an avalanche sweeping away the south side camp I at the entrance to the Western Cwm. One Sherpa suffered spinal injuries and a Polish climber had broken bones in his foot, but amazingly no-one was killed.

Very high winds were forecast for the second week of May. We'd been warned to weight down our tents, both inside and out, with large rocks. A group of our Sherpas had gone up to drop most of the North Col tents and all those at camp II. Only three Himex tents at ABC had been left standing.

Chuck and Charlie were already back up at ABC, aiming to spend a night at the North Col in a bid to catch up with the rest of the expedition. Charlie, in his nightly radio transmissions back to base camp which were now his only means of communication with his wife Mary, reported that the winds were vicious up there. They failed to materialise down at base camp, but the forecasters and the enormous plume roaring off the summit suggested that gales of at least 150kph were blasting the top of the mountain.

The winds weren't due to drop until May 16, but the Norwegians, in a leap of faith driven by their desire to reach the summit on their national day of May 17, left for ABC on the 10th.

Guide Andy Taylor, known to everyone as Frog, was suffering badly up at ABC. Dean went up to replace him and Frog came back down to base camp to try and shake off the chest infection that was weakening him daily. Narly was in a similar state. Sissel and I were also coughing badly. Terry recommended salt water gargles and steam inhalations for all of us and we'd sit with towels draped over our heads, faces suspended over bowls of steaming water laced with eucalyptus oil from Mary's capacious alternative therapy kit.

Jez, one of the few who'd escaped the cough, was in the tent next to mine. I heard him noisily blowing his nose one morning. "God, there are boulders coming out of my nose", he called through the walls of the tent to me. "Me too", I said. "Are your boulders red?", I asked, knowing that mine were. "Mmm, yes", he said, obviously having examined the contents of his tissue. "Sounds like an episode of Dr Who, doesn't it. Dr Who and the Red Boulders."

We were doing less and less exercise. Even the slightest uphill exertion would set off hacking bouts of coughing that left us exhausted. We had come back to base camp supposedly to strengthen ourselves for the final summit push. But several of us, including me, seemed to be getting weaker by the day. My muscle-tone, built up so meticulously in the gym and the pool and out on the hills, had literally vanished. The only muscles that were still very obviously in residence were the intercostals, those running between the ribs, which complained vehemently with every cough.

Several other expeditions had got out of base camp altogether, including Russ's south side team, who had chartered a chopper and flown back to Kathmandu for a week. We were all desperately jealous and sat in the mess tents dreaming up schemes to follow fireman Brett to Thailand for a few days to fatten ourselves up while we waited for the weather to change on the mountain.

In between the steaming and the dreaming, the yellow team watched DVDs on Duncan's laptop. Mogens' computer provided the entertainment for the red team. The two Guy Ritchie movies, Lock Stock And Two Smoking Barrels and Snatch proved particular favourites. Jez and Dean went around camp quoting liberally from them. Questions about the movies even featured in the second of two pub quizzes that Jez and I organised in a bid to keep everyone sane during the wait for the weather. I think we probably drove them even further towards madness.

Peg and I took some time out from the claustrophobic atmosphere of base camp to visit the remains of the monastery further down the valley. The ancient lama, whose even more ancient mother was now apparently thriving under

Terry's care, came out to greet us as we clambered up to a tiny courtyard, whose sole occupant was a flagpole topped with prayer flags.

He offered us an almost completely toothless grin and the gentle double-handshake and bowed head so typical of the Tibetans. We were invited into the room that obviously doubled as both his reception room and bedroom. Two men who had been eating with the lama were ejected from their seats. Yak butter tea was passed to us, steaming and stinking in thankfully tiny glasses. Every time I took a sip, the lama would top up the glass. Peg wisely refused to drink hers.

We asked if we could look round and the lama nodded, leading us back into the courtyard and up a short flight of steps into a gloomy and featureless room. He beckoned for us to follow as he disappeared through a trap-door in the floor. Peg and I looked questioningly at each other, but then followed him. As I edged down into the dark on invisible steps, he extended a bony, leathery hand, guiding me down into an Aladdin's cave.

Illuminated solely by butter lamps, the tiny cavern contained an altar, where incense burned alongside offerings to the gods. The lama took my hand again and, lighting the way with the weakest of torch beams, gestured for me to duck my head before ushering me to a large smooth boulder in one corner.

He stroked the stone and motioned for me to do the same. I could feel indentations, but it wasn't until I heard him say "Buddha" that I realised this was an enormous Buddha handprint on the rock. A footprint, tiny by comparison, was on the other side of the cave.

The lama gave us rice and we threw it in the air at the altar as he blessed us. And then he took us outside for a magical tour of more caves – caves created by thunderous rock-fall that had left spaces between the massive boulders, and subterranean caves deep beneath the rock walls at the side of the valley. Prayer scarves and votive offerings were strewn in piles. After squeezing through one particularly narrow gap, the three of us lay on our stomachs looking out at the crags that rose steeply from the valley floor. The lama pointed to a lone rock pinnacle rearing towards the heavens. "Buddha finger", he said.

And the lama, the gentlest of creatures, stroked our hands and our faces as we felt our spirits being reborn. The heartache of Joe's death had been lifted from me. We emerged, blinking, back into the sunlight, clutching the rings he had given us, worth nothing but worth all the world.

But our spiritual preparation made no difference to the mountain. She still wasn't ready to receive us. On May 12 we all piled into an ancient open-topped truck and headed off for a picnic, stopping en route to visit a school that Russ had built for the local children. That night he called us all together and told us that a four-hour weather window would open in a couple of days' time, but then the forecast was dire until the 27th. No forecast was available beyond that and there was nothing to suggest – except hope – that the winds would drop even then.

"The Tibetan calendar has two Aprils in it this year, that's why it's so cold", he told us. "But we'll go up to ABC in case we need to make a dash for it. I'm going to send the Sherpas up tomorrow."

The Sherpas left the following day, Friday the 13th. The puja fire was re-lit on the chorten and the Sherpas left camp chanting prayers and throwing rice into the air as they walked.

The Sherpas' departure didn't stop us worrying about the continued bad weather. Russ was even talking about having to extend the expedition. I confided my fears to Lachhu. "Don't worry Didi", he said, calling me by the Nepali name for big sister, used to convey respect but also affection. "We have time. We have food, we have gas and we have 99% hope."

And he reminded me about the Big Three that would make sure we got up the mountain, Big Boss Russ, Lachhu himself and Phurba Tashi, the sirdar, whose strength on the mountain has become almost legendary. "Last year Phurba fix new ladder on Second Step, went back to camp III for sleep and then went to top next day", Lachhu told me. Two years before that, Lachhu continued, Phurba had climbed Everest twice in one week and then went home to Kumjung and had twin sons. I never discovered whether the homecoming coincided with the conception or the birth itself.

Lachhu and I sat chatting companionably in the tent. He was usually so busy he didn't have time to spend with anyone except his staff, but his face would always light up with a 100-watt smile whenever he saw the clients. Ever the journalist, even when I was being a housewife in Tibet, I asked him about his background.

"I am cross", he said. Seeing my forehead crease with a perplexed frown, he explained. "My mother was a Sherpa and my father a Hindu." His father had died when he was three and he was sent out to work at the age of 10. Totally self-educated, Lachhu now speaks six languages. He's also a dab hand at cards.

He told me he had two children, the result of an unexpected marriage the day before he was due to go to on an expedition in 1992. "My mum was very old by then. I had my passport, visa, plane ticket, everything ready to go to Pakistan the next day. But my mum took it all and said I couldn't have it back until I got married. 'I need your wife here', she said. She already had a girl organised so I got married at 10 o'clock the next morning, went to the airport at 12 o'clock with my mum and left my wife at home. I came back two months later and then we had a big party."

Two years later he started working for Russ, eventually working his way up to become one of the Big Three. He obviously holds Russ in high esteem, but still looks back fondly on his days as a cook boy. "Kitchen boy is best job", he said. "Washing pot, cleaning pot, finish. No decisions about what to cook. No headache." He grinned as he got up to go back to the cook tent to make decisions. And to make dinner.

He even made a cake, complete with candles, for my birthday the following day. "Happy Borth Day Groniya" was piped in icing across the top. Lachhu also handed me a bottle of Famous Grouse whisky. "Didi, share share", he cautioned, before he and Russ whirled round the table in a hilarious Nepali dance, with Russ stopping to plant a birthday kiss on my cheek mid-dance.

As well as my birthday toast, we could have used the whisky to celebrate French pilot Didier Delsalle, who had landed a helicopter on the top of Everest for two minutes that day, although his claims were subsequently disputed. Or we could have raised a glass to American Ed Viesturs' Annapurna summit two days earlier which completed the last of the 8,000-metre mountains, all climbed without oxygen. Instead, we used the Famous Grouse solely for medicinal purposes that night.

Even Jez, the joker in the pack, was concerned about our summit chance and told me he'd spent two hours in his tent one afternoon, "communing with Qomolangma" asking for good weather. I knew that he'd been plugged into his iPod, because I'd heard him singing his version of tunes rendered almost unrecognisable by his caterwauling. I hoped the mountain goddess was tone deaf.

But she must have heard someone's prayers, or at least Russ did, because we left for ABC two days later. But not before we indulged in last showers, the equivalent of the condemned man's final breakfast. We could have showers at ABC, but it was so much colder up there, it wasn't an attractive proposition.

The showers, a primitive portable hand-pumped device filled with water in the cook tent, had been a bone of contention earlier in the expedition. With one toilet and shower tent for each of the teams, we had worked out a roster that seemed to keep everybody happy. But when we came down from our first trip to ABC at the end of April, we discovered that the yellow team's shower tent – my shower tent – had been overrun by Italians.

The 12-strong Italian team was there as back-up for the wonderfully named Bruno Brunod, whose aim was to establish a new speed record for an Everest ascent and descent. The 43-year-old mountain runner and his support team, made up mostly of mountain guides from the Aosta valley, had sponsorship from Vitesse for the bid.

The D at the end of Bruno's surname is silent. Alas his compatriots were anything but and I endlessly found them singing in our shower. Or wandering around in the shower tent in various states of undress. But it wasn't just the double frustration of scantily clad males being dangled before me and the shower being dangled just out of reach too. It was the fact that the shower tent wasn't only for ablutions, it also contained the official toilet.

Russ is a stickler for ensuring that his expeditions have as little impact as possible on the mountain environment. So although an outdoor cross-gender urinal is used by everyone, with liquid waste permeating through the rock's natural filtration system, solids are confined to the toilet barrel. From the North Col up, al fresco rules apply, but all human solids are taken off the mountain from ABC and base camp.

Not being able to use the shower or the toilet could have caused a major breakdown in international relations. Especially when it transpired that the Italians weren't even supposed to be using our toilet facilities as they were only satellite members of the Himex team.

At one point I was so desperate that I even considered using one of the 12 individual toilet tents that had been erected for a neighbouring expedition, which was carrying out a study measuring the intake and output of each of its members. But the Italians were so charming that, once we'd actually managed to get into the shower, we forgave them.

The day after our arrival at ABC Russ called us together for a meeting. "There is a small window on the 21st and 22nd, but there's too much risk of losing digits and even toes", he said, as we all sat crushed into the yellow team mess tent. "I won't risk your lives or my Sherpas. Temperatures will be –30 at best and there'll be 60kph winds. You guys would last 10 minutes if anything goes wrong." And then he dropped the bombshell we were all dreading, but hoping never to hear. "I can't guarantee we're going to get a summit attempt this year."

After breaking the bad news to his team, Russ then had to face the climbing equivalent of a firing squad – angry expedition leaders who were demanding to know why the Himex Sherpas hadn't fixed the ropes to the bottom of the summit ridge. They were baying for blood. And for details of Russ's weather forecast. He wasn't prepared to part with either and told the crowd gathered round the Himex chorten exactly what he'd told us. He wouldn't risk the lives of his Sherpas in such conditions.

The controversy was aired on the Everest websites and Russ, who had agreed to mastermind the rope fixing, was vilified on several web pages. But he refused to back down, telling the other teams that there was plenty of rope at high camp if they wanted to go up and fix it, but his Sherpas wouldn't be part of the workforce while the storms raged.

The weather higher on the mountain remained unrelentingly dreadful. Conditions were not as horrific as the storm of 1996, when eight climbers had died in a single night and a total of 15 lives were lost in the deadliest year in Everest history. But there seemed to be no sign of the weather easing for us. We were desperately waiting for the weather window, a brief period when the approaching monsoon would push the jet stream north, leaving the calm conditions that would allow us up to the summit. The weather window that, up to now, had refused to open long enough to allow anyone even close to the top.

The Norwegians, reduced to just half of their original 12, had missed their chance of a national day May 17 summit, but four of them went up the following day, only to be blown back down again. Morale plummeted. And then news came through that there had been a serious avalanche on Annapurna. Italian Christian Kuntner, a colleague of our Team Vitesse friends from the Aosta valley, had been killed while tackling his 14th and last of the world's 8,000 metre peaks. Twenty-fours after that, our confidence took a further knock when Chuck, who had been struggling to get back to full health after his bout of pneumonia, told us that he was going home. He looked desperately thin and his face was grey with fatigue. He knew it was the right decision. And so did we, but we were sorry to see him go.

But spirits at ABC rose again the next day when word came through that 43-year-old Spanish climber Rosa Fernandez had claimed the first summit of the year. She had gone for the narrow window and had squeezed through, reaching the top at 10.40 in the morning of May 21 with Dawa Sherpa. That date was to be a memorable one for more than just Fernandez, however.

Amongst others bagging the summit that day were two of the Russian/Seven Summits team, Slovenians Viktor Milnar and Marko Lihteneker. The younger of the two, 38-year-old Viktor reached the summit at 12.30, meeting his colleague on the descent about an hour from the summit. But he was never to see Marko again. The 45-year-old, an experienced climber and a member of his national mountain rescue service, ran out of oxygen either on the summit or on the way back down. His body was found by a Chinese team the following day.

Marko had been on the summit with a Bhutanese climber, Karma Gyelt-shen. He too had run out of oxygen and the pair stumbled back down the summit ridge, knowing that they were dying. Marko lost the battle for life at the bottom of the snow ramp above the Third Step, but Karma pushed on, willing himself to survive. Dangerously hypoxic and close to death, Karma met a Korean climber who told him that there was an oxygen bottle next to him. Karma looked down and there was the oxygen, lying next to a body. The Korean had died on the mountain the previous year. The oxygen saved Karma's life.

Before Marko's death had been confirmed, there were rumours at ABC that two climbers were missing close to the summit. The first was Marko, the second was said to be French Canadian Jocelyn DuFour. The 33-year-old geophysicist had reached the summit early on May 21, in fact earlier than Rosa Fernandez according to his own reports. He too ran out of oxygen on the descent but managed to stagger down to high camp where he collapsed into a tent.

His wife was celebrating her birthday at home in Calgary on the day her husband reached the top of the world. But the following day, news of Jocelyn's death was posted on one of the mountaineering websites. The report said that his body had been found in a tent at 8,300 metres. But by then the "body" had got up and had struggled back down to the North Col, where he borrowed one of the Jagged Globe radios to get a message through to his Monterosa team mates – and his wife – that he was safe.

In a continuation of the emotional rollercoaster that typifies big mountain climbing, on the same day that Alan Hinkes was celebrating becoming the first Briton to complete all 14 of the world's 8,000 metre peaks when he summitted the 8,587 metre Kangchenjunga on May 30, the Indian Air Force were mourning the loss of one of their team on the north side of Everest. Squadron Leader Chaithanya had reached the summit at 9.45 that morning, but had fallen in deteriorating weather on the descent. His body was never found. A solitary crampon in the snow was the only reminder of his passing.

Team morale in the Himex camp took another dive, but there were good news stories coming off the mountain too. All five of the Norwegians had summitted on May 29 and a Tibetan Sherpa, abandoned at camp II by the Chinese team on their descent from the top, was found in good spirits by two of the Himex Sherpas sent up to rescue him. The Tibetan was snow blind, but although he accepted the proffered food and oxygen, he rejected all offers of assistance. "Eyes broken, body strong", he told his would-be rescuers.

We were living vicariously through all these reports as we waited for our chance to go for the summit. But while we feasted on the stories, we still had to keep our focus on the summit. We kept our fitness and acclimatisation levels topped up with a trek across the Lhakpa La, the beautiful pass that crosses beneath the Kangshung Face and opens out to reveal stunning views of Makalu. It was a glorious day. And Peg and I had another wonderful outing up to the ice wall. Just the two of us and the north side of Everest. It was perfect. We'd been told that big mountain climbing is a retrospective sport, only to be enjoyed after it's all over. But there was nothing retrospective about our enjoyment that day.

But none of us were enjoying the waiting. Whoever it was who said the worst part about climbing Everest is the bed sores hit the nail on the head. Nerves were fraying by the time Russ called us all in for another meeting to say that a bigger window had been forecast for June 3 and 4.

"It's still a long way off and it could change, but this is what we've been waiting for", he said, with the first sign of a smile we'd seen in days. "But we're on a once-only chance. This is it."

He'd had discussions with the guides, he told us, and had split the teams into two groups. Bill and Woody were to be in charge of the first team, with Dean and Narly at the helm for the second. Russ read out the names and I could see that Peg and Soren were not impressed to be put in the team going for the second date. The pair remonstrated with Russ immediately after the meeting. I had assumed Peg would be going with the first group, but at least it meant that now we could share a tent on the summit push. But then I heard Soren telling Woody that he'd be sharing with Peg. I couldn't believe it.

It was ridiculous to be upset, but the endless waiting and the draining of physical and mental reserves had left me more sensitive to perceived slights than I realised. Peg and I had been room-mates on the way to base camp and had been firm friends since. I felt betrayed and hurt. And what made the sense of betrayal worse was that everyone else was already paired up with tent partners.

Russ had been warning us about the bodies that we would encounter on summit day, saying that there were around 27 above high camp, four of which we probably couldn't avoid seeing. I wasn't the only one unnerved by this information and now, at my most vulnerable, I was suddenly completely on my own.

Dean and Woody told me later that Russ had no intention of leaving me on my own. He was going to arrange for a Sherpa to share my tent. It did very little to soothe my feelings. I was about to embark on the scariest undertaking of my life and I'd be in the company of a total stranger. Not only that, but a stranger who couldn't speak my language and who wouldn't even know my name. And at the end of five days would probably still be calling me Didi, which had sounded so endearing at base camp, but wasn't going to be what I needed when I was at my lowest ebb.

I pictured myself on summit night, trying to chase away the demons, the demons of the bodies Russ had just told us we'd have to face and even step over.

My already vivid imagination was running riot and I tried to banish thoughts of the dreadful Everest statistics and how easy it would be to become one of them. Who would comfort and console me when such thoughts threatened to derail me? I knew I was over-reacting and behaving like a spoilt child, but my nerves had been stretched to breaking point with the wait.

I slept badly that night, but my resolve strengthened the next day when Chieko admitted that she too was having doubts. "This Everest", she said to me, "it's very big. I'm feeling nervous and I don't know if I can stay strong for six days." She was worried about the bodies, but I told her we all were, we just had to stay focused. And as I talked to her I felt my own strength returning.

Russ had nominated Karsang as my Sherpa for the summit push. Son of the legendary Ang Rita, Karsang had already summitted Everest six times, but had been forced to turn back with Paul Hockey the previous year. With his dark hair and tiny shades, he looked like a cross between Yoko Ono and John Lennon. I assumed that Russ's comment that Karsang would have to wash his feet before he got into the tent was a joke. Everyone roared with laughter, but I discovered at camp II that it was no joke. No joke at all.

But, even now, the weather stalled us yet again. Russ called us to a meeting under the prayer flags and this time we knew we were facing the possibility of abandonment, even though the Sherpas had headed up the mountain the previous day. The expected weather window had shifted, Russ told us, and we were now looking at June 4 and 5 as possible summit days. The previous latest Himex summit had been June 2.

"There are two things I can do", Russ said to a gathering that was holding its breath as one. "I can say the expedition is over and get you back to Kathmandu by the 9th, or I can say let's wait and we can try for the 4th and 5th. But that's our last try", he emphasised. We collectively exhaled with relief at the reprieve. There was no question of anyone wanting to head back to Kathmandu.

But supplies of everything, particularly gas for cooking and heating the mess tents, were running desperately low. "We're right down to the end of our supplies", Russ warned, "but a little bit of discomfort means we can stay a few days longer. It'll be minor discomfort for major gain." Nobody disputed that. And no-one was going to quit now when the mountain, finally, seemed to be opening her arms to us.

As we counted down the hours over the last two days prior to departure, we spent a lot of time looking through Russ's high-powered telescope, watching other smaller teams on their summit push. "Is that the one you use at the North Col when the team are on the hill?", Kiwi Mary quizzed Russ. He nodded. "Oh, the one with cross-hairs in it?", I asked. "Yeah, why do you think there are so many bodies up there", Russ joked and then added, "and how do you think Hockey lost his arm?"

Peg and I had reached an unspoken truce and, that night, as the two of us were collecting toilet rolls in the tent, a voice in the dark said "Peg" quietly. The Antipodean tones definitely weren't Kiwi. It sounded like Hockey, but it turned out to be Australian Duncan Chessell, who had switched to another expedition after a fallout with Russ. Even in the light from our head-torches we could see that he looked dreadful. He told us he'd gone for the summit the previous night, but had been forced to turn round at 8,300 metres with breathing problems. Stronger than most of us, he had been humbled by the mountain.

It was hard saying goodbye to the first team the next morning. With four deaths already recorded and so many strong climbers limping back to camp, it was like watching soldiers going off to war. I was nervous for them, but their departure also brought our moment of reckoning closer. Once they were gone we had no excuses left. The procrastinations were over. Rucksacks had to be packed, but every item had to be evaluated. Was it worth the extra weight? Trying to decide what to leave out was the toughest part. Nobody stayed up late that night.

Shivering as I slid into my sleeping bag, I decided to leave my down jacket on until I warmed up. I fell instantly asleep and woke, two hours later, with my down jacket and my head-torch still on.

II

Countdown To The Summit

June 1

We were breakfasting in the red mess tent the next morning when Russ came in. I could tell by the look on his face that this wasn't a social call. Jez had told me before he'd headed off to the North Col about the pre-climb briefing they'd been given the previous morning. He'd said it had been pretty hard hitting. True to form, Russ didn't pull any punches with the second team either.

After going through the oxygen flow rates that we would be using on the very varied terrain higher up the mountain, he urged us not to spend too long on the summit. "You'll be wasting valuable time and valuable oxygen", he cautioned. "Remember, when you reach the top you're only halfway. Most people die on Everest coming back down. You must have at least 25% of your energy left. If you don't you're going to die. It's simple."

The nervous chatter and excited banter of breakfast a few minutes before was gone. We sat in silence. Nobody looked at anyone else. Russ was the sole focus of our attention.

"Remember, what you're doing is dangerous. It's difficult and you can die. Don't take it lightly. The mountain won't go away, it'll still be here next year. Success is coming back here alive, with all your toes and all your fingers. You must make some effort yourself in making the right judgement call. I can't make those judgements for you. Be cautious. Be aware. There's no second chance here, no rescue. If you make a mistake you die."

I looked round at the stony faces of my team-mates. Peggy was crying quietly. Several others weren't too far off it. Anxiety thickened the air.

"Any questions?", Russ looked round us all. "Can we go home?", I queried mischievously. Gales of laughter dispelled the tension and Russ ruffled my hair in a rare display of emotion and something akin to affection. It was unlike him to be so demonstrative, but my deliberately crass question had diffused a tense situation.

He went on to tell us not to take too much food. It would weigh us down, we wouldn't eat it all and we'd have to carry it back down off the mountain, he said. And then he returned to the serious stuff.

"If you stop feeling your toes and fingers, don't carry on. Frostbite comes on and you don't feel it. If you start to stumble, ask yourself, 'can I feel my feet'. And don't forget, you'll be more prone to frostbite if you don't drink, because your blood will be thicker."

He brightened visibly. "Let's go for it", he urged. Then, aware that nerves – frayed by such a lengthy wait for the weather window – were now taut to the point of snapping, he smiled his crooked smile and said: "I'm probably the most nervous of all of you!"

And with that he was gone, leaving us to digest some of the most important information we were ever likely to be given. The atmosphere in the tent felt chilly, so we spilled out into the sunshine to get some heat back into our bones.

Despite the tenor of Russ's talk, I felt oddly calm. The nerves I'd felt the previous day when the others were leaving were now gone. I was ready for this challenge and, whatever the outcome, I knew I would give it my best shot. My body was pitifully thin. I just had to hope that my mind would be strong enough to make up for the muscle wastage caused by such a lengthy stay at altitude. I had a suspicion – built on wishful thinking – that as long as I could maintain my focus, my willpower would carry me through.

I remembered Whetu's words on that final night in Kathmandu after we'd come back from Cho Oyu. "Everest has a way of getting inside your head", he'd told me the previous October. "You have to go with the mindset, 'I will get to the top'. If you have any doubts at all the mountain will magnify them." It was a mantra that was to carry me through many moments of self-doubt. I will get to the top, I told myself endlessly. I never allowed the thought of failure to enter my head.

I set off for the North Col on that morning of June 1 filled, not with the sense of foreboding I had expected to feel, but with a cautious optimism that I hoped would stay with me right to the very top of the world. Already bubbling with excitement, I was buoyed up still further when a male voice rang out, "Grania!"

I whirled round, having no idea where the voice was coming from or who it belonged to. It called again and I scanned the neighbouring tents and those scattered further down the moraine, closer to the rapidly diminishing glacier that was already beginning to show signs of the thaw. "Who's that?" I bellowed back. "Humphrey", came the voice and then I spotted him, waving frantically from the Monterosa camp way down below me. It was a pretty impressive feat to recognise me from that distance.

"Are you going up?", he questioned. "Yes, what about you?" I quizzed back. "Summitted on the 30th", came the reply. "Fantastic", I shouted, feeling my own energy and confidence rising at the news of Humphrey's success. "Congratulations!"

I yelled down that I had no contact details for him. Could he come up and leave them with Russ later? He said he would and I headed on up towards Crampon Point with the sound of his good luck wishes echoing in my head. It felt like the best possible omen that one Irish person had already made it to the top of the mountain from Tibet. And I was determined to make it two. It was only on my return to Dublin that I discovered that another Irishman, Gavin Bate, had almost made it two in one day. Climbing without oxygen, Gavin reached the bottom of the Hillary Step on the south side on the same day as Humphrey was summitting from the north.

Peg and I chatted as we plodded up the familiar rocky terrain towards the remnants of the Chinese camp. "That was pretty tough stuff from Russ, wasn't it", I said. "Yes", agreed Peg, "I was crying." "I know, I saw you." "I cried all the way up Denali", she went on. "They didn't know what to do with me." It was hard not to sympathise with her, even though I was still raw from what I viewed as her indifference to my feelings over the tent sharing issue.

Minor upsets were put into perspective shortly afterwards when we met a member of the Indian Airforce expedition which had lost one of its team on his return from the summit. There had still been no news in the search for the body. We spoke briefly and the man's sadness at the tragedy was all too evident. He said he'd pray for us and went slowly on his way

We weren't in any rush, so we kept the pace leisurely as we went up towards Crampon Point. Narly caught up with us as we were pulling crampons, ice axes and harnesses out of the blue barrels where our gear had been stored for so long now. "Some fella left a message for you, Grania", he said. Humphrey had obviously come straight up from the Monterosa camp to leave his phone number with Russ. I hoped I'd have good news for him the next time we spoke.

As I tightened my harness and strapped on my crampons I knew I wanted to savour every minute of this adventure. I could come back again another year, but I would never be able to repeat this first time and I wanted to make sure I could retain every little detail in my mind.

Lost in my own thoughts, I hadn't seen a stranger coming up towards us. He stopped to talk, telling us he was an Austrian mountain guide and was climbing the mountain as part of Swiss leader Kari Kobler's international team. He was slower than the other members of the expedition, he said, and they'd gone on ahead without him. As we climbed up onto the glacier he and I fell into conversation. His fellow Austrian had gone home the previous week, he told me, abandoning his summit attempt because of stomach problems.

I introduced myself and he responded by telling me that his name was Christian Eiterer and that he owned a hotel in Ischgul. I said that although I was listed as an Irish housewife on the climbing permit, I was really a journalist. He was just telling me that this was his first attempt on Everest as I looked back over my shoulder to see that we were already some way ahead of Peg, Narly and Charlie. "Yes, it's my first attempt too", I said, looking round at him. "I'm hoping to be the first Irish woman to summit from the north side." Christian was thrilled at the idea. "So no Irish wives have gone to the top on the north side", he said with delight, whacking me with his ski pole a couple of times for emphasis.

As we walked along companionably, side by side where the narrow track permitted it, he told me that he had managed to break the sole of his climbing boots clean in half. Jon Gangdal, leader of the Norwegian expedition that had summitted on May 29, had lent him his boots for the summit push. When I told him my own boot saga, he was highly entertained at the thought of my boots making their own way up the south side while I climbed the north side but, like me, he was disappointed that my south side boots had already abandoned their attempt.

We stopped at the bottom of the fixed ropes, where Sissel and half-Irish New Yorker Kevin Goldstein were already taking a break. Charlie, Peg and Narly arrived shortly afterwards and I introduced Christian to them as they flopped down into the snow and pulled out their water bottles. We were all feeling the effects of long-term living at altitude and didn't want to get dehydrated with another four more days' climbing to go before summit day.

Narly didn't hang around for long. After warning us not to take a break anywhere there was a danger of avalanche or ice-fall, he strode purposefully off towards the ropes, clipped in and headed up the slope. He rapidly disappeared out of sight. After chatting for a while, Christian said he was going to go on too. He was followed shortly afterwards by Kevin and Sis. The pair clipped into the fixed line and started their ascent.

I gave them all a bit of time to move on up the hill and then set off after them. It felt so good to be on the move at last, away from ABC and with our sights now firmly set on the summit. All the doubts of the last two months had now been replaced by a sense of eager anticipation and a determination to get to the top.

I headed on up the increasingly steep snow slope towards the ice wall. Another climber was retreating slowly down the hill. As we came level with each other, we stopped to chat. I asked him how it had gone up there. "I turned round at 7,900", he said disconsolately, before heading pitifully slowly on down the ropes. He was only just disappearing out of sight as I reached the lip where the snow flattened out at the bottom of the ice wall.

My Sherpa, Karsang, was already there, squatting comfortably in the traditional pose that the Sherpas seem to be able to hold for hours without seizing up with cramp. Two more Indian Airforce team members had just abseiled down the side of the ice wall and stopped to talk to me, sitting down in the snow just as Peg came up to join us. I offered my condolences on the loss of their team-mate.

GETTING CLOSER: On the way to base camp I had the perfect opportunity to point out my goal.

FAMILY LIFE (top left): me holding onto baby Kate, with twin sister Megan behind me and elder sister Sarah at the back; top right: twin rivalry, me on top of Meg; right: my parents, Dilys and Jerome, on their wedding day; above: my 19-year-old nephew Joe, a victim of sudden adult death syndrome, who died five weeks before I was due to leave for Everest; far right: my competitive riding days were brought to a halt by two serious injuries.

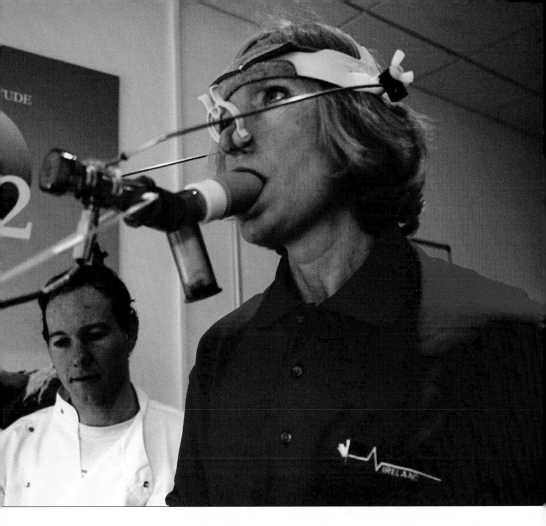

IN TRAINING: facing page (top): me and Brendan O'Brien of SORD Data Systems, taking a break from the Tesco's freezer, where we subjected the Hewlett Packard technology to the type of cold it would be facing on the mountain; above: being put through my paces during a fitness analysis with sports physiologist and manager of Peak Centre Ireland, Carl Petersen; left: rock climbing in France, with Mont Blanc in the background; far left: on my first trip to Nepal where I was declared both best walker and best party animal.

TIBETAN LIFE: **facing page (top left):** the Chinese remeasuring team failed to record the definitive height of Everest on this new monument at base camp; **centre:** the local brew; **top right:** purveyor of antiquities in Lhasa; **centre right:** Buddhist monks' footwear outside the Drepung monastery in Lhasa; **above:** the 26 metre high gilded statue of the Future Buddha in the Chapel of Jampa at Tashilhunpo monastery in Shigatse; **left:** Tibetan mother and child; **far left:** our bus just squeezed across this bridge on the way to base camp.

PART OF THE GANG (top left): Himex base camp manager, Lachhu Bastnet; **top right:** Tibetan Karsang and me on the 22 kilometre trek up to ABC; **centre right:** my Sherpa Karsang, who rescued me when I ran out of oxygen on the descent; **right:** expedition leader Russell Brice; **above:** Irish climbers Noel Hanna and Lynne Stark, who were forced to abandon their bid for their summit when Noel developed altitude related eye problems; **above centre:** the Himex women - Monica Weil Kalozdi, me, Sissel Smaller, Chieko Shimada and Peggy Foster. **Facing page:** prayer flags catching the breeze during the base camp puja.

A sensational view down the Rongbuk glacier on the descent from the summit of Everest.

GETTING TO THE TOP (top left): rehydrating is an important part of success on the mountain; **top right:** using the Hewlett Packard iPAQ to send stories and pictures back to *The Irish Times*; **right:** climbing the ice wall on the way up to the North Col; **above:** Sherpas sorting out the oxygen before the final summit push. **Facing page:** Himex climbers on the snow ramp at the top of the Third Step, between 90 minutes and two hours from the summit.

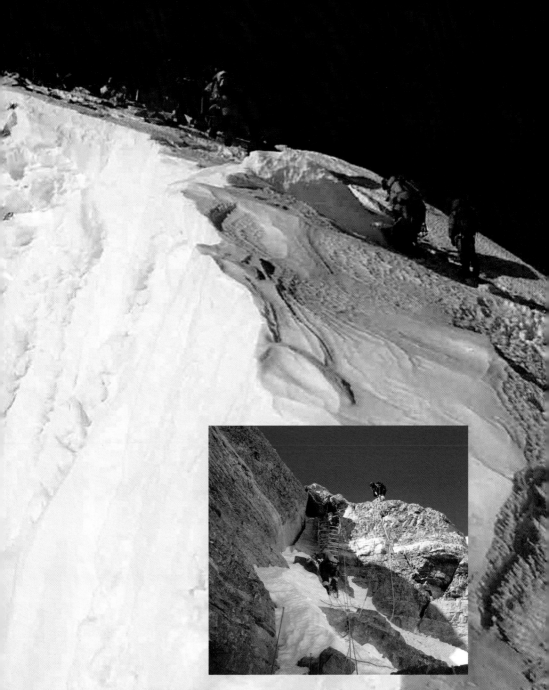

MAIN PICTURE: June 4, the first Himex team reach the prayer flag draped summit. If any of the team had strayed too close to the edge they would have plummeted down the Kangshung Face on the left or the North Face to the right. Falls down either would result in certain death. I reached the top the following day in much gloomier conditions. **Above:** descending the ladder at the Second Step, one of the most character-forming moments of summit day. On the way up the mountain the Second Step is climbed in the dark. (Photographs: Bill Crouse copyright)

SUMMIT DAY (top): a picture that could have been taken anywhere, but is actually me standing on the misty summit of Everest on June 5, 2005; **above left:** Donegal climber Humphrey Murphy, who reached the summit on May 30 and has toys belonging to his two children, Zak and Altan, in his mouth; **above right:** one-armed Australian climber Paul Hockey, who nearly died on the descent; **right:** rather clearer conditions for a Dublin photo-shoot on my return from the mountain.

As I clipped into the ropes before starting my ascent of the ice wall, I saw a third member of the Indian team rappelling down to my left. I could see one of his crampons was far from secure on his boot and, the next second, it shook itself free and hurtled down the wall straight towards the others I had just left. "Below", I yelled out. Quick as a flash, Karsang stuck out his boot and arrested the crampon in full flight. It was a masterly piece of goal-keeping.

I turned my attention back to the ice wall, where the amount of traffic meant that there were now far more steps hacked into the face, making the ascent much easier than when we'd first tackled it so many weeks ago on our initial acclimatisation trip up to the North Col.

Things had changed quite dramatically further up too. The ladder was still over the first crevasse, but a snow-bridge next to it had obviously become the main route, rendering the ladder redundant. And there had been a high level of activity just above the ladder, where enormous chunks of ice had come rocketing down the face and now lay strewn across a large area of snow. It wasn't a place to hang around.

I moved more slowly as the incline increased, partly due to the exertion required but also because I was conscious of the fact that I needed to conserve plenty of energy for the demands that would be placed on my body over the next few days. I was close to the top of the steepest section when Christian suddenly leaped into view from above, grabbed my hand and hauled me up the last few metres. It was totally unnecessary, but an act of pure chivalry and showmanship. Kari and the other members of his team sitting outside their tents thought it was hilarious.

"You know he has two daughters, a pretty wife and a hotel in Ischgul?", one of them said to me. "He told me about the hotel, but oddly enough he didn't mention the wife and daughters", I replied, to more laughter from Christian's team-mates.

I still had to cross the double ladder over the wider crevasse just below the North Col and prayed I wouldn't fall off in front of Kari's team. I negotiated it cautiously, gripping the double ropes that formed wobbly handrails, but at least provided some sense of security. As I took the final step before reaching the far side, I heard a cry of "Grani". Looking up I saw the Russian team leader Alex Abramov coming down towards me. He'd never got to grips with my name, but the warmth of his greeting reinforced my belief that the mountain engenders a camaraderie rare in other walks of life.

Dean caught up with me just before I reached the Himex camp. "You're on fire today", he said to me. It was just the boost I needed. Dean had used the same expression the day we went across the glacier at Lhakpa La, when I knew myself that I was moving well. But this time those same four words boosted me like nothing else had during all the previous weeks and I arrived into camp full of confidence about the challenge before me.

I stripped off my crampons and harness and then went to the tent I assumed I'd be sharing with Karsang. "Will I get some snow", I offered. "No, you relax", Karsang replied, disappearing with a sack and a shovel. Returning shortly afterwards with a sackful of freshly cut ice, he emptied some into a saucepan, lit the gas and balanced the pot delicately on the stove. Picking up one of the dual-purpose plastic bowls that function as both mugs and plates on the mountain, he carefully wiped it out with toilet paper to make sure it was clean. And then blew into it. I hoped I wasn't going to pick up some bug when my reserves of strength were already compromised by such lengthy exposure to altitude.

Having made sure I'd got enough water, he then told me that he and two of the other Sherpas would be sleeping in the store tent, so I'd have the tent to myself for the night. Knowing that we'd be sharing from then on, I thought he'd probably be more comfortable in the company of his fellow Sherpas. But he'd no intention of leaving me just yet and set about cooking noodle soup for the two of us. I felt bad telling him I didn't want chicken stock. I didn't know if his English, shaky at the best of times, would understand vegetarianism, but he took the sachet of vegetable soup I handed him from my pack and made chicken-free noodle soup for me.

Until that moment I had no idea that monosodium glutamate could taste so good. They say hunger is a good sauce, but obviously altitude – which usually suppresses appetite – was an equally good sauce that day.

After I'd finished, Karsang poured more water into my bowl and then left me listening to reports on the radio that someone had been seen on the summit at five o'clock. Russ reckoned the climber would be back down to the First Step by seven, but it seemed dangerously late to be so high on the mountain.

I could hear Chieko talking to her Sherpa Dorjie in the neighbouring tent.

"What's it like at camp III?", I heard her ask. "Very, very, very windy", came the rather disconcerting reply.

It was a long and cold night, but I slept better than some of my team-mates. Charlie, who seemed to have made such a good recovery, became increasingly unwell as the night wore on. Some time after midnight he attempted to wake tent mate Antoine, but he was sleeping soundly and couldn't be roused. By one o'clock Charlie knew he was in serious trouble and finally managed to wake the slumbering Frenchman who, very unwillingly, got out of the tent to go in search of assistance from one of the guides.

Antoine's calls woke me as he went past my tent. "Dean, Charlie needs oxygen", I heard him shout urgently in his thick French accent. There was a flurry of activity, a cylinder of oxygen was found and taken to the sick New Zealander. With Charlie settled on oxygen, silence returned to camp.

June 2

I woke at six and, having lit the gas, threw chunks of ice into the saucepan and put it onto the stove to melt. While I waited for the pot to come to the boil I ate an Alpen bar and thought of Jez describing in glorious technicolour how he'd thrown up on his first trip to camp II after eating one of the muesli bars.

With the sun yet to reach the tents, the biting cold meant it took almost an hour for the water to boil, but it was worth the wait. The bowl of drinking chocolate tasted so good. Fed and rehydrated, I even managed to take some of the vitamin pills that Jenny had so painstakingly counted out on the eve of my departure. I was thrilled with myself, but the feeling of delight didn't last long. Brushing my teeth shortly afterwards, I pushed the toothbrush too close to the back of my tongue, triggering the gag reflex. Next thing I knew, my entire breakfast was making a rapid reappearance out of the back of the tent.

My vomiting episode was minor. But the expedition was over for Charlie. His pulmonary oedema had returned during the night and he had no choice but to go down. I went over to his tent to say how sorry I was. I could see from the look in his eyes that he was totally devastated. It must have been desperately difficult for him to watch us all leaving and know that his dreams of the summit were now exactly that, just dreams.

Jagged Globe leader David Hamilton was on the radio shortly before eight, telling Russ that it was extremely windy at the 7,900 metre camp III. "Two of your store tents are badly damaged", he said. "My guys are trying to save them for you. We were hoping to go up to high camp today, but I think conditions are too bad." It wasn't encouraging to hear that the higher camps were still being battered by the wind.

By 8.45 I was ready to leave. After checking my crampons were firmly strapped on, I hefted my pack onto my back and started on the long haul up to camp II. The terrain from the North Col to camp II is very straightforward, but the endless snow slopes rapidly sap energy, particularly on the steeper sections.

I led for a good while, but every time I decided to stop for a drink, the sight of a long string of climbers straggling up the fixed lines behind me urged me on. I didn't want to get stuck behind anyone. I'd already overtaken one pair of climbers, but they'd caught up while I was having a breather. They unclipped and went past only to slow down again, causing frequent hold-ups, but I felt there was no point us constantly overtaking each other so I stayed behind them.

At least the delays gave me a chance to look around at the staggeringly beautiful views to my right. Unknown snow-covered peaks strained towards the sky and, ahead of me, towering over them all, was the summit of Everest, black and sombre in comparison. It looked so daunting and so huge. What on earth was I doing taking on such a vast endeavour, I asked myself. It was way outside my scope and experience.

I immediately banished such negative emotions, focusing instead on how lucky I was to be in such an amazing place and on such an incredible journey. Lucky too that the weather seemed finally to be turning in our favour. Brilliant sunshine sparkled off the clean, snowy wastes around me, with only the blue of the fixed lines and the occasional dot of colour of a climber's down suit far ahead breaking the white expanses. The winds that had made our last trip to camp II such a nightmare had disappeared, although the plume off the summit gave evidence of much worse weather higher up the mountain.

Aware that I needed to stay hydrated, I sat down on the snow for a drink. Paul and his Sherpa Nima joined me and I suggested that Paul should go on and take the lead. He was quite content to follow me, he said. Somewhat reluctantly I hauled myself to my feet, turned around to face the hill again and ploughed on, feeling the pressure more now that I had people right behind me.

The plodding seemed to go on forever but, at last, I could see familiar red tents perched at the very top of the snow slope, just before the start of a rocky section that seemed to vanish skywards. One team had pitched their camp higher up amongst the rocks but, for once, the Himex tents were the closest.

The wind, which had been absent for most of the ascent from the North Col, had started to build again. By the time we got to camp, it had worked itself into a frenzy, buffeting us with such force that it threatened to knock us over. The wind had wreaked havoc amongst the cluster of tents, leaving shredded pieces of fabric flapping noisily in the breeze as the skeletal remains clung desperately to the snow.

By now the wind was so strong that we had to stay clipped in right to the very door of our tents or risk being blown straight off the mountain. With so many tents ripped to shreds by the gales, it was hardly surprising that there weren't enough to accommodate us all, but Karsang had already established himself in one, so I battled my way up to it, collapsing in an exhausted heap outside the vestibule.

After unbuckling my crampons and dragging off my harness, I crawled into the tent and flung myself onto one of the sleeping bags. Later, as I sat sipping from a bowl of hot mango drink, I heard Dean trying to sort out the sleeping arrangements. Two team members were still without a tent and sleeping mats. I was glad I wasn't last into camp.

Sissel had established herself in the tent behind mine, but was still waiting to be joined by tent-mate Kevin. Paul and Nima were on the other side. Snuggled in between the two, my tent was probably the least exposed to the elements, but it was still being continuously pummelled by the winds.

Karsang and I shared a Cliff bar and I must have dozed off after eating as, when I woke about 20 minutes later, Karsang had gone. I made myself a big bowl of noodle soup – it was to become my standard fare on the mountain – and had just finished it when he reappeared carrying two bottles of oxygen. The canisters gave a satisfying hiss as we screwed them onto the regulators and, having established that the bottles were full, we set the flow rate and then fitted the masks to our faces, sucking in the oxygen deeply.

Karsang settled back on top of his sleeping bag and, within seconds, was asleep. It didn't take long for me to follow suit. I've no idea how long we slept, but I woke just as Karsang was sliding out of the tent. I took off my mask and, as I turned off the oxygen flow on the regulator, my nostrils were assailed by the smell of gas. I sat up rapidly, turning round to look at the stove out in the vestibule. The wind gusting in through the tent flaps as Karsang went out had obviously extinguished the flame. I hastily turned off the gas, thinking how ironic it would be to be gassed when attempting to climb the highest mountain in the world.

Karsang returned shortly afterwards, just as my body decided it was fully rehydrated. My bladder was crying out for attention. I hadn't taken off my boots so I opted for an al fresco pee. "Be careful, be careful", Karsang warned me as I climbed out of the tent and was hit amidships by a huge gust of wind. I rapidly clipped into the rope and shinned down the incline to try and find a suitable spot. But the combination of the wind, the flapping remains in the tent grave-yard and my determination not to let go of the rope meant that peeing was impossible. I managed to undo the zip on my down suit, but that was as far as it went.

I abandoned the unequal struggle, zipped up and heaved myself back up the rope, deciding I'd attend to matters from within the safety of the tent. I'd heard too many stories of climbers being killed in the mountains while answering the call of nature and I had no intention of being added to the statistics.

"Too windy", I said to Karsang as I scrambled in through the tent flaps. Once inside I ostentatiously got out my pee bottle in the hope that Karsang might discreetly leave to give me some privacy. But he had no intention of moving. We were going to be sharing a tent for at least four nights and the pee bottle was obviously going to be put to quite a lot of use during that time, so I simply asked him to turn away.

He silently turned his back on me and I hurriedly stripped off my down suit and dragged multiple layers of undergear down to mid-thigh level. Employing an art I'd perfected over many nights at BC and ABC – but never in front of an audience – I carefully positioned myself over the not very capacious neck of the bottle. It felt like the longest and noisiest pee in the world. Karsang kept looking stoically towards the front of the tent throughout.

Apart from peeing, or listening to someone peeing, there's very little in the way of entertainment at the higher camps. Sissel and I intermittently made attempts at conversation, but it was hard to make ourselves heard over the noise of the wind, even when we shouted to each other through half-open tent flaps, so eventually we gave up. I tried taking some pictures through the flaps of the view back down to the North Col, but huge white clouds were bubbling up and obscuring all but the highest peaks.

I went back to listening in on the chat on the radio. Shortly after four o'clock, David Hamilton reported that the winds had died down at 8,300 metres and that things were looking good for a summit push at midnight. His pessimism of that morning had been misplaced. Russ said that he'd have another forecast at about five if David wanted to call back. "Oh, and your doctor's come down, but didn't use his radio all day." Fred Ziel, who had lost the tip of his nose to frostbite on a previous expedition, had obviously been out of contact throughout his descent after abandoning his summit bid, so it was good to hear that he was safely back down at ABC.

My attention drifted in and out of focus, but it was brought round sharply just after five o'clock when Karsang pulled off his boots. The rancid smell was so overpowering the lining of my nostrils felt like they were burning. Praying that I wouldn't regurgitate my noodle soup, I grabbed my mask and clamped it to my face with indecent haste, holding it in place with one hand while I frantically turned on the flow of oxygen with the other. Russ hadn't been joking about the foot washing.

Just before seven o'clock I heard a male voice outside the tent. "Knock, knock." It was Dean doing what he called his "last thing" check on everybody to see we were all okay. "Last thing" made it sound as though it was midnight, but late nights on mountains bear no resemblance to late nights at sea level.

June 3

I woke at seven the next morning after almost 12 hours of really solid sleep, feeling stronger than I had done for some time. Karsang was already awake and had the stove going. But the wind was threatening to blow out the flame and, at one point, gusted so strongly that the stove itself nearly blew over.

If we were going to get any drinking water into us, the only way the stove was going to be safe was if it was brought inside the tent. Karsang cleared a space in the middle of the mats and set the stove down. I warned him that the pot wasn't on squarely, but before he could move it, the whole thing toppled over, flooding the tent with water.

We were in the midst of mopping up the mess when Russ's voice crackled through on the airwaves, giving the forecast to his two Himex team leaders Bill and Dean and to Kari. Wind speeds were dropping, he said, but were still strong. Kari said he thought he might send some of his weaker climbers down.

I'd already eaten breakfast, but Karsang said he would eat later, having nothing apart from a sachet of instant butter tea that he'd bought in Lhasa. "All the Tibetan Sherpas use", he said, offering me a taste of the rancid smelling liquid. I took the tiniest sip, knowing it would be disgusting. It was, but I told Karsang it was delicious. "Very good", I lied.

As I was readying myself for departure, Karsang caught sight of my Black Diamond head-torch, one of the bits of gear included in the sponsorship package from the Great Outdoors in Dublin. "It's good", he said, as he picked up the head-torch and examined it minutely. Telling Karsang that he could have the head torch when I left – if I'd had a spare I would have given it to him on the spot – I then asked him if he could turn away. I needed to strip my bottom half so that I could tape my knees. I could sense that Karsang was filled with curiosity. What could Didi possibly be doing now? He pulled up his hood so that he could see nothing, but I noticed a couple of minutes later that the hood was down again.

With my knees securely strapped, I zipped myself back into my down suit, struggled into my boots and pulled on my harness. Checking to see that I'd left nothing behind, I tightened the drawstring on my backpack, closed the outer buckles and swung the pack over my shoulder before crawling out of the tent.

The wind hit me full force and I retreated back into the vestibule to put on my crampons, uncomfortably aware that today was all about rock. The combination of crampons, rock and wind was not a good one. At least on snow or ice, the crampons would provide some purchase, a solid foothold to withstand the worst of the wind. But there was no such comfort on rock. A loss of balance caused by the buffeting of the wind would be dramatically magnified as the crampons skittered across the impervious surface of the rock.

But even getting to the rock from the relative safety of our snowy camp was a battle that morning. I stood up cautiously, but the force of the wind was so strong that I had to crouch down again and hold onto the guy-ropes to negotiate the step off the platform our tents were pitched on. As I turned to clip into the fixed line just below, I saw Sissel just emerging from her tent. She snapped a quick photo of me.

Conversation was out of the question, but even thoughts were blown away, quite literally, moments later as I turned uphill, facing right into the teeth of the gale as I inched my way towards the massive jumble of rock that led to camp III. A narrow path on the right-hand side of the first outcrop led up to a jagged cluster of rocks. Clambering up them at sea level would have been the work of seconds and, even at this height, would have been nothing on a calm day. But every time I went to launch myself up the first step, a gust of wind would throw me off balance and I'd have to start again. It was frustrating and stamina sapping. Within minutes of leaving camp I was exhausted.

Planting both feet firmly on a level patch of rock, I stopped to try and catch my breath. Turning round to look back down towards camp still less than 100 metres below me, I expected to see a queue of fellow Himex members stacked up impatiently behind me. But, headed by Sissel, they were strung out on the rope, all struggling as much as me in the difficult conditions.

I attacked the task with renewed vigour and three moves brought me up onto another level area surrounded by huge rocks that offered momentary respite from the wind. Encouraged, I forged ahead up a narrow gully that led to a right-hand turn up steeper but less rocky ground. I hauled myself up, catching sight of two yellow-suited climbers some distance ahead of me.

I had got into a rhythm by now and was enjoying this part of the climb. It was really little more than scrambling. But the extreme altitude made it so much more demanding, mentally as well as physically. As I scanned the rocks for cracks and fissures big enough to take my crampon points, I was glad I'd spent a half-morning dry tooling in Scotland. I knew that the First, Second and Third Steps above high camp would be far more taxing, but I was now working well on this rocky terrain and it gave me confidence for the much greater demands of summit day.

I caught up with Paul and Nima taking a break. After snatching a quick drink, I went on and, not much further ahead, passed Fujibayashi and his Sherpa, Lhakpa Tshering. The pair tucked in behind me and, on easier ground, we all climbed together for a while, but it wasn't long before Dean came steaming past us all, heading strongly on towards the camp that was still out of sight above us.

Following in Dean's wake, Narly was now hovering on my tail, so I stepped aside to let him through as well. But the pace being set by Dean was too much for Narly, weakened by non-stop coughing and the resultant rib damage. No sooner was he past me than he slowed right down, leaving me snapping at his heels, itching to be back out in front. Less than 10 minutes later he dropped down onto a rock and, without speaking, waved me on past. He didn't seem in any mood for sympathy so I seized the opportunity to take over the lead again.

There was a fair bit of downward traffic by now and we were continually having to stop to allow descending climbers past. A man ground to a halt in front of me, seemingly incapable of working out how he could get by. I extended a hand, which he took gratefully, but then stopped again when he came level with my shoulder. I asked the only question that occupied all our minds by now. "Did you get to the summit?"

He looked wearily down the rocky horror he still had to negotiate. "With my friend", he said, breathing hard, "we got 30 or 40 metres from the summit, but we were too tired." It seemed desperately close to the target to abort the mission, but I assumed it must have been 30 or 40 vertical metres from the summit when they made the decision to turn round.

Just behind him, a woman was being helped down by three male companions. Her vacant gaze rested briefly on my face, but there was no recognition of a fellow human being or attempt at a greeting. Tubes running into her nostrils were supplying badly needed oxygen. More solid support was provided by the two men, around whose shoulders her arms were draped. She was in a bad way. We stood aside in silence and let the party through.

I was flagging psychologically by now. Seeing so many strong, fit climbers looking totally shattered had unnerved me and my own pace suffered as a result. But my spirits were given a timely fillip when I caught sight of a flash of red. Moments later as I came up to a massive boulder that diverted the rope up to the left, I saw what was unmistakably the top of a tent only about 100 metres away.

I hadn't the energy to up my pace in celebration and there were still climbers coming down that intermittently halted my progress but, shortly afterwards, I scrabbled my way up the final incline and there were the tents bearing the familiar Himex logo.

Tents were dotted around irregularly, pitched anywhere that was vaguely flat. There was one, some distance away from the others, teetering on the edge of a serious drop. It clung precariously to the rock, looking as though the slightest breeze would send it scudding down the mountain. I had no intention of occupying it and saw, with some relief, that Karsang was already installed in much more secure looking accommodation.

Secure it may have been, but it was also stuffed to the gills with Sherpas. Karsang was entertaining. Along with his three visitors, Karsang was breakfasting or lunching, it was hard to tell, on a strange mud-coloured lumpy concoction that all four were spooning enthusiastically into their mouths. It was only when I was offered some that I discovered it was black tea and cornflakes mixed together.

The tent may have been crowded, but at least it was as sheltered as it was possible to be on the flanks of a wind-scoured mountainside, 7,900 metres above sea level. I put my oxygen mask on and, as I tried to find room to lie back on my sleeping bag, I thought about how oxygen really is the life-blood of the high-altitude mountaineer. I felt fine without it when I wasn't moving, but knew that it would help my recovery and give me more energy for the climb up to high camp and then the summit push tomorrow night. Of course there are the purists who can and do tackle the biggest peaks without supplemental oxygen, but they are few and far between. For a novice like me oxygen wasn't just a treat, it was a necessity.

One of those purists, Mogens, was at that very moment gearing himself up for his summit attempt in a tent only metres away from mine. The Dane's familiar voice came through on the radio, talking to Russ, who was now in position at the North Col camp, from where he would oversee operations throughout the two Himex summit days. Both Mogens and the Italian mountain runner Bruno Brunod were on programmes tailored specially to suit their oxygen-free ascents.

The visiting Sherpas and Karsang had all vacated the tent by now and I could feel my nerves beginning to kick in as I thought about Mogens and Bruno without oxygen and about the rest of the Himex team heading for the summit later that night. I needed something to distract me.

Karsang returned. He smelt strongly of cigarettes, known in the Himalaya as "Sherpa oxygen". He quickly turned to the more traditional oxygen, however, putting on his mask and turning up the regulator. Lying down on his back with his hands folded behind his head, he instantly fell asleep. I was horrified, not that he was asleep, but that he was sleeping with his feet towards the mountain. One of the myriad Sherpa superstitions forbids adopting such a position, which is considered irreverent to the mountain goddess.

But then I realised with relief that Karsang had his knees bent, meaning that his feet weren't pointing towards the mountain, they were firmly planted downwards. Even in sleep he adhered to traditions.

Just after five o'clock, Dean came to the tent. His "last thing" checks were getting earlier. I'd heard Antoine's name mentioned on the radio, so I asked Dean about him. "He turned round about 50 metres from camp II", Dean confirmed. "He's not very good on his feet and was being blown around, so he turned back." Remembering that morning's struggle against the wind immediately after we'd left camp I could understand the Frenchman's decision to call it a day.

I knew that some of the Jagged Globe clients, including Sibusiso Vilane, had spent 90 minutes on the summit that morning. Ranulph Fiennes wasn't amongst them. Even though the legendary explorer had completed seven marathons in seven days on seven continents just months after heart bypass surgery two years earlier, he was concerned about putting his heart under further stress and had turned round an hour after leaving high camp.

Karsang, who had gone out while I was talking to Dean, returned with a freshly filled snow sack, dropping it into the vestibule before going back outside. As I put the pot on to boil I could hear him chatting close to the tent. He came back in shortly afterwards, bringing with him two new Sherpas. The pair settled themselves down in the cramped vestibule, so I sat up to make room for the visitors and told them to come into the tent itself.

Only one of them came in, leaving the other one sitting alone out in the vestibule. Karsang told me that the Sherpa now in the tent had been on Cho Oyu with us last year. To my shame I didn't recognise him.

As Karsang poured out hot water for his guests I hoped he wouldn't use my bowl. I had put it in the side pocket of the tent wall behind me, so he would have to ask me for it. Thankfully he had enough bowls for the visitors. "You want chocolate?", he then said, turning to look at me. "Yes", I nodded, handing him the precious bowl. He executed his usual blowing routine, poured the chocolate powder into the bowl and then sneezed straight in on top of it.

I don't mind if I get ill afterwards, I thought, but please don't let me get ill for the next three or four days. Let me at least get a chance at the summit.

June 4

I woke early after a very restless night. I'd heard David Hamilton say on the radio that Sibusiso was missing and hadn't heard any news of his arrival at camp before I went to sleep. I was worried about him. I was also nervous about our first team on their way up the final and most challenging part of the mountain. I turned on the radio at six to hear the news that Jez and Bill were both on the summit. The pair had broken away from the rest of the Himex team at the Second Step.

Reports were coming in so thick and fast by now that it was difficult to keep up. Richard, David and Woody had all summitted, as had Phurba and four other Sherpas. Soren, who had been switched into the first team at the last minute, was 100 metres from the Third Step and Monica was not far behind. Ishi, who hadn't reached high camp until six the previous night, was only at the First Step. Some time later, when Ishi finally reached the Second Step, Russ told him he was going too slowly to make it to the summit and back down safely. He turned him around. It was the second time in 12 months that the summit had eluded the Japanese climber.

At 7.40 Mogens was on the radio, saying he was calling from high camp. He'd turned around at the top of the Exit Cracks before the First Step, he told Russ. "I've a foot as cold as a deep freeze, but it's not black yet, so that must be a good sign", he said. "I've got a slight pulmonary thing going on as well. I want to keep all my digits, so I'm going on oxygen to come down."

Dean came in on the radio. "He's a smart man. Conditions were never right for going without oxygen. It's too cold."

Meanwhile Mogens' compatriot Soren was making slow but steady progress towards his goal. He was well adrift of the rest of his team, but reports came back that he still had enough oxygen left to get him up to the summit and back safely. Russ urged him to keep going and reports came through later that he'd reached the top somewhere around nine o'clock.

Russ couldn't actually see any of his climbers from his perch on the North Col, where it was snowing heavily. His high-powered telescope was rendered useless in the whiteout. But the snow seemed to be affecting only the lower part of the mountain. We were basking in cold but glorious sunshine at camp III.

Just before eight an Italian voice came through on the radio, confirming that Bruno had made the decision to stop above camp III. It had been an impressive enough feat to have run all the way up from base camp but, without oxygen, he was simply too tired and too cold to continue. He was now back at camp II and two of his support team, Stefano and Claudio, were going on to the summit.

I was getting out of the tent shortly afterwards when a voice some distance behind me said, "Peg?" Turning round I saw two climbers, both clad in dark down suits, on the far side of camp. One of them was Sibusiso. Thrilled to see him so obviously safe and sound, I called out for Peg and then asked Sibusiso what had happened. "Did you summit?" "Yes, at 6.30 yesterday morning", he replied, just as Peg appeared out of her tent. "I heard David saying that you were missing between high camp and here." "No, I got back here at about six last night."

He was beaming now, revealing incredible white teeth in a wraparound smile. "I know you guys are going to do it", he said to Peg and me. "I'll pray for you." Since my prayers for Sibusiso's safe return had been so spectacularly answered, there seemed to be hope that his would be similarly successful.

Returning to my tent to prepare for our departure for high camp, I found Karsang in a spectacularly bad mood. "You ready?" he demanded of me grumpily, before commenting beadily, "All members ready".

Without saying another word, he made it abundantly clear that he had no intention of letting me brew any more water, even though I had intended drinking more before we left. But I knew I would need him on my side when we started out for the summit that night, so I decided it was best to avoid a confrontation. I started packing up.

"Which gloves best?", I asked him, using the monosyllabic questioning so beloved by Russ and which seemed the best way to break through the language barrier. I held up two of the North Face options, the rugged gloves I'd been wearing since we'd left the North Col, which looked like the result of a mating between a ski glove and a motorcycle gauntlet, and the down mitts that I had only worn in camp up to then.

Karsang pointed sullenly at the mitts. "Yes", he said. I put the mitts out on my sleeping bag, before stuffing the rejected pair into the top of my backpack so they would be easily accessible if I needed to switch if the weather warmed up.

Under Karsang's stonily silent gaze, everything I did seemed to take longer than usual. I put out a black balaclava to wear, promptly lost it and then spent several minutes frantically searching the similarly black depths of the sleeping bag for it. I eventually found it where I'd put it initially, under my backpack.

The delays were infuriating Karsang. I could feel his anger building, which just made me more nervous and uncoordinated. I scooped everything else up and stuffed it into my backpack so I could get away from the oppressive atmosphere of the tent as quickly as possible. Strapping on my crampons, usually the work of a minute, seemed to take forever. It wasn't something I wanted to rush, however. I had no intention of losing a crampon now. It could spell the end of my expedition or have far more serious repercussions.

But there was another delay and one that I couldn't – and didn't want to – avoid. Mogens had just arrived down from camp IV and was sitting outside my tent having a rest before continuing his descent. I gave him a big hug and said how sorry I was that he'd had to turn round. "I wanted to keep my toes", he said, before adding, with a wink and a boyish grin, "I'll be back". I hoped I could be as sanguine about it if I was faced with the prospect of having to abort my attempt on the summit.

Mogens kissed me on the cheek and wished me luck. "I'll say a prayer for you", he said as I got up to go. It was incredible how much more religious we had all become the closer we got to the summit.

Finally I was ready to make a move out of camp. Setting my regulator at two,

I heaved on my backpack and pulled on the mitts. But it was warmer than I thought and the balaclava was uncomfortably claustrophobic with the oxygen mask. I knew I'd have to wear it for the actual summit push, but I decided I needed to be comfortable now and I didn't want to drain my energy reserves by getting too hot. I peeled off my mask, ripped the balaclava from my face and doubled it over to make a hat. Replacing it on my head, I then put the oxygen mask back on. Now I really was ready.

Without looking back at Karsang I headed for the fixed lines, feeling unsettled and nervy. Those feelings were almost immediately intensified when I went to clip in to the rope. Any dexterity I had previously had for such a simple task seemed to have evaporated overnight. And putting my jumar onto the rope proved even more impossible.

It was the mitts. Without the use of my fingers as separate entities my hands seemed to have been rendered almost useless. I should have remembered from summit day on Cho Oyu. I knew I would have to change back to my gloves, but the thought of having to take off my oxygen mask again and remove my backpack was more than I could bear. I turned round in the hope of finding Karsang, infuriated, behind me, but he was nowhere to be seen.

The part of my brain enabling me to make a choice had apparently been surgically removed overnight. Would I carry on with the mitts or would I take off all my gear and find the gloves for myself. I was paralysed with indecision. I had finally forced my befuddled brain to realise that I would have to take off my mask and search for the gloves in my backpack when Karsang appeared behind me, radiating disapproval. "I can't work with these mitts", I said. "Can you find my gloves for me?" He had the gloves out in a flash, snatched the mitts from my hand and rammed them into the backpack. I took the hint, hastily dragged on the gloves and set off up through the rocks.

Only about 100 metres ahead of me I could see two climbers, both in red down suits, sitting on a rock. By the time I caught up with them, one had got to his feet and gone on. The one left sitting alone was Kevin. He looked shattered. "I've no energy", he told me. "Nor me", I said, realising that the other red-suited climber must have been Dean, who had been trying to persuade Kevin to keep going.

I could see Kevin was struggling with the decision. "Don't give up now", I said to him as Karsang stomped passed us. "You've come this far, you've got to keep going." He nodded, but without conviction and although he did get to his feet and started plodding along behind me, I had very little confidence that he would keep heading in an uphill direction. His heart just wasn't in it any longer and I had a feeling that the lure of base camp would prove stronger than the pull of the summit.

I was torn between the desire to stay with him and the need to keep going. I was aware that if I slowed down too much I would lose my own impetus. Apologising for my apparent callousness, I told Kevin I was going to have to go on ahead.

After negotiating a series of gullies, I got back into my own natural rhythm, but it felt incredibly slow in comparison to my speed at lower altitudes. It wasn't long before I heard the sound of crampons scraping on rock behind me. I turned round and was delighted to see a red down suit, assuming it was a revitalised Kevin. But it turned out to be Piers, an Australian climber who had been forced to abandon his traverse attempt from the Nepalese side of the mountain and had joined us at ABC just before the summit push. I moved over to let him past. Peg, who'd been sharing a tent with Piers, followed in his wake.

The three of us climbed together in companionable silence as the route took us up a slightly steeper incline, where patches of snow that hadn't been scoured by the wind clung tenaciously to the down-sloping terrain. The snow made a welcome change after two days on rock, but it was very patchy and we frequently felt our crampons scraping on slabs just beneath the thin veneer of snow.

We had been passing a trickle of descending climbers for some time now, but the next one I saw had none of the exhilaration in his face that we'd seen on the features of two of our Himex colleagues, Richard and David when they'd stopped to tell us of their summit success. The man was slumped against a prominent rock, shaped like the prow of a battleship. It had the look of a sacrificial altar and the climber was clinging to it as though his life depended on it. He took off his goggles as we approached and all I could see were two totally blank, soulless eyes. I asked him if he was alright, but got no response.

Piers and Peg had already gone ahead, so I went on, wondering if there was anything I could do to help the exhausted climber. I turned round to see if he had moved and, to my relief, saw him walking desperately slowly after team leader Kari Kobler. It wasn't until the next day that I heard of the death of one of Kari's German clients from a heart attack only metres away from his tent at camp II and knew it must have been the same man.

There was a pretty solid traffic jam on the final snow slope up to camp IV. Piers, Peg and I tagged on at the end, but when Karsang caught up with us he ignored the rope and continued climbing about 10 metres to the left of us. He'd already had one fall early in the expedition when he hadn't clipped in on the snow slopes up the North Col. I hoped he wouldn't have another.

As the pace got slower, I took off my oxygen mask and called ahead to Piers. "What's the hold-up?" "The Japanese", he said simply. "Don't put too much weight on the rope", he shouted back to Peg and me. "It's holding everyone all the way to the top." It was a sobering thought. If someone did fall they'd probably take all of us with them.

The snail's pace as we approached the 8,300 metre camp gave me a chance to reflect on the fact that this was an altitude record for me. My previous high was the summit of Cho Oyu, its massive bulk visible above the clouds when I looked over my right shoulder. That was 8,201 metres, but I'd only been there for about 10 minutes. Now I would be staying 100 metres higher until 11 o'clock tonight and then, if everything went according to plan, climbing another 548 metres to the highest point on earth. It was a daunting prospect.

Also daunting was the thought that, somewhere below us on the steeply terraced broken rock to our right and invisible from where we were climbing, was a makeshift grave. Five members of a 1999 expedition had painstakingly piled rocks over a body that, until it had been found by Conrad Anker, had lain undiscovered for 75 years. It was George Mallory, killed in a fall three-quarters of a century earlier. But the mountain still refused to give up the camera that would have determined whether Mallory and his climbing companion Andrew Irvine had reached her summit before they both fell to their deaths. It remains a mystery buried, like the camera, on the unforgiving flanks of Everest.

As we straggled into high camp, all of us weary and feeling the effects of the altitude, I was scanning what I could see of our route to the summit. Knowing it would be dark when we left camp, I wanted to be able to memorise as much as possible beforehand. I realised with a hollow feeling that it was still an unbelievably long way to the top.

I laboured up the final shallow incline towards the tents, passing an exhausted looking Fujibayashi. Chieko was just ahead, making her way up to a tent pitched high up on the left-hand side of camp. I continued on through a narrow gap between two other tents, glancing in through the open flap of the one to the right. A pair of crampons, still strapped to their owner's boots, stuck out of the entrance. Gudman was written across them.

"Soren", I called out, kneeling down so I could peer into the gloom within. There was a grunt from inside the tent and its occupant heaved himself up onto one elbow and looked out at me. "Well done", I said, "fantastic! How do you feel?" "Fucked", he said eloquently, looking at me with bloodshot, unfocused eyes. "But I'm very, very happy", he added, with a vague attempt at a grin before slumping back down onto the rolled up sleeping bag he was using as a pillow.

I was just about to move on in search of Karsang, when Jez's head popped up from the far side of the tent. "Sorry Jez", I said, "I didn't see you there. Congratulations!" "Thanks", he said, with something more approaching a smile than Soren had been able to manage. "It's a very peculiar feeling", Jez continued. "It hasn't really sunk in yet. Just eat and drink and you'll make it."

The pair were too shattered for further conversation and I was conscious of the fact that I needed to do exactly as Jez had suggested, rehydrate first and then get some food inside me. They wished me luck as I pushed myself up off the rock, looking round camp for Karsang. I glanced up to my left and saw a dingy grey tint perched precariously on the scree. It seemed to be the worst sited of the entire camp, set on a sharply raked angle that threatened to send the tent plunging down the mountainside at any minute. Karsang was sitting cross-legged outside it.

Resigned to the fact that there didn't seem to be any alternative as every other tent was occupied, I dragged my uncooperative limbs up the slope. "Very bad tent", Karsang said glumly, without getting up. His humour had obviously not improved.

However bad the tent looked from the outside, it was nothing to what greeted me when I finally managed to get inside. One sleeping bag and a single mat adorned the interior, but the surface of the floor was tilted at an alarming angle. I crawled over to the mat, which had been flung to the back of the tent, stripped off my backpack and lowered myself gingerly into what I naïvely hoped would be a vaguely horizontal position.

Not only did the tent slope precipitously downhill, but the mat also concealed a series of steep steps. It was like trying to lie down on a staircase. There would be no sleeping in this tent, I thought, knowing that Karsang and I both needed to get as much rest as we could before our departure for the summit, now only a matter of hours away.

I radioed through to Dean and asked him if Karsang and I could move to another tent. Dean wasn't sure there was an empty one, but I pointed out that Jez and Soren were in one down near him and that they would be heading back to camp III soon. Could we move into that one when they'd gone, I asked. "Don't see why not", Dean said agreeably.

Karsang had disappeared, when another Sherpa arrived bearing a Nepali flag and a sleeping mat, obviously both for Karsang. Later that afternoon Karsang told me that the flag had been to the summit 10 times with his father Ang Rita and he had taken it to the top six times himself. He was obviously hoping it would be 17 times in total by tomorrow morning. I hoped so too.

I was conscious of the fact that I was badly dehydrated. My throat felt as though I was swallowing razorblades, although surprisingly the cough that had tormented me at base camp and ABC seemed to have eased as we went higher.

I looked out of the tent to see Monica and Jean just starting their descent to camp III. Monica looked totally wiped out, barely able to put one foot in front of the other. Jean, as solicitous as ever, was helping her. Tom wasn't to be seen, but I was sure he was somewhere close, video camera at the ready to capture everything on film.

I wanted to rush out and congratulate them on their summit. I knew how much it meant to Monica and I knew how much it would mean to the hordes of family and friends that were gathering in Kathmandu to welcome her down. But she looked so shattered and so fragile that I thought I'd wait until I saw her back at ABC. Hydration was my most important mission for now. And moving to a better tent.

Ten minutes later Karsang was back and, for the first time that day, looked almost good-humoured. His features had softened and he looked more like the Karsang I'd grown quite fond of lower down the mountain. "We move", he said, with an air almost of triumph in his voice.

I lost no time in gathering up my gear and pulling on my boots. Dragging my backpack after me, I crawled out of the tent and headed downhill towards the one where I'd been talking to Jez and Soren. Jez had already gone, but Soren was still standing outside the tent and I could see he was trying to muster the strength to embark on the long trek back down to camp III.

As I got closer to him I could see his lips moving, but there was no sound coming out of his mouth. "Hold on, I can't hear you", I said, noticing how wretched he looked. His lips were painfully cracked and his eyes were even more bloodshot than when I'd seen him earlier. He was totally drained.

"Have you got any water?", he asked me croakily when I got down level with him. I shook my head, suggesting that he asked Sissel, who was within earshot in the next-door tent. He looked blankly at me, then crumpled slowly to his knees. I thought at first that he'd collapsed, but then realised he was simply too weak to do anything other than fall into Sissel's tent.

I heard her talking to him as I turned back towards the tent Soren had just left, grateful that it was finally vacant. I groped my way in through the open flaps, but the tent was far from empty. It looked as though there had been an avian massacre inside. White goose-down feathers were everywhere – the contents of much of Soren's down suit, which had obviously got ripped on the descent from the summit. Jez said afterwards that by the time Soren got to camp III, he was effectively wearing a wind suit. Virtually all the stuffing had leaked out on the way down.

The downy covering on everything was only a mild irritant. At least I was in a tent pitched on the flat, I thought to myself as I prepared to settle in. How wrong could I be? It certainly wasn't anything like as bad as the one I'd just left, but there were huge holes underneath the ground sheet and, when Karsang came in, he suggested I should take the downhill side so that he could use the one flat area for the stove.

I moved over and immediately sat on a large, sharp rock poking through the mat. That was momentarily uncomfortable, but much worse, there was a yawning chasm right where I wanted to put my head if I was going to adhere to Sherpa rules and sleep with my feet away from the mountain. With the summit push now less than seven hours away, the last thing I wanted to do was antagonise the mountain goddess. I looked around for something to fill the hole. Two oxygen bottles, my ice boots and my backpack were required to level it off with the rest of the tent.

As I waited for the water to boil on the stove, I ate a couple of protein bars. I told Karsang that I wanted to wake at 9.30 so that I could rehydrate as much as possible and eat a bowl of noodles before we left. I asked him if he had an alarm on his watch. "No", he said, "but I don't sleep." As I settled down shortly after seven I hoped he would wake me on time.

The combination of worry about sleeping too long and nerves about the final climb into such unknown territory meant that sleep eluded me totally. I lay there sleepless for a long while, sitting up periodically and trying unsuccessfully to rearrange my "pillow".

I tried to imagine what it would be like on the way to the summit. We'd spent so long glued to the telescope at ABC watching other climbers battling their way through the winds as they struggled up the steep snow slopes towards the final rocky pyramid and the crowning summit ridge. But we were so far removed from the action that it was like watching a movie. It didn't give us a real feel for the route we were about to embark on.

Even though my eyes were shut, I couldn't switch off my brain. My mind was racing, with thoughts and questions tumbling around in my skull. I was never going to get to sleep. Unexpectedly, I was too hot and had to unzip my sleeping bag to cool myself down. I hadn't expected to get overheated at such extreme altitude, but it proved that all the insulating layers under my down suit were doing their job.

I must have fallen asleep shortly afterwards. When I woke some time later, Karsang was moving about the tent and I could hear the hiss of the gas stove. He'd obviously put snow on to melt already. I assumed he would wake me at 9.30, so let myself drift back into that half-sleep where I was aware of things going on around me but not fully conscious.

Karsang must have turned his radio back on, as the next thing I heard was Russ asking Dean if everybody was up and getting ready to leave. I looked at my watch and, to my horror, saw that it was already after 10.20, almost an hour after I'd planned on waking. I sat up quickly, realising that with only just over half an hour before our scheduled departure I wouldn't have enough time to drink and eat as much as I needed to. Already feeling flustered, I hurriedly started to get myself organised.

Karsang filled a bowl with hot water and passed to me. It was too hot to drink so I put it down on one of the few flat areas in the tent and, handing Karsang a sachet of vegetable soup and a packet of noodles, asked him if he would make me some noodle soup. While he started to cook, I dragged on my harness, checking to make sure everything was buckled correctly before I started to put on my boots.

Russ had given me a pair of battery operated boot warmers to make up for the disappearance of my Millet boots on the south side expedition. The specially designed insoles had wires, covered in plastic tape, designed to go from the heel and up the inside of the boot. The operating dial was on a wire cradle designed to clip onto the top of the boot. As I struggled with the batteries and dial I thought of Russ warning us on the morning of our departure from ABC to make sure our toes and our fingers were warm before we left camp on the push for the summit.

"Don't go out with cold fingers and toes – they won't get warm", he cautioned. He then stunned those of us that had climbed with him before by saying: "I don't care if you put holes in the mats, don't put your crampons on outside." It went totally against the grain to put on crampons inside the tent, but I had no intention of risking frostbite.

I'd organised my backpack before going to sleep, putting in a spare balaclava and my down mitts to use if I got really cold. I knew I wouldn't be able to climb anything technical while wearing the mitts, but at least I could put them on to warm my hands if they got dangerously cold. My goggles were also easily accessible so that I could put them on as soon as the sun came up. I didn't want to risk snow-blindness.

I had spare batteries for my head torch and for my digital camera. I also had a disposable camera for use if the digital camera froze. Both cameras and my water bottle would be kept warm zipped up inside my down suit, along with protein and carbohydrate bars and carbohydrate gels for instant energy.

I checked to make sure the Irish tricolour was in the top compartment of my backpack and found it neatly folded, snuggled next to a laminated sheet of A4 paper given to me by my IT coach Brendan O'Brien before I left Dublin. It bore the message – SORD Data Systems, Extreme IT. Brendan had asked for a picture of me holding it on the summit. Looking at the flag and the sponsor's message I couldn't quite take it in that this was it – I was about to embark on the final leg of a journey that would hopefully take me to the top of the highest and most famous mountain in the world.

III

The Final Push

June 4/5

The months of training and preparation had all been geared towards this moment. All the work that other people had put in, all the support everyone had given to me was focused on getting me to the summit. Now the onus was on me to perform. It was a weighty burden. I suddenly felt terribly alone and terribly vulnerable.

Such thoughts weren't helping me get ready so I refocused on the present. I carefully unscrewed the regulator from the top of the oxygen canister I'd used for sleeping, saving it as a reserve for the way back down to camp III later. I hefted a fresh four-litre cylinder onto my lap, attached the regulator and then started to tighten it. The violent hiss of escaping oxygen made me jump and I hastily screwed the regulator tighter to stop the noise. After checking to see that the valve was registering a full cylinder I turned back to the business of dressing and trying to eat noodle soup at the same time.

It must have been well after 11.30 by the time I finally crawled out of my tent, pulling on my hood as I stood up. As predicted by Russ, I was late but, despite the urgency I could feel coursing through me, I still made sure not to leave crampon holes in the mats as I got out of the tent.

It was incredibly dark outside. There was no moon and the stars were also concealed by cloud. It was oddly unnerving to be setting off in such inky darkness, with only a thin shaft of light coming from my head-torch to illuminate my surroundings. The last time I had climbed like this was on Cho Oyu over eight months ago. I'd done plenty of climbing in the interim, but only in daylight hours. Now, in the loneliness of the night, I was already higher than the summit of Cho Oyu and I still had an unbelievably long way to go before the sun's rays would start to break up the night. And I was completely on my own.

Camp seemed to be depressingly deserted. The rest of the team must be well ahead by now, I thought to myself. Looking up towards the summit, I could see the bobbing lights of my fellow climbers. Although I knew the general direction that I was aiming for, I could see no sign of the fixed lines that would lead up to the Yellow Band, and everyone else was so far ahead that it was impossible to tell whether I could head straight after them or whether I had to take a more circuitous route.

I struggled over the sloping rocky terrain, stumbling over my crampons and almost falling as I tried to head in a right-handed diagonal path towards what I assumed was the route. It seemed an infinity before the beam of my head torch finally picked up the blue line of a rope and I clipped into it gratefully, knowing now that at least I was on the right track.

I upped my pace slightly and my crampons crunched on the scree, occasionally skidding awkwardly off a large rock and causing me to lurch sideways to regain my balance. Obscured by my oxygen mask, I couldn't see my feet or what I was treading on. I felt clumsy and uncoordinated. And I was getting uncomfortably hot. I pulled my hood off and felt the chill night air striking through my balaclava, but the cold seemed to refocus my energy.

I've no idea how long I was plodding across the shingly surface, but by now I was on a distinct path with a rocky handrail on my left and a drop to my right. I didn't want to think about how steep or how long the drop was and kept my eyes trained on the route ahead. On the odd occasion I did look to the right, the beam of my torch vanished into blackness dark as a pint of stout.

Some time later I saw two lights not far ahead. I was catching up on someone, but it was a while before I got close enough to realise that it was Fujibayashi and his Sherpa, who were making tortuously slow progress up the mountain.

The pair stood aside to let me past and, shortly afterwards Karsang caught up with me. Even though we didn't speak the companionship was comforting and I felt my confidence increasing. I remembered Whetu's words back in Kathmandu almost exactly eight months ago and reminded myself that this wasn't just my summit bid, this was going to be my summit day.

The first piece of steep terrain came at the Exit Cracks, a series of narrow gullies that put me on notice that there was going to be some real climbing ahead of me. It was slow and painstaking work finding footholds, but it was more fun than the tedious trudge on shallower terrain and I knew it also meant that there was at least some height gain, even if it was only marginal.

I knew that Green Boots, the name given to the only visible part of one of the numerous corpses that litter the mountain, lay somewhere near the Exit Cracks. Thankfully I didn't see the remains of the Polish climber, but I was focusing my concentration so much on the climb that I would only have seen anything that had appeared directly in front of me.

Much to my surprise Peg joined me shortly afterwards. I had assumed she was the owner of one of the tiny lights way ahead, but she apparently had left camp even later than I had. Like me, she was having to work hard to keep going. "I'm exhausted", she said soon after joining me. "Me too", I agreed.

We seemed to be moving desperately slowly, but we were some distance on from the Exit Cracks when I heard Fujibayashi calling in to Russ on the radio to say that he was turning round. He was complaining of chest pains and exhaustion. It sounded like he'd made the right decision to abandon his summit attempt.

In the dark I could sense rather than see a sizeable rock buttress rearing up in front of me. The First Step is the initial one of three steps and the beginning of the serious climbing on the summit push. I watched as Karsang started on the bottom section. The battery in his head torch had died early on, so he was really only climbing by braille. Even though it was familiar territory to him, it can't have been easy. I tried to train the beam from my torch onto the rock face, but Karsang's own shadow meant that it would only have been of marginal help. I hoped that at least it might cast some light on footholds, even if it didn't illuminate anything higher.

There was an awkward move early on and Karsang, obviously handicapped by an almost total lack of visibility, spent some time finding a suitable crevice for his crampons before he hauled himself up. Things seemed to get easier after that and, aware that I would be providing even less light to Karsang if I stayed too far behind, I started on up the face.

I manoeuvred myself into position and managed to get my left foot high enough to make the move I'd just seen Karsang execute. It was quite a stretch, but nothing like the one under the mantle shelf at Dalkey Quarry where my climbing buddy Shane Cleary had told me there was a perfect foothold next to my left ear. That had been at sea level however and I'd been climbing in rock shoes. Now, at over 8,300 metres, wearing ice boots and crampons and in the dark, this was a far more intimidating proposition. As always, once I'd committed myself to the move, it was easier than it initially appeared. Breathing heavily from the exertion I moved on up the rock to join Karsang at the top.

It had started to snow lightly and, as I looked skywards to check on the progress of my fellow Himex team members way above me, the flakes caught in the beam of light from my head torch. It was colder now and I pulled up my hood, tightening the drawstring to keep the snow off my face. Even though the bottom half of my face was covered by my oxygen mask, it was still too dark to wear goggles and the hood provided some protection for my eyes.

The terrain had levelled out and the flatter ground gave me a chance to recover from the climb up the First Step, but it also made for depressingly slow progress towards the summit itself. The snow was heavier now and I could sense that the traverse we were on was horribly exposed. I knew that the north-east ridge fell away down the Kangshung face to the left and the North Face to the right. I didn't want to think of the consequences of a fall here.

Peg had caught up with me again and stayed on my heels for a while, before asking if she could go past. She overtook me just before the traverse got seriously narrow, but she was moving at the same pace as me so we stayed together for some time.

It was distinctly colder by now and our slow pace didn't help, but my body temperature remained stable as long as I kept my hood up and the drawstring tightened. I knew once the sun rose it would warm up, but dawn was still a long way off.

We had been going for probably another half-hour when Peg suddenly stopped and said bluntly, "I can't go on". I was totally stunned and thought it was just a momentary lapse. Peg was one of the strongest and most experienced climbers of the entire team. She couldn't be contemplating turning round now. But she was deadly serious. "I'm exhausted. I can't go on", she said again.

"You can't stop", I said, "you've come this far, you've got to keep going". I suggested we should have a drink and a carbohydrate gel to boost our flagging energy levels. She said nothing, but walked on for another 10 metres or so, before suddenly flopping down onto a large rock and then sitting there with her head in her hands. Even in the dim light of my head-torch I could see she looked totally shattered, both physically and mentally.

I took out my water bottle and handed it to her. I couldn't bear to watch her distress, so I turned away from the mountain, gazing into the darkness of infinity below me as I squeezed a sachet of carbohydrate gel into my mouth. The sickly sweetness of the gel was cloying, but I knew its energy giving properties would kick in rapidly. Peg passed the bottle back to me and I took a swig out of it. I didn't know whether she'd drunk from it or not, but she ate nothing, even when I offered her another sachet of gel.

Without looking at me, she mumbled almost under her breath, "I'm turning round" and started to cry quietly. I was appalled. She really was serious. I snatched the oxygen mask off my face, put my arm round her and told her she'd be fine, just to keep going for a little while longer until she settled back into her rhythm again.

She shook her head. I could see she had already resigned herself to the fact that she was going down. I looked up in the direction of the summit, still swathed in darkness, and could see the lights from our team mates way in the distance. Following my cue, Peg looked up too, but that just seemed to confirm in her mind that she was going no further.

"Talk to Russ", I suggested. She sat up slightly and pressed the button on the side of the radio, putting in a call to the Himex headquarters at the North Col. Without preamble Peg told Russ that she was thinking of turning round. "Where are you?", he queried. "Just above the First Step. How much further is it to the summit, time-wise?", she asked.

"Probably at least another five hours from there", Russ said. "I can't make up your mind for you", he went on, but he must have known from the weary resignation in Peg's voice that her summit bid was over. There was a pause before Peg said simply, "I'm coming back down". She was crying harder now as she turned to look at her Sherpa. "I'm sorry", she said.

I tried to comfort her, but she was inconsolable. It was her second time on Everest and still the summit eluded her. Would she ever get a third chance? Did she even want a third chance? I could almost see the questions whirling around in her head.

And there were plenty of questions whirling round in my head too. Self-doubt began to creep in. Was I right to continue if someone as tough and experienced as Peg was turning round? After the problems with her oxygen mask on the south side two years ago, did she know something I didn't?

I wanted to stay with her to try and console her. I knew she was shattered, but if I stayed I was going to find it very hard to get going again. I was within a heartbeat of telling her that I'd come back down with her, but then I remembered why I was doing this. I wanted to climb the mountain for me, of course, but more importantly I wanted to climb it for Joe and for the two charities that I'd pledged to support. I had to keep going.

I told Peg that I would have to leave her, but I'm not sure it registered. I kissed her on the top of the head and went on. I didn't dare look back. I knew the sight of her misery would draw me back to her side and I'd end up heading down the mountain. I couldn't afford to look round.

It was probably almost as tough a decision as the one Peg had just made. She had given the mountain her best shot. I was determined to do the same. I wasn't finished yet.

But I very nearly went back and joined Peg shortly afterwards when I heard the plummy tones of Russ's friend Henry Todd on the radio, speaking from the south side of the mountain. Henry said there had been an "incident" that he didn't want to discuss on the radio. He'd call Russ on the satellite phone, he said. Henry didn't need to say any more. It was obvious someone had died and it was fairly safe to assume that it was one of Henry's clients.

I didn't learn the details until much later in the day, but I had already heard enough to know that, including Kari's German client, this was the sixth death on the mountain this year. I was tempted to turn off the radio. I didn't want to hear any more bad news. I needed to focus on the task ahead of me. Henry

Todd's report, combined with Peg's departure, had shaken me badly.

I clung to Whetu's words like a mantra. "I will climb this mountain. I will climb this mountain", I chanted to myself as I forced myself forward.

As I made my way along the traverse, I wondered where Mushroom Rock was. Russ had told us to change oxygen cylinders there, leaving the half-empty one for the descent and putting on a fresh one. The new one would last all the way to the summit and back, providing we used it conservatively.

Karsang, who was some way ahead of me, showed no signs of stopping and, in the darkness, I doubted that I'd recognise Mushroom Rock, especially as Russ had said it didn't look like a mushroom at all. I took off my mask and called to Karsang to wait. He stopped and, when I caught up with him, I asked where Mushroom Rock was. He didn't seem to understand, but muttered something incomprehensible and went on again.

I assumed we hadn't reached it yet, but the next thing I knew we were at the bottom of an imposing buttress, almost 30 metres high. In the beam of my head-torch I could just see the outline of a ladder about halfway up. The Second Step. Obviously I'd passed Mushroom Rock without knowing it.

"What about the oxygen?", I asked Karsang. "We were supposed to change cylinders at Mushroom Rock." "I look after", he said, as he started climbing up the bottom section of the step. It was apparent that he had no intention of stopping to change cylinders. I put my faith in him and followed him up the rock face.

After a few big stretchy moves up a series of ledges, I found myself in a narrow gully between the cliff face and a large smooth-faced boulder on my right. Karsang was in the process of scaling this and, just as I got to the bottom of it, his foot skidded off the only blemish on the boulder. I had to snatch my hand out of the way to prevent it being skewered by his crampons.

He hauled himself up again, using his knee as an extra aid and, with one deft movement, was up on top of the boulder. My head torch illuminated his face as he peered down at me. "You come", he said, before vanishing upwards into the darkness.

I dragged myself up to where Karsang's crampon had failed to find sufficient grip on an almost invisible flaw in the rock. I had little hope of succeeding where he had failed and, just as I allowed that negative thought to enter my head, my crampon skated off the face and I ended up dangling inelegantly on the rope inches above where I'd just started from.

I began the process again and this time used my knee as I'd seen Karsang do. It felt clumsy, but it worked and I grabbed the top of the boulder and hauled myself up to straddle it. I sat for a couple of minutes getting my breath back and used the opportunity to look around for Karsang. He was standing over to the left and slightly above me, waiting at the bottom of the ladder.

Once he'd seen I was safely up the previous section of the climb, he began to scale the ladder. As he went up I glanced over at the old ladder that had been put in by the Chinese in the mid-1970s. It looked impossibly rickety and I was glad that a new aluminium version had been put in place the previous year.

I turned my attention back to Karsang and was surprised to see that he was already at the top. Clipping in to the blue rope running up to the right of the new ladder, I grabbed the two sides and put a tentative foot on the first rung. The ladder felt decidedly wobbly. "Be careful", Karsang called down from above. I had every intention of being careful. I'd heard too many stories about disasters on the Second Step and, although the darkness masked the dangers, I knew how horrendously exposed this part of the climb was.

Making sure that the rung was positioned in the middle of my crampons, I moved up to the next step. It was surprisingly easy. I'd expected it to be a lot more awkward, but I was rapidly on the top rung looking across to where Karsang was waiting in a small alcove over to my right.

It was quite a long stretch to get across and I remembered stories of climbers rigid with fear and unable to relinquish the safety of the ladder and commit themselves to this exposed move. Even though I couldn't see it, I could almost feel the enormous drop to my right. I immediately banished thoughts of a fall that would be measured in kilometres rather than in feet and extended my right leg across to the niche. Before I could change my mind, I shifted my weight onto my right foot and launched my body across the airy divide.

There were still several more hazardous moves to make to reach the top and I was wary of getting my crampons caught up in the tangle of old frayed ropes left from previous years. Karsang had already vanished over the lip and, with this small summit in sight, I propelled myself upwards in pursuit of him. I didn't like to think what it would be like getting down the Second Step on the descent.

There was much easier terrain at the top of the step and we spent quite some time on an almost flat rocky path before hitting the first boulder-strewn snow-field. I'd heard frequent dispatches from other members of the team, relaying their whereabouts back to Russ. But I was loathe to radio back to the North Col and let Russ know that I'd only just gone up the Second Step. I was terri-fied he would tell me I was going too slowly and turn me round.

After Peg and Fujibayashi had both headed back down, I was still convinced that I could see the beam of a head torch following me some distance behind. But it was only when I heard Narly's huskily breathless voice on the radio that I realised I wasn't suffering from high altitude hallucinations. Russ listened to Narly's almost whispered report that he was at Mushroom Rock and then told him to turn around.

I felt as though there was an unseen creature whose jaws were snapping at the stragglers above high camp and I was next in line. Fujibayashi, Peg and now Narly. How much longer would it be before the creature's teeth sank themselves into one of my ankles and dragged me back down the mountain? I decided not to radio Russ until I was closer to the Third Step.

I can scarcely remember the transition from dark to light but, as I plodded on across the snow-field, I realised that dawn had broken. It was a revelation to be able to see more than just what was illuminated by a narrow shaft of light from a head torch. But the whirling spindrift kept visibility down to a minimum and I wondered just how much I would be able to see if I did make it to the top of the mountain.

I couldn't even see my goal at that stage. The only thing I could see clearly was the fact that Karsang was a good distance ahead of me, depressingly far ahead and getting further away by the minute. Unless he stopped to wait for me soon, he would rapidly be as out of sight as the summit itself.

Aware that I was struggling with the pace, he stopped momentarily and turned round to look at me. It seemed like the perfect opportunity to stop for a rest. If he saw me sitting down on the snow he'd presumably stop as well. My tactics worked perfectly. Although he didn't sit, Karsang did at least abandon his relentless pace onwards and upwards, standing motionless, a dark shape against the stark white of the snow.

I dragged my water bottle out of its cosy nesting place inside my down suit, unscrewed the cap and took a big slug. The water, boiling when I poured it in at high camp, was now cold and soothing as it hit the burning soreness that used to be my oesophagus. I wondered how long it would be before the water froze over, thinking of how many climbers ended up carrying bottles of ice up to the summit of Everest. I took another drink and quickly put the top back on the bottle, shoving it inside my down suit before the cold got a chance to wipe out my drinking supply.

I needed a rapid source of energy too, but couldn't face another of the carbohydrate gels. I delved down into the capacious pockets of my North Face fleece and pulled out a Musashi protein bar. If it had been left in an outside pocket it would have frozen into a teeth-shattering block, but my body heat had kept the chocolate-covered bar pliable. I took a large bite, leaving teeth marks like a dental impression in the pink insides of the bar. I welcomed the sugary rush.

Karsang, even from a distance and in poor visibility, was able to convey his impatience to get going again, so I dragged myself to my feet and started trudging up the slope towards him. He didn't wait until I caught up with him, but turned and headed on as soon as he saw me moving.

The snow had momentarily eased off and I was able to see a bit more of my surroundings as I followed in Karsang's footsteps. It made me feel like Good King Wenceslas's page, although I don't think Wenceslas wore crampons. A snow bowl dropped away to my right and, to my left, scalloped cornices marked the edge of the ridge. It was definitely not a place to wander off course.

Karsang had stopped up ahead and was looking down close to the edge of one of the cornices. I prayed it wouldn't give way and send him plummeting down the Kangshung face. As I got closer to him, he turned and walked on ahead.

The updates on the radio continued relentlessly. With the weather closing in again, Sissel was concerned about the lack of visibility. "If I go on to the summit, will I be able to see the route back down again?", she asked anxiously. Russ told her to keep going. "You'll have no trouble finding your way back", he said.

It didn't seem too much later that I heard Dean reporting that he and Chieko were on the summit. Chieko and her Sherpa Dorjie had left some time around 10 o'clock the night before. Moving slowly, they were caught by Dean, but he tempered his pace to match theirs and the three of them reached the top around six in the morning. Five minutes later I heard Sissel's voice saying that she too was on the summit. I didn't hear him radio through to Russ, but apparently Piers reached the top soon afterwards.

I still couldn't even see the summit, but I knew it was a long way off. I had yet to tackle the Third Step, but at least that was now only just ahead of me. And it was a relief to see that it was really only a series of giant boulders tumbled on top of one another, which required scrambling rather than serious climbing.

Already I could see Karsang at the top of the step and it didn't take me too long to join him. As I laboured on across gently sloping terrain towards the final steeper snow ramp up to the dohedral, I could hear Dean talking to Russ on the radio. Prompted by Russ asking Dean if he knew where I was on the hill, I decided that it was time to declare my whereabouts. As soon as the pair had finished talking, I radioed through to Russ that I was almost at the bottom of the snow slope.

"Okay Grania, keep going", Russ told me, before asking what sounded like could I see Bill. "Bill?", I queried. "No, Bill", he said indistinctly again, "the one-armed bandit." "Oh, Paul. No, I can't see anyone. It's pretty bad up here", I said. "Just keep going", he reiterated, "you've got about another hour and a half to go."

The news couldn't have been sweeter. My goal was still out of sight due to the poor visibility, but at least it was now within reach. My spirits lifted and I felt a surge of renewed enthusiasm. I was going to make it!

But the mountain wasn't going to surrender her summit to me that easily. Just as I was contemplating the possibility of success, I saw what I had been dreading from the moment I left ABC on the summit push. Stretched out on the snow, still some distance away, was a long, vivid red object. I knew immediately what it was. The body of Slovenian climber Marko Lihteneker, lying on its back, frozen onto the mountainside.

I felt my pace slowing. Every step I took was bringing me closer to the corpse and I didn't want to see it. I could remember Marko from base camp when he was a vital, strong human being. His limited English meant I had never spoken to him, but I'd seen him conversing with his Russian-speaking colleagues on my frequent visits to the Seven-Summits team. I had been in their tent the day he and Viktor Milnar had left ABC. Russian team leader Alex Abramov told me afterwards that he had warned Viktor that it was too risky going for the summit in such unstable weather conditions. They should wait for a better window.

Viktor and Marko decided to ignore the expedition leader's advice and went on. Tragically, Marko never returned to ABC. Claimed by the mountain, he had been left to lie alone in his icy grave, a grave marked by nothing except the body itself.

Karsang had stopped about five metres from the corpse and stood, looking down at it. I thought it odd behaviour, knowing how superstitious Sherpas are about dead bodies, but any emotions were concealed behind his oxygen mask.

Marko's lifeless arms were flung back above his head, his naked hands frozen into terrible claws, through which the fixed line had run until the previous day when our first team leader Bill had removed it. Even though the rope no longer rested between the waxy digits, it still ran hideously close to the corpse. I unclipped and stepped a few feet to my right where the downhill rope lay in the snow. Clipping in to that I moved on until I was level with the body, trying desperately to keep my eyes focused on the route ahead. But it was impossible. No matter how much I tried to look away, I could feel my gaze being dragged back towards the poor creature who had breathed his last on that very spot.

With a prayer for his soul half-formed in my head, I forced myself past until the sides of my goggles took on the role of blinkers and I could no longer see the red form beside me. But I couldn't erase it from my mind and, totally unnerved by now, I wondered if I was signing my own death warrant by continuing on up the mountain. If an experienced climber like Marko had perished why did I think I could cheat death in my bid for the summit? And if I did make it to the top, would I suffer a similar fate on the descent?

I could see now why so many climbers had told me that success on Everest was due more to mental strength than stamina or physical fitness. I needed my mantra more than ever. You're not going to die and you will climb this mountain, I told myself firmly.

The gradient had started to increase as I moved up onto the snow ramp itself and I could see a party of climbers moving slowly down the rope towards me. The gap between us took an eternity to narrow. I was struggling uphill, but they seemed to be having almost equal trouble descending.

As the group got nearer to me I recognised Dean at the front. We stopped to talk and I could see Chieko behind him looking totally wasted and being short-roped down by her Sherpa, Dorjie. I congratulated them, but Chieko looked at me with unseeing eyes, seemingly unable to take in anything I was saying.

I asked Dean how much longer it would take me to get to the summit. "Probably another couple of hours", he said. I was appalled. "But Russ told me an hour and a half and that was a while ago", I said, in a voice that even I could hear was pleading Dean to revise his estimate. But he just wished me luck and started on down, leaving me in a state close to shock. I didn't know if I had the energy for another two hours of climbing and, even if I did, how would I know that I still had the 25% in reserve that Russ had said we would need for the descent.

I watched as the rest of the group went wearily past me, giving the thumbs up to Sissel and Piers as they came level with me. Oddly, despite my misgivings, I wasn't tempted to join them. From nowhere, a new wave of determination had temporarily wiped out my doubts. But it wasn't long before they resurfaced as the power of the mountain re-established its hold over my mind.

The visibility deteriorated still further and, as I peered into the gloom, the only thing I could see ahead of me was Karsang. The whole of the mountain was swathed in fog and, as far as I knew, Karsang and I were the only climbers still going up. Thoughts of the 1996 disaster crashed unbidden into my head. On May 10 of that year, climbers had summitted late but in apparently perfect weather conditions, unaware of the storm brewing up below them that was eventually to leave eight people dead, including two experienced expedition leaders, Rob Hall and Scott Fischer.

Doubts about the advisability of continuing my bid for the summit began to magnify themselves. I began to question myself again. What was I doing? Why was I continuing an ascent in obviously worsening weather? If I went any higher up the mountain and a storm hit, there would be no possibility of rescue. Karsang and I would have to try and fend for ourselves, but the most likely outcome was that we would die.

But then I realised that Russ would not have let us leave high camp if there was any possibility of a storm. His weather forecasts were usually incredibly accurate and his own knowledge of the mountain's fickle moods would allow him to spot potential trouble. The whiteout conditions meant that he wasn't able to see Karsang and me through his telescope at the North Col, but his years of experience would enable him to detect dangerously changing weather patterns by watching cloud formations and the plume coming off the summit. I realised that the fatalistic thoughts were the mountain trying to turn me round.

As I reached the top of the snow slope, with the Great Couloir plunging unseen down to my right, I could see Karsang disappearing towards a rocky out-crop. I recognised the dohedral I had heard Russ mention so many times. But, as I moved up to join him, a new horror caught my eye. Slightly to the right, I could make out the top half of a climber in a yellow down suit slumped just below two large rocks. Not another body, I thought, knowing that one of the Koreans had perished somewhere near this buttress the previous year. I had to steel myself to walk on past the hooded form.

Karsang, aware that I was slowing down yet again, turned and called out something and, to my horror, the 'corpse' moved. It turned out to be one of the Himex Sherpas, who I later discovered was waiting for Paul to come back down from the summit with Nima. The fright at seeing a dead man move was rapidly replaced by delight that this wasn't another corpse. The mountain had just been playing tricks on me.

I greeted the Sherpa with a warmth born of relief and turned my mind back to the summit. Karsang had disappeared around a large rock and I quickened my pace to catch up with him. As I rounded the rock I saw Karsang some way ahead on a narrow rocky traverse. I didn't even think to look down at the drop to my right but I could feel it was pretty exposed. It wasn't until I was on the descent and had time to look around me that I realised just how exposed it was.

By the time I was halfway along the narrow ledge, Karsang had started up a steep section above me to the left. It was soul destroying to see him constantly vanishing like an elusive butterfly that constantly flutters just out of reach. I eventually got to the jumble of rocks that formed the final summit tower. The rope I was clipped into was tied off in an impressive array of knots. Unclipping my safety line, I clipped in to the new rope before transferring my jumar for the ascent.

My energy levels were seriously depleted by now. I could feel my determination wavering and prayed silently that Russ's estimate of how much further I had to go was closer to reality than Dean's. I looked up at Karsang. He was less than 15 metres above me. "How much further to the summit?", I asked, aware that I sounded like a whingeing child.

"Ten minutes", Karsang said. "Summit just up here."

My jaded spirits almost soared. Ten minutes! I could do another 10 minutes. And then I'd think about the descent.

IV

Top Of The World

I dragged my exhausted body up the rocks to join Karsang, who had his back to me and was leaning against a massive boulder. He turned as he heard me approach and watched as I heaved myself up the last step. "Summit", he said, pointing to the right. I turned and there, not much more than 200 metres away, was the highest point on earth. A snow dome draped with Tibetan prayer flags, which dripped down its side like a multi-coloured version of the drizzle icing my grandmother used to put on her lemon cakes. It was magical. I was totally stunned by the sheer beauty of the mountain and the unexpected proximity of my goal.

As I set off up the final summit ridge behind Karsang, I remembered Russ's warning to be careful here. Dean's words also echoed in my head. "If you trip on the summit ridge you're gone." Without the comfort of the fixed lines I felt vulnerable and exposed. Beautiful scalloped cornices marked the edge of the ridge, but there was no temptation to inch closer and peer over. The cornice could break away at any moment and send me hurtling down the Kangshung Face. And the massive North face plunged into oblivion to my right. There was a well-trodden track going straight for the summit and I made sure not to stray from it.

As I inched my way towards the grail, I realised with surprise that there were two climbers on the summit itself. Even though I remembered Russ asking me earlier if I'd seen Paul, it hadn't crossed my mind that he was ahead of me. It wasn't until I got closer to the pair that I recognised the familiar outline of one of them. Unless there was another one-armed climber that I didn't know about, it had to be Paul Hockey and his Sherpa Nima.

I dragged myself up the final few snow steps and suddenly, dramatically, I was there. Paul and I were hugging and kissing, but I was almost in a trance. I couldn't quite believe that this was it. After the interminable weeks of waiting, I was finally standing on the summit of Mount Everest. I radioed through to Russ, but discovered later that the waning batteries meant I could only receive not transmit. My Himex team-mates waiting for news further down the mountain were becoming increasingly anxious about my welfare.

The 15 minutes I spent on the highest point on earth were both the shortest and the longest minutes of my life. Like a drowning man, life flashed before me. But it was my nephew Joe's life that I saw, not my own. As I waited for Nima to finish taking what seemed like endless pictures of Paul with various sponsors' logos, time stood still. The fog cocooned us from the world outside. If there had been any sounds up there they would have been muffled. Despite the wind, the place seemed hauntingly still. And hauntingly spiritual.

And I cried. Big fat tears welled up in my eyes and spilled down into my goggles as I remembered why I had done this, why I had gone through the months of exhaustive training and why I had pushed myself to my physical and emotional limits and beyond. It was for my nephew Joe. And although I felt his loss even more keenly in this beautiful but lonely place, I could sense his presence. He was with me on that summit, just as he had been with me every step of the way on the ascent. And I was comforted. Again.

As I sat down in the snow I saw an oval memorial plaque to a dead climber. It was a salutary reminder of just how many others had paid the ultimate price in their bid for the ultimate high, but it was also a reminder that we still had a long descent ahead of us before we were safe.

As I thought about the climbers that hadn't made it back down, I watched Nima taking pictures of Karsang with his Nepali flag, marking Karsang's seventh trip to the summit and the flag's 17th.. I needed pictures to record my first.

As soon as Nima had finished with Karsang, I pulled my digital camera out from the warmth of my down suit and asked him to do a picture of me with the

Irish flag. I also got him to take the requested shot of me with the SORD Data Systems logo, before I took the camera and snapped one of Paul with the Australian flag. It was one of those lucky shots that captured the very essence of big mountain climbing.

He still has his oxygen mask on, but has pushed his goggles onto his forehead and the picture shows him with a heavy frost fringing his eyelashes. There is a thick white cord of ice tumbling out of his mask where the condensation from his breath has frozen. The Australian flag is fluttering in front of his body and the backdrop is a white infinity. The photograph was to feature on the front page of one of the Australian papers a couple of days later when the press got wind of Paul's incredible achievement and how close he had come to death on the descent.

I then handed the disposable camera to Nima and he took several shots of me and Paul and one of Karsang with the Nepali flag before giving the camera back. I have absolutely no recollection of where I put it after that. I assumed I'd stuffed it into the front of my down suit but, as I stood up to leave, I had a niggling feeling that I didn't have it with me. I gave a cursory glance back at where I'd been sitting, but saw nothing on the snow. The SORD Data Systems poster had gone, presumably taken by the wind. There was no sign of the camera. It was only when I checked inside my down suit on my return to camp III much later that day that I discovered I had disposed of my disposable camera somewhere on the summit.

Thankfully my digital camera produced the goods, although the weather meant that any landmark that would confirm the picture's validity as a summit shot had disappeared in the mists. Like the moon landing photographs, my summit picture could have been taken in a studio. An orange down-suited climber, goggles and oxygen mask obscuring the face. An Irish tricolour whipped away in the wind. No mountain backdrop gives a clue to its location. The background is a blue-tinged mist. But the three photographs that survived on my digital camera will always be precious to me because they are reminders of the day I stood on the highest point on earth and thought of my nephew Joe and the terrible waste of a young life.

But the photographs also bring back memories of Paul's struggle to descend and how lucky he was to survive the ordeal. "Summitting is mandatory, getting back down is optional", he'd joked at base camp and ABC, turning the old climbing adage on its head. His words came scarily close to being prophetic on summit day.

Paul's Sherpa Nima was anxious that we shouldn't delay any further once the photographs were done. If there had been any sort of view I would probably have wanted to stay longer, to extend the moment and to feast on the 360 degree panorama of the surrounding peaks, to marvel at the curve of the earth on the distant horizon. But it was pointless to remain in such poor conditions and I was conscious of how demanding the descent was going to be on our already exhausted bodies.

I had been surprised to see Paul without his goggles on when I first reached the summit, but his decision to take them off for his photographs turned out to be a big mistake. Instead of putting them inside his down suit, he had simply pushed them up onto the top of his head. The condensation that had formed inside them from his body heat had rapidly frozen over. Initial attempts to clean off the skim of ice had only partially worked and Paul just couldn't see through the goggles properly.

I looked more closely at Paul, who was sitting back down on the snow while Nima tried cleaning the goggles again. His skin looked grey and his frost-rimmed eyes had a terrible lifeless look about them. I was concerned about snow blindness. Paul was already looking completely wasted. He didn't need any other issues to compound the problems he was going to encounter trying to descend with only one arm. He needed to get down off the mountain without delay. I'd seen how quickly Charlie had deteriorated at ABC and Paul looked like he was heading rapidly in the same direction.

He got to his feet wearily and started moving slowly down the summit ridge, stumbling in Nima's wake. I was immediately behind him and could empathise with Paul's faltering gait. The adrenaline that had got me to the summit had totally gone now and been replaced by a hollow feeling of sheer exhaustion. I didn't feel completely in command of my own legs. It was a totally alien sensation. I needed far more concentration now to keep going but, even though I was focused on my own descent, I couldn't help noticing that Paul seemed to be struggling more than I was.

When we reached the big boulder at the top of the dohedral, the yellow suited Sherpa that I had thought was a corpse was sitting there, obviously waiting to help get Paul down. Nima stopped and Paul immediately flopped down onto the snow for a rest. I sat down beside him, grateful for the chance of a break, no matter how brief.

Paul held his oxygen mask away from his face so that I could hear him and asked me to get a small bottle out of the top of his backpack. When I unzipped the bag I found a white plastic medicine bottle almost totally covered with black heavy-duty duct tape. I passed it to Paul who tried, without success, to open it.

He gave it back to me and asked me if I could open it for him. "What's in it?", I asked, as I tried to remove some of the masking tape so that I could unscrew the top of the bottle. "Ashes", Paul answered and I remembered that he had told me something early on in the expedition about scattering someone's ashes on the summit. "Nima wouldn't let me do it on the summit", Paul said, as though he'd read my mind.

I gave up trying to take off the tape. Without removing my gloves I couldn't find the end of it, so I told Paul there was a Swiss army knife in the top of my backpack. As he rummaged around trying to find it I racked my brains trying to think whose ashes these were. I knew Paul had told me about it and assumed they were the remains of his mother, who had died of cancer the previous September. He told me several days later that they were the combined ashes of the parents of a woman who had contacted him before his departure from Cairns, offering to pay 5,000 Australian dollars to his children's cancer charity if he would take them to the summit.

Paul eventually found the knife and I opened out the largest blade and tried to lever off the tape. It wouldn't move. I held the bottle and knife up to each of the three Sherpas in turn, but they refused to even try. I couldn't decide whether they were just being uncooperative or whether – if they were aware of the identity of the bottle's contents – their superstitious natures wouldn't let them touch a canister containing human remains.

I attacked the bottle with renewed fervour, but the effort required was substantial. Then, just as I started to make inroads into the plastic tape, I realised that the way I was holding the bottle meant that the slightest slip would send the blade straight through my gloves and into my wrist. Bleeding to death so soon after summitting Everest would be more than mildly ironic, I thought to myself, as I moved the bottle to a safer position.

My efforts finally bore fruit and I ripped off the tape and opened the bottle. I handed it to Paul and he awkwardly got to his feet. He walked about a metre or so away from me and then I could see rather than hear him muttering something. His words were whipped away by the wind before I could identify them, but I imagine they were prayers for the souls of the couple, both climbers, whose remains he now threw into the air. A gust of wind caught them and they disappeared like smoke towards the heavens so close now above our heads.

I could see that Paul, for all his rough and tumble exterior, was moved and knew he would be thinking of his mother and the other members of his family, including his father and his step-father, that had been lost to cancer. It was a hugely emotional moment.

V

Edge Of Life

The Sherpas were keen to get going now. The new Sherpa attached a sling to the back of Paul's harness so that he and Nima could short-rope Paul down. He was still walking under his own steam, but now had the double security of being attached to a Sherpa front and back.

After clipping into the rope, the trio started the descent of the rocky dohedral and I tucked in behind them, with Karsang once again bringing up the rear. But progress was tortuously slow and I could sense Karsang's frustration. As I stepped down onto the narrow ledge to start on the traverse back towards the snow field, I glanced down and it was only then that I realised just how exposed the traverse was. The ground dropped away in a tumble of rocks straight down the North Face, with the clouds boiling way below us. There would be no surviving a fall here.

I wasn't given too much time to think about it, however, as Karsang was nudging me to keep moving. Paul and his two Sherpas were already inching their way painstakingly along the ledge, but it didn't take me long to catch up with them. With the drop on his left, Paul was obviously uncomfortable not being able to keep a hold on the fixed line and whenever he lost his balance, he had to swing his left arm right across his body to snatch at the rope.

The rapid movement meant that his crampons, no longer square on the rock, were in danger of skittering off over the edge. We were all clipped into the fixed line and, if Paul fell, unless his two Sherpas could hold him, he would take us all with him as the rope ripped out. It was a sobering thought.

Equally sobering was the fact that my hands were getting colder by the minute. It was the first time I had been affected by the cold since leaving high camp, but the pace wasn't fast enough to keep me warm. Paul and his Sherpas had stopped in front of me, so I took the opportunity to shake my arms and slap my hands against my thighs in an attempt to keep the blood circulating and ward off frostbite.

I could feel rather than hear Karsang muttering behind me, but the ledge was too narrow and the exposure too great to risk trying to get past Paul. He was getting dangerously slow now, but I could do nothing except wait and hope that he would be strong enough to keep going. If he didn't, we were all in jeopardy.

After what seemed like an eternity we finally reached the end of the ledge and I knew that we were within a few metres of the snow field, terrain that Paul would find much easier. But just as we got level with the rock where I'd seen the resurrection earlier when the seated corpse had turned into a living Sherpa, Paul stopped.

"I'm going to talk to Russ", he said, tugging his radio out from inside his down suit. Pressing the button on the side of the radio, he talked without preamble, staring at his feet as he spoke. "Russ, I'm in trouble." As he said it he raised his eyes to look at me. The life had already gone out of them. He was close to giving up.

"Is Grania with you?", I heard Russ ask. "Yes", Paul told him. "Put her onto me." Paul handed me the radio and I quickly spoke into it. "Russ, it's Grania here", I said. "Get your arse down that mountain quickly or you're going to run out of oxygen", he barked at me.

It was his usual blunt style, but I'm sure Russ was fully aware of the significance of what he was saying. He knew there was very little I could do to help Paul and he didn't want a double rescue on his hands. Ordering me down the mountain had a dual effect. It meant he would have one less person to worry about and it effectively gave me permission to leave Paul. Without that I would simply have refused to abandon him.

With the decision made for me, I handed the radio back to Paul. "Good luck", I said, squeezing his shoulder. "I'll see you back down there." I tried not to think the unthinkable but I was painfully aware that this could be the last time I set eyes on him.

It was desperately difficult walking away from him. I felt it was an act of betrayal, but I knew that Russ had major contingency plans in place in case any of us got into difficulties and would rapidly deploy the troops to try and get Paul off the hill safely.

Paul was still talking on the radio as I clipped into the fixed line and headed down the snow slope as quickly as my exhausted legs would allow. Just as I'd been unable to look back at Peg when I left her on her rocky perch above the First Step, I didn't dare risk turning round to look at Paul. I wasn't running away from him, I was trying to escape from the omnipresent threat of the mountain.

Paul had just enough life left in him to keep going for a while, but he was going to need a lot of help, particularly on the down climb of the Second Step. I just hoped the rescue team would reach him before the fight went out of him and he gave up completely.

Alone with Karsang again and weighed down with worry about Paul, I was dreading the thought of having to go back past Marko's body. I was already desperately fatigued and I didn't want the sight of the corpse to leach away the last of my stamina. I knew it would be just as horrific as it had been at first sight, but at least I was prepared for it this time.

The red of Marko's down suit once again drew my eyes straight to the corpse, but the initial shock factor had been removed and I was able to walk past without having to fight a compulsion to look more closely. Even so it was a relief when I had passed it and knew that I wouldn't have to see it again.

As I sank down onto the snow for a rest once Marko's body was well behind me I noticed for the first time that the visibility had cleared dramatically and at last I was able to see some of the surrounding mountains. There were still clouds way below, but I could see some of the taller peaks beginning to break through the billowing white masses. But I wasn't going to be given a chance to sit and enjoy the view. Even as I pulled out my water bottle for a drink, Karsang was telling me that we needed to keep going.

I hastily gulped down some water and wearily pushed myself up off the snow, knowing that Karsang was right but wishing I could stay put, even though

I'd been told by other climbers that there was no point in stopping to rest as the body can't replenish itself at such extreme altitude. I wrapped the fixed line round my right arm and continued my stumbling descent, feeling the burn in the front of my thighs at each step as I struggled to stay upright.

Scrambling down the Third Step added to my exhaustion, but at least it wasn't technically taxing. I knew that the Second Step would be a very different proposition. There was still some way to go before I had to tackle that, however, and I knew that the level of fatigue I already felt would be even greater by the time I got there.

The terrain was straightforward for a good distance now, but my co-ordination was substantially diminished and I had to concentrate to master even such a basic task. Tripping over my crampons now wouldn't put me in any immediate danger, but I was aware of how rapidly a simple slide could turn into an unstoppable fall.

To my eternal shame, the only time I thought about Paul and his battle with the mountain was when I heard Russ talking to him or messages of support from other Himex team members on the radio. Russ, in a series of brilliantly pitched dispatches, used all kinds of psychological weaponry on him. "Come on Paul, think of your family back at home", Russ said. He didn't need to add the rest. What will your family do without you if you die on the mountain? The unspoken words hung heavy in the air, heard by everyone listening in on the Himex wavelength.

When that tactic clearly wasn't working, Russ told Paul in the bluntest language that he was a fool for even trying to climb the mountain, hoping that Paul's anger at the insult would make him determined to prove Russ wrong. It was clear that Paul's willpower had waned to a dangerous degree. Russ was going to need to use every weapon in his armoury to get Paul down, even if it meant abusing him verbally to get Paul to fight back.

I had a battle on my hands too. I had the worst part of the descent still to do, but my brain was now as exhausted as my body. My mind and my body were unravelling. Decision-making would have been seriously difficult, but there were no decisions to be made. I simply had to keep on moving, making the descent as quickly but as safely as possible.

The snow-field, which had provided easy footing, eventually gave way to rock but it was flat for a good distance and I kept pace with Karsang on this straightforward terrain. I was only too aware that the Second Step was looming, but its proximity was brought into unexpected focus when the top half of a red down suit suddenly appeared directly in front of Karsang.

We stopped and waited for the climber to heave himself up over the lip of the step and, after taking a couple of steps away from the edge, he stood, breathing heavily, just in front of me. He was bearded and seemed to be looking straight through me with a pair of dull brown eyes.

"Are you on your own?", I asked him, seeing no sign of either a fellow climber or a Sherpa. He stared blankly at me. "Are you going to the summit now?", I tried, thinking that it was very late to be heading up to the top of the mountain. That elicited no response either, but I couldn't tell whether he was too tired to make any attempt at communication or if he just didn't understand my questions. Still with the same glazed look in his eyes, he turned and continued his silent ascent.

When I reached camp III much later in the day, Sissel told me she was convinced she'd seen a ghost at the First Step, describing the very creature that I had watched on his listless trudge up the mountain. It wasn't until the following day that I discovered from Russ that, far from being a ghost, he was an Eastern European climber that nobody knew very much about except that he was endlessly trying to borrow equipment from other teams.

He seemed to be climbing unsupported, claiming that the other members of his expedition had left ABC and headed down to base camp, abandoning him as he was heading up on his final summit push. His late departure from high camp was brought about by a desire to be the last summiteer of the 2005 season and the latest ever recorded. It was only then I realised that, were it not for him, that accolade would have been accorded to me.

When I turned back to look at Karsang I saw that he had already started down the Second Step and had almost disappeared, with only his head still visible above the edge. I moved forward and looked down the drop. By then Karsang had climbed down to the top of the ladder and was starting his descent. I could hear the click of his crampons on the aluminium rungs. He stopped when he saw me.

Climbing up the Second Step in the dark meant I hadn't been able to see the full extent of the exposure. Now, even though the clouds way, way below obscured some of the drop into infinity, I could see that there was nothing between me and those clouds. The cost of even the smallest mistake here would be my life.

As I clipped into the rope I was painfully aware that the sense of security it provided was, to a very large extent, a false one. If I fell the rope might save me from hurtling all the way down to the glacier, but even if I only fell to the bottom of the rope I would still probably be killed. A favourite expression of my father's flashed into my head. He always described difficult situations as "character forming". This undoubtedly was a real character former.

I turned my back on the drop and tentatively put my left foot down over the edge. It was a blind leap of faith. I felt like I was stepping into an abyss. The jutting snout of my oxygen mask made it impossible to see my feet and I groped around blindly with the toe of my boot, hoping for a crevice big enough to hold my crampon points so I could lower myself down for the next move. Not for the first time that day I was acutely aware of my own mortality.

Unnerved, I snatched my foot back up to the safety of the ledge and glanced down over my left shoulder at Karsang, still standing on the top of the ladder. There was no way he could make the move for me. I had to do it myself. Taking a deep breath, I lowered my foot again and this time felt my crampon grate on a crack in the rock. I forced the points into the shallow crevice and, to my relief, they held.

Gingerly, I transferred my weight down onto my left foot and was moving my right foot down off the ledge when I felt it snag against something. I peered down as best I could over the top of my mask and, to my horror, saw that the crampon points were caught in the tangle of old ropes draped down the rock face.

Instantly my mind conjured up images of Ishi's Japanese friend Shoto Ota, who had been killed after getting entangled in these same ropes on her way down from the summit a year ago. She'd broken her neck in the fall and had been found dangling with her crampons still entwined in the jumble of ropes.

Aware of the dangers, I knew I couldn't wrench my foot out in a bid to free my crampons. Any sudden move would send me plummeting straight off the face. I warily tried to untangle the tattered ropes with my right hand, but every time I freed one, the jagged crampon points would get caught in another.

I could feel the muscles in my left calf starting to twitch, the precursor to the familiar "hammer legs" that afflict nervous or exhausted climbers stalled on the crux of a route. Even in my short climbing career I had surmounted far more technical situations than this one, but felt that I was now facing the crux to beat all cruxes. One false move and I would be dead.

It seemed to take a lifetime to wriggle my crampon free of the clutches of the shredded rope, but finally I disentangled it and got my right foot down level with my left so that I could stand square to the rock face and take a moment to compose myself. My usually solid nerves were as frayed as the ropes I'd just extricated my crampons from.

Now all I had to do was reach across to the small alcove in the face and then make the stretch across to the top rung of the ladder. Karsang, obviously confident that I didn't need his watchful eye to execute these final two moves, was already halfway down the ladder. It was a relief when, just moments later, I felt my left crampon scrape against the aluminium of the top rung and I could clip into the blue rope that descended down the right-hand side of the ladder.

But I had only gone down three steps when I was suddenly stopped in my tracks. Looking up I saw that my safety line was caught up in the horizontal rope at the top of the ladder. My brain was almost too weary to take in the information. I climbed back up, unclipped to free the sling and hastily clipped back in again before restarting my descent. In less than a minute I was down at the bottom and following Karsang to the big boulder I had shinned up so inelegantly in the dark.

I had expected that we would rappel down from where the ladder ended, but Karsang was down-climbing this too. Using a cross between arm rapping and down-climbing I managed to negotiate the rest of the Second Step, but it wasn't a technique I was comfortable with. I was relieved to get to the bottom, but my relief didn't last long. As I turned round I saw that we would be on pretty exposed terrain for a considerable distance.

I sat down on a rock and pulled my water bottle out from my down suit. It was much warmer now and I could feel myself getting more and more dehydrated. The water was cool on my tongue, but there was precious little left in the bottle, so I allowed myself only one mouthful before recapping the bottle and replacing it in its nest inside my suit.

Russ had told us in his final talk before we left ABC that Mushroom Rock didn't really look anything like a mushroom. Having missed it in the dark the night before, it was a welcome landmark on the way back down. And Russ was right. It didn't look like a mushroom at all, it was just a rock out on its own. There were a number of oxygen bottles lying on the snow next to it where ascending climbers had left half-full bottles and those on their descent had discarded their empties. As well as the orange Poisk bottles from Himex members, there were numerous blue and red cylinders. The red ones, which I'd seen scattered on other parts of the mountain as well, had Indian Air Force scrawled on them in large uneven letters.

As the ridge became increasingly narrow I could see between the dips in the cornices on the right that some of the neighbouring peaks, including Makalu and Kangchenjunga, had managed to break through the gloom and were now poking their heads above the clouds far below. Knowing the propensity of cornices to break off and send climbers plummeting to their deaths, I refrained from going closer to the edge for a better view.

My rest periods were becoming more and more frequent now and I was finding it harder to get to my feet each time. I still had the First Step and the Exit Cracks to negotiate before the long sloping final run back down to high camp, where I could at least rehydrate before embarking on the slog to camp III and sleep.

Once again Karsang opted to down-climb when he got to the First Step and although I would infinitely have preferred to abseil off, I meekly followed suit, too tired to object. There were so many old ropes coming down the step that it was difficult to know which one to clip into. Even when I did find the blue rope put in place by the Himex Sherpas it didn't guarantee a smooth passage as it frequently got hopelessly tangled up with the old ropes, requiring me to unclip and clip back in underneath the knotted mass.

I tugged on a thick dark brown rope to see if it was securely attached. It seemed safe enough, but I wasn't keen to entrust it with my entire bodyweight, so I climbed down using both the blue Himex rope and the thicker brown one for added security. I descended rather faster than planned at a couple of points. It gave me a jolt when I realised that if one of those slips had turned into a fall

I was too drained of energy to try and save myself.

The ropes on the Exit Cracks were even more snarled up. I frequently found myself in the middle of a twisted coil of multi-coloured ropes, at one stage having to reverse back up a step to unravel myself from the spaghetti-like loops. It was only afterwards that I realised I had managed to go both up and down the Exit Cracks without catching sight of Green Boots' body.

I now had just the long rocky slope back down to high camp to negotiate, but my legs seemed unable to hold me up any longer. I kept stumbling and falling down the scree. Moments after I had scrabbled my way back onto my feet, I would repeat the process, exhausting myself still further each time.

Karsang was always at least 50 metres ahead, but he finally stayed put until I had caught up with him and then told me to take off my oxygen mask. I had been so concerned about running out of oxygen on the way up, but had only checked the valve a couple of times on the way back down to make sure I was still getting air. Karsang pulled the old bottle out of my backpack and replaced it with what I assumed was a reasonably full bottle.

He turned to pick up the empty bottle that was lying next to him on the snow, but lost his grip on it and it rolled away from him, picking up speed as it went. Before he had a chance to try and save it, the bottle bounced over the lip of the ledge and hurtled down the slope. It was well away from the climbing route, but I still prayed that it wouldn't hit anyone as it flew down with wicked velocity. Its speed was a stark reminder of how quickly a body would plunge down the same route.

I went on ahead of Karsang for a while, but it wasn't long before he overtook me again. As I came to the point where Karsang had branched off to the left, dropping off the north-east ridge, I saw one of the most welcome sights of my life. There below me, still a good distance away but clearly visible, was the higgledy-piggledy scattering of tents that marked out high camp on the scree slope.

By now Karsang had become like some Will O The Wisp creature, darting on ahead of me but never close enough to be caught. Every now and then he'd disappear from view, but I'd scramble down a cluster of rocks or round a giant boulder and there he'd be, sitting like a little leprechaun waiting for me.

It didn't seem to matter how long I trudged on for, the tents never seemed to get any nearer. It was soul destroying, but my memories of summit day on Cho Oyu kept me going. I knew that, even though I was shattered, I would make it back to camp. I didn't want to think about the next stage, about having to head on further down the mountain to the relative safety of camp III. I would take it one step at a time.

Eventually I could make out human figures moving amongst the tents and gradually I could distinguish faces as I got closer to camp. I could see Karsang already squatting down talking to the other Sherpas and drinking what I assumed was his favourite butter tea, but he had disappeared by the time I staggered, drunk with exhaustion, into camp and flopped down next to the nearest tent.

Dean had just come out of his tent further down the slope. He waved up at me and I tried to shout down to him that I'd come and see him as soon as I'd had a drink, but my throat seemed to have closed over and no sound came out. But human contact had an amazing effect on me. Even before I had been handed a bowl of steaming water by one of the four Himex Sherpas whose sole job on summit day was to melt snow I felt renewed. The water was pure nectar.

I downed three bowls in rapid succession, amazing myself by chatting to the Sherpas as though I'd just done a walk in the Wicklow hills. Their warmth reminded me of smiling cook boy, Kul Burdhu, who had greeted me on my return from the summit of Cho Oyu with his usual two-handed grasp of welcome. "Have you been upstairs, Didi?", he had asked me then.

I learnt all four of the Sherpas' names and swore to myself that I would remember them so I could thank them properly for their life-giving support when I saw them back at ABC. I even arranged to meet them for a party at base camp. But my addled brain had forgotten their names and even their faces before I'd got down to camp III and there was no possibility of recall.

I stood up feeling unbelievably strong and walked over to Dean's tent without a trace of the lurching gait that had carried me down from the summit. I crawled inside and flung myself down on a sleeping bag. Dean was slouching, semi-recumbent, across the top end of the tent.

I asked him if I could use his satellite phone. He nodded and handed me the phone and I keyed in the mobile number for my PR man, Tom McCormack which, with amazing foresight, I had written on one of the four pages I had torn out of my notebook to use as my summit diary. The phone clicked and, after a long pause, I heard it ring a couple of times before Tom's voice came on the line.

"You're talking to the first Irish woman to summit Everest from the north side", I said simply. I couldn't have asked for a better reaction. Tom had always believed that I would reach the summit. Before I'd left for Tibet he would talk about the "victory tour", never even considering the possibility of failure. But the continued stretch of bad weather and the endless waiting had unnerved him and I could hear both delight and relief in his voice as he yelled his congratulations down the line.

I asked him to send out a simple press release stating that I had summitted just before eight o'clock that morning, 3.45a.m. Irish time. This wasn't a burst of publicity seeking vanity. I wanted everyone at home to know about my success in the hope it would spark off an influx of cash for the two charities. I had no idea that I would feature in the headlines on all the television news bulletins as well as in newsprint.

I ate half a protein bar while Dean and I chatted. I asked him how Paul was. "He's coming down slowly, but he's going to have to stay up here tonight", Dean said. He went on to tell me that he'd just rung his partner Boz back home in New Zealand to tell her that he'd summitted but would be sleeping at 8,300 metres to keep an eye on Paul once he got down. Boz knew how the Death Zone above 8,000 metres had earned its name and wasn't impressed, but Dean had assured her he'd be alright. I wondered silently if Paul would be alright too.

Talking about the dangers of sleeping at such extreme altitude had obviously reminded Dean that I should be heading down to camp III. "It's time you started moving", he said. I was enjoying just being able to lie there talking. The last thing I wanted to do was get up and start on down the mountain again. But Dean had no intention of letting me stay any longer and pre-empted all argument by radioing down to Russ that I was just leaving high camp. I had no choice but to re-gather my thoughts and my gear and crawl back out of the tent.

"See you back at ABC tomorrow", I said as I left. "And good luck with Paul."

Just as I was heading back towards the tent I'd left little over 15 hours before, I heard Dean calling out to me, "Oh, Karsang says he'll collect any stuff you left in the tent", I could procrastinate no longer. I had to get started on the final, and probably the toughest, challenge of my summit day.

I had gone only 50 metres when my legs buckled underneath me and I fell. My restored energy levels had drained away before I even got out of camp. I dragged myself upright again and set off downhill, welcoming the change to snow not far below. It was a much more forgiving surface for jaded legs.

It was now a glorious day and I could see the massive bulk of Cho Oyu peering over the clouds. I knew in mountaineering terms Cho Oyu had no great status apart from its height, but it seemed to my novice eye to be an impressive mountain to have under my harness. Now I could claim two 8,000ers in the past eight months during a climbing career that spanned all of 15 months. I felt phenomenally lucky to have achieved so much in such a short space of time, but knew that my high altitude dreams – particularly of Everest – would not have been realised without Russell Brice.

Buoyed up by this sense of achievement, I began to feel stronger again and the prospect of getting down to camp III didn't seem quite so arduous. I turned to look back at the summit behind me. It already seemed extraordinarily distant and I could scarcely believe that I had stood on that tiny triangle silhouetted against the blue of the sky, free, for once, of the familiar plume.

Camp IV was no longer visible and there was no sign of Karsang, who was obviously still resting before heading on down after me. It felt good to be alone on the mountain with my thoughts. I sat down on a rock, took off my mask and fished out my water bottle. It was only then that I realised I'd never even thought of asking the Sherpas at high camp to fill it up for me. I hadn't checked my oxygen either, but the significance of that didn't strike me until later.

I took out my digital camera. There was still no sign of the disposable and I just hoped that it was only because it had slid out of reach inside my suit. I snapped off a couple of shots of the mountain panorama laid out in front of me. Under a vivid blue sky, wispy clouds clung to the snowy summits and, far below me, I could see the glacier snaking between the lower dark chocolate brown slopes. The knife-edge ridge on Changtse that runs down to the North Col was directly in front of me, but the Col itself was obscured by the lip of the rocky ledge I was on.

The wind had died down completely and I was surrounded by silence. I could have sat there for hours, relishing the peace and beauty of the mountain environment, but I knew that I needed to get a lot lower before I was out of danger. I replaced my oxygen mask and checked the valve on the tube to see I was still getting air. The small clear section of tubing reminded me of a spirit level. The valve was where I expected it to be, right in the centre, showing that there was still a strong flow of oxygen.

Although I felt much stronger than I had on the descent to high camp, I knew my legs weren't capable of carrying me much faster than I was going. But it was some time before I heard Karsang's crampons scraping on the rock behind me. I stopped to let him go past, but he gestured for me to stay in front.

"No, I'm fine, you go on without me", I said, and I meant it. I was quite happy to be alone and at one with my surroundings. Without saying a word, Karsang passed me and headed on down the rocky trail. He was no sooner out of sight than my oxygen ran out.

Supplemental oxygen is a boon to high altitude climbers. A tiny minority are strong enough to climb without it, but for the rest, oxygen has made the biggest and most challenging mountains accessible. Its use is almost as controversial as the birth of the commercial expeditions, with the purists scorning both. But, without supplemental oxygen, many of the world's greatest peaks would remain out of reach to all but a tiny handful of elite climbers.

The one major drawback is that, when it runs out, the contrast is huge. A climber on an oxygen-free ascent has gradually acclimatised his or her body to the thin air, but the climber who runs out of supplemental oxygen suddenly finds what is effectively their life-support system cut off. They have acclimatised themselves to the lower altitudes, but their bodies are not accustomed to the higher elevations.

I re-checked the valve and it confirmed what I feared. There was no sign of the valve in the clear section of tubing, meaning that there was no oxygen getting through. I took off my mask and breathed the fresh – but thin – mountain air.

I wasn't left gasping like a goldfish. I knew I could survive for a limited time without oxygen, but it was going to slow my descent drastically and I certainly didn't want to spend too long on the mountain without it. It was even more important now that I got down to camp III without delay.

With no batteries left in my radio, I couldn't contact Russ or Karsang to request a new bottle. And I knew that nobody else would be coming down behind me. Dean was waiting up at high camp to look after Paul, and Karsang was the last of the Sherpas to descend. I was on my own and would have to fend for myself. Thankfully there was nothing technical ahead of me, but the rocky terrain would require considerable care if I was going to negotiate it safely.

I was determined not to let the lack of oxygen affect me psychologically. I knew that I could get down to camp III without it, but I was going to have to use all my powers of concentration to get my wasted body to respond. There was one bright spot, however. Without the oxygen mask blocking my view, I could now see my feet.

The deterioration came so slowly that I didn't even notice it creeping up on me until, suddenly, my legs just wouldn't obey any commands. Even the simplest step down was a huge task and all too frequently would result in me falling as my limbs buckled underneath me.

I took one tumble that would have looked spectacular if there had been anyone around to see it. I was attempting to climb down between two large boulders when, without warning, one of my crampons skidded off the rocks. Before I had time to try and save myself, I found myself plunging headlong between the two slabs of rock, landing awkwardly on my side with my right arm pinned underneath me.

I lay there winded, aware that my arm was hurting. I sat up gingerly. My elbow had taken the full brunt of the fall, but a speedy check with my left hand revealed that there was no serious damage done, except to my down suit. Every time I moved a cloud of soft white feathers puffed out of two huge gashes in the sleeve.

I was lucky. I could easily have broken my arm or, much worse, my leg. Without radio contact, I would have had no means of raising the alarm. How long, I wondered, would it have been before anyone noticed I was missing and sent out a search party? And would the rescuers have arrived before exhaustion and oxygen deprivation added me to the grim statistics and allowed the mountain to claim me for her own.

I only discovered later that my metal water bottle had saved me from more serious injury. When I was filling it in camp that evening, Sissel pointed out a huge dent in the side. Obviously it had struck a prominent rock in the fall. If the bottle hadn't been inside my down suit, my ribs or breastbone would have taken the full impact.

At least the boulders that had caused my fall provided the leverage to get me back onto my feet again. Heaving myself upright, I stood for a while trying to get my breath back and waiting for my heart to stop hammering in my chest. Expedition doctor Terry O'Connor had told us before we left ABC that the prolonged exposure to altitude resulted in a thickening of the blood, meaning that the heart had to work doubly hard to pump it round the body. I resolved to take more care for the rest of the descent. Having successfully reached the summit, I didn't want to injure or even kill myself with a fall on terrain that wouldn't normally cost me a thought at a lower altitude.

My elbow was sore, but my confidence was more severely bruised. The solitude that I had been so enjoying now hung over me like a threat. And every rock seemed to be lying in wait, its polished surface refusing to offer any purchase to my crampons and threatening to send me skidding off my feet again.

My wariness slowed my pace even more, but I was still endlessly stumbling and half-falling, making ever more demands on my body as I attempted to right myself. My lungs were screaming out for oxygen but there would be no respite until I got to camp.

I had thought I was tired coming back down from the summit, but that was nothing compared to this. I was literally having to will my legs and feet into making the next move, coercing them into taking the next step that would bring me closer to my goal.

My down gear was making me desperately hot and I was also parched with thirst. Whenever I came across a clean patch of snow I sank down into it, scrabbling at it with my fingers and shovelling it into my mouth. It was like the best ice cream I'd ever tasted.

Finally I could make out splashes of colour that marked the tents down at camp III. But the surge of energy I thought this welcome sight would elicit just never came. My body and my mind were simply too drained to respond. The last vital reserves of energy had gone.

I must have been literally within 100 metres of camp when I fell again. It was more of a slide than a fall, but I hadn't got the energy to save myself and I found myself sitting on the scree when, a split second before, I had been walking. From this angle I could no longer see camp, which also meant that no-one in camp could see me.

I had finally, genuinely hit the wall I had heard marathon runners talk about and, as I looked round at the mountains, I realised that I didn't care any more. I was simply too tired to worry whether I lived or died. My body had had enough. I closed my eyes.

VI

Rescue

I don't know how long I sat there, but when I opened my eyes again I saw Karsang climbing up towards me, carrying a bottle of oxygen. I feebly waved a hand in his direction. "I've run out of oxygen", I whispered, as he squatted at my side. He said nothing, but immediately unscrewed the regulator from the empty cylinder and attached it to the new one. I heard the rush of air as the oxygen hissed out from the top of the bottle, feeling an almost Pavlovian response to the noise.

I pulled the mask up to my face and sucked in as much air as I could in one breath. I felt the oxygen flood into my lungs, but it was a while before its restorative qualities took effect. I leant against Karsang's shoulder for support, half-expecting him to pull away at the unusual physical contact, but he remained still and I felt soothed by his presence. We sat there without speaking for what must have been at least 10 minutes before Karsang shifted himself, getting ready to move.

I had felt so weak before his arrival that I hadn't expected to be able to get to my feet unassisted. But the oxygen had given me renewed strength and, when Karsang got up, I stood too and followed him – pitifully slowly – down the last few metres into camp.

Sissel and I shared a tent that night. "What happened to you?", she asked after I'd gulped down the bowlful of water she'd just handed me. "Why did it take you so long to get down?"

When I said I'd run out of oxygen, she told me that she had radioed through to Russ well over an hour beforehand to say that Karsang and I were both back in camp. She had assumed that I was only just behind the Sherpa and didn't want to block the airwaves more than necessary during the battle to save Paul high up the mountain.

When an hour had passed and I still hadn't arrived, Sissel had got out of her tent and looked up towards high camp, expecting to see me on my way down. The route was completely deserted. Concerned, she went to Karsang's tent and had to wake him to ask where I was. He shrugged an answer, but he got out of the tent and, stopping only to pick up a bottle of oxygen, came straight up the hill to find me. It was a timely intervention.

I was amazed how quickly I bounced back. Sissel and I drank as much as we could and ate some chocolate and I could feel my energy levels rising. Apart from my brief phone conversation with Tom McCormack, it was the first time I had really allowed myself anything approaching celebration.

"Do you realise we've just climbed Everest?", I said to Sissel, who responded with a grin that mirrored the huge smile on my face. We could talk of nothing else, comparing notes about different parts of the climb and our emotions on the summit.

While Sissel had been talking, I had finally summoned up the energy to take off my big heavy ice boots. Incapable of any more strenuous movement, I had flopped back onto the sleeping bag, almost filling the tent with downy feathers as the contents of my sleeve came billowing out of the gaping holes caused by my fall.

I knew that the toes on my left foot were rubbed and wasn't surprised to discover blisters on the two smallest toes. Sissel handed me a packet of baby wipes and a fresh pair of socks. She even managed to produce some blister plasters. The wipes felt fabulously cool against my hot skin. Clean feet, clean socks and padded plasters to cushion my blisters. How good the simple things in life felt.

My body was coming back to life now. At last the rehydration techniques had worked. I needed to pee, but my pee bottle was either with Karsang or still up in high camp. I never actually saw it again and ended up using an empty lemon powder tin as an alternative when I got back down to ABC. It was disconcertingly noisy to use.

I had no such luxuries at camp III and knew I'd have to go outside and face the elements. I had no intention of putting my climbing boots back on, but we were on a solid rocky ledge and there was no wind, so I thought I'd be safe enough in my yellow and black North Face down booties. I wasn't going to be straying too far from the tent.

Luckily it was still beautifully sunny, because I was going to have to strip from the waist down. My down suit had a crotch zip that went all the way from front to back and would have been perfect for use with the Freshette, a sort of flattened cup device with a removable tube that is designed for use by women climbers so that they can urinate standing up. Unfortunately, my Freshette – ordered online in mid-February – arrived the day after I left for Kathmandu. It's still sitting, unused, in a drawer at home.

The crotch zip would also have been ideal if all my undergear had been fitted with similar openings. But the five pairs of thermal leggings were elasticated at the waist and needed to be pulled down, something not easy to achieve through a crotch zip. I'd tried lower down the mountain where the air was thicker. Even there I couldn't do it, so what hope was there at 7,900 metres, after the toughest 24 hours of my life and my longest ever exposure to extreme altitude. I decided not to even try.

After finding myself a reasonably flat area right outside the tent, I simply unzipped the top of my down suit and pulled everything down. My legs were surprisingly compliant to the order to squat, but I didn't want to stay in this Sherpa style position for long in case my limbs seized up. Getting the job done as quickly as possible, I wielded another of the ubiquitous baby wipes, pulled up and zipped up all my clothing and opened the flap of the tent.

As I crawled in on hands and knees, I was dimly aware of some unidentifiable liquid cascading down my neck, but it was Sissel who realised exactly what it was. "Get out Grania", she shrieked at me, "you've pissed in your hood and it's going all over the sleeping bags!"

We laughed so much I was grateful that it was my now empty bladder that had caused all the mirth, otherwise the bottom half of my suit would have been soaked in the unusual marinade, not my hood.

It took a while to clean up the mess, but I couldn't get rid of the smell of urine from my down suit. While the sun was still up it was pretty warm in the tent and that didn't help. I felt desperately self-conscious of the smell. Every time I rolled over in my sleeping bag that night I was convinced I could catch the stale scent, even though it couldn't possibly have permeated my oxygen mask.

Sleep was surprisingly slow in coming that night. Even when I did doze off, I re-climbed the mountain so many times that I woke up exhausted. It was still dark, so I groped round in my sleeping bag until I found my head-torch. Feathers fluttered everywhere. Switching on the torch, I shone the beam onto my watch. Ten past two. No wonder I was still tired.

I shifted my weight onto my left, unbruised elbow and sat up, shining the torch onto my regulator. I was out of oxygen. That's obviously what had woken me.

I unscrewed the old bottle and replaced it with a half-empty cylinder that was lying next to me in the tent. I knew there wasn't enough in it to get me down the rest of the mountain the next day, but it would do to sleep on. With my mask back on I rolled over and fell instantly into a deep sleep.

Sissel left early the next morning, but I had no intention of rushing. We had all day to get down to ABC. I was looking forward to the snow slopes down to the North Col, because that would mean the end of crampons on rock – for this expedition at least. The next rock I would meet would be the moraine after Crampon Point. My crampons would be in my backpack by then.

But I still had over an hour of scrambling down the tumble of rocks that I had so relished climbing up. It was hard to believe that it was only three days since we'd battled against the wind to go up these same rocks to get to camp III. Three days since Antoine had thrown in the towel shortly after leaving camp II. Two days since Kevin had turned back just above camp III. And it was only yesterday that I'd stood on the summit with Paul. It felt like a lifetime ago.

Looking down towards Changtse, I could see the entire descent laid out below me. It looked a desperately long way, but I was feeling so much stronger than I had the day before that I was confident I wouldn't have too much trouble. I didn't have the same confidence about Paul though. He had been due to leave high camp at about the same time I was setting off from camp III, 400 vertical metres below him. Thinking about all he'd been though yesterday and having heard Dean on the radio saying that he'd had a very rough night, I knew he wasn't out of danger yet.

I made my way down through the rocks as quickly as I could. Even though I didn't feel hungry I knew I needed to eat. The thought of real food down at ABC spurred me on, even though the strength in my legs had waned rapidly after my departure from camp III.

As I neared the snow line right above camp II, I could see the tiny dots of other climbers heading down towards the North Col in front of me. The first of these was already almost at camp I. I assumed it was Sissel, who had obviously made astonishingly good time on her descent.

But then my eye was caught by an unfamiliar outline just ahead. A long roll of some sort of cloth lay neatly on a ledge between the rocks up to my right. I couldn't work out what it was initially, but then realisation hit like a punch. It was the body of Kari's German client, Dieter Kramer.

I seemed to have picked up the Sherpas' superstitious beliefs about dead bodies and didn't want to look too closely, but I saw enough. The body had been rolled up in an old tent, covered completely except for one thing. A gloved hand stuck poignantly out from under the nylon fabric. Another life wasted in pursuit of the ultimate dream. Even here the clutches of death were still strong. I hurried on past.

I scrambled down a narrow rocky gully before dropping onto the stony, uneven track that sloped down to camp II. Vivid memories rushed into my head of how we had struggled up here, shoulders hunched against the elements and clinging to the rock to prevent the wind blowing us over.

A noise behind me broke my thoughts. I turned to see Karsang clambering down towards me. I stopped to wait for him and, for once, it was him who sat down first for a rest. I found a flat rock next to him and sat down.

I pulled my battered water bottle out, unscrewed the cap and offered the bottle to Karsang. To my surprise he took it. Normally he always declined. As he put his lips to the top of the bottle and tipped back his head to drink, I thought with amusement about how paranoid I'd been on the way up the mountain. I was so terrified of picking up some sort of bug and now here I was, watching Karsang drinking from the bottle that, in a couple of minutes, I was going to be drinking from too. And I didn't care.

Karsang handed me back the bottle and, without a second thought, I took a couple of swigs before replacing the cap and asking him to put the bottle into the outside pocket of my backpack. I was keen to get going again, so as soon as the bottle was securely housed, I stood up and told Karsang I was going to keep moving. He nodded, but didn't move from his perch, so I turned and headed across the final short rocky stretch.

It was a relief to feel my crampons biting into snow and, moments later, my pace speeded up as soon as I left the rock behind. With the blue down-rope wrapped round my right arm, I moved confidently down a slope that had seemed exhaustingly steep on the way up.

I could see two yellow-suited climbers way below me. They seemed to be spending more time sitting down than descending. They were too far away for me to see whether they were sitting talking or taking a silent break after the strain of the past few days.

I decided to take a break too and, just above a join in the rope where I knew my safety line would prevent me executing an unplanned glissade, I sank down onto the snow. As I looked over at Changtse on the far side of the North Col, I saw a single gorak soaring high above me, silhouetted against the bluest of skies. It flew in decreasing circles as if it was homing in on me, but then flew off downhill towards the North Col.

But as I watched the bird, it doubled back and flew in a straight line up from the Col towards me. When it was directly overhead, it stopped, hovering above me, its vast ragged black wings fully extended to catch the breeze. It seemed to hang there for an eternity, but then, uttering one harsh caw, it dipped its wings and flew off.

I knew beyond all doubt that it was Joe. But I couldn't decide whether the raucous croak was one of triumph at my success on the mountain or if it was a call of farewell from a spirit that had done its work. I never saw another solitary gorak for the rest of the expedition.

I sat in silence for a while, watching as the bird got smaller until it was only a black speck and then, suddenly, was gone. But there was no pang of loss. I felt a deep sense of calm. Almost in a trance, I got to my feet and carried on down the slope towards the two climbers moving slowly beneath me.

I turned to see where Karsang was and saw him coming down the snow towards me. He was carrying a crampon in his left hand.

"Broken", he said succinctly, as he came level with me and showed me where the strap had snapped. I was glad for his sake that it hadn't broken the previous day when we were on the way to the summit or, worse, on the way back down. He sat down on the snow and started tying the crampon back onto his boot with a long piece of orange cord. The tangled mass of knots reminded me of the jumble of ropes I'd got caught in coming off the Exit Cracks. But the repair job didn't last long.

When we got back to the North Col I was surprised to see a semi-naked Himex guide, Andy aka Frog, inside the store tent as I flopped down on the snow-ledge outside. Dragging on a tee-shirt as he came out towards me, Frog croaked his congratulations and kissed me on the cheek. He sounded terrible.

"I didn't expect you to be up here. I thought you were going to be ABC manager", I said to him, returning the kiss. I'd long since stopped expecting him to turn into a prince.

Through a prolonged and hacking bout of coughing, he attempted to tell me that Russ had asked him to come up to the North Col to help while we were all on the summit push. He finished his explanation by hawking up a lump of phlegm, which he then spat unceremoniously into the snow. Far from turning into someone of royal extraction, he seemed to have become a yak man.

After a feast of digestive biscuits and rubbery cheese triangles, I stripped off my down suit, replacing it with my waterproof over-trousers and jacket. Karsang was already packing up, so I buckled on my harness and then sat back down on the ledge to put on my crampons.

I led the way out of camp, crossing the double ladder for the last time and without any great feeling of regret. But as I headed on down the snow slopes I was conscious of the fact that I might never see any of this again. I stopped to gaze around at the incredible scenery, peering into the blue cavities of ice caves and watching the shadows of clouds as they scudded across the snow.

I suddenly didn't want to leave this magical winter wonderland and its majestic beauty. But then I thought about hot food, real food. And showers. And a proper bed. And I started walking again.

I was amazed how much of a thaw had taken place. The slopes had deteriorated dramatically and the snow now had the consistency of granulated sugar. It was heavy work ploughing down through it, but it was harder for Karsang. The running repairs on his crampon had given up permanently above the ice wall and he'd continued the descent on only one.

I unclipped from the fixed line at the bottom of the final slope, clipped my carabiner onto a gear loop on my harness and trudged over to where I had left one of my trekking poles six long days ago. Despite the thaw it was still standing upright in the snow.

By the time I had stumbled back down the moraine from Crampon Point, my legs had turned to jelly, the wobbly sort that hasn't quite set properly. Ducking under the prayer flags strung between the Sherpa tent and our mess tent, I walked into camp. Now I was the soldier returning from battle.

VII

Euphoria And Homecoming

And what a welcome I got. Even before I had got to the comms tent there was a queue of four men waiting to hug me. I fell, almost literally, into the open arms of first Bill, then Woody, Jez and finally Russ. Jez's words in particular will always stick in my mind. "You don't look like you've done anything", he said. My thespian genes, what my mother calls Dr Footlights, were obviously working overtime.

I went over to my tent to drop off my backpack before I went to see everyone else. I flung my trekking pole onto a rock, knelt down and opened the outside zip. When I unzipped the inside flap, with a feeling akin to opening the door to my own house after a long period of absence, the first thing I saw was a rock in the middle of my sleeping bag, holding down a piece of paper. It was a note, scrawled hurriedly on a scrap of paper torn from a notebook.

"Sorry I missed you. Didn't realise you were so close, I would have called over and abused your facilities. I will be thinking of you on the fifth and willing you on. The best of luck and also my regards to Peggy and hope all goes well for her too." There was a phone number, an email address and a squiggle of a signature that I recognised as Humphrey only because there was a very obvious H at the beginning and something resembling a Y bringing up the rear.

I was desperate to get out of my climbing gear and at least have a baby-wipe bath. The shower would have to wait. Stripping off all the layers of clothes resulted in the usual avalanche of flaky, dead skin. That no longer appalled me, but I was shocked at what nakedness revealed. It was as though body snatchers had been at work, stealing my familiar body while I was up the mountain and replacing it with an unfamiliar and unwelcome form.

I could have played tunes on my ribs. My arms and legs were just bones with a thin layer of skin covering them. All the muscle I had so carefully developed in the gym was gone. Jutting hip and pubic bones accentuated a now concave stomach.

I had expected to be thin. I knew that never before had I been forced to delve so deeply into my physical and mental reserves, but this state of apparent malnutrition horrified me. I realised that it was purely my willpower that had carried me to the top of the mountain. My muscles were too wasted to have contributed much. It was only muscle memory that had got me to the summit. That and the memory of Joe.

Everyone converged on the mess tents early that night. As I set up my iPAQ and bluetooth keyboard I was conscious of the excited chattering that was going on all around me as the others swapped their summit day stories. But I didn't really hear any of it, tuning in only when someone directed a question specifically at me.

It wasn't that I was lost for words. I had plenty to say, but I was saving the emotions I wanted to express for *The Irish Times*. I started to type and, despite the background noise, the words spilled out of me just as the tears had on the summit only the morning before. I had wanted to write a joyous, triumphant piece, but it wrote itself totally differently. It was a truly heartfelt outpouring and the response to it took me completely by surprise.

It was the piece that seemed to have the most impact on friends and on readers I had never met. Text messages, emails, phone-calls and cards that I got afterwards nearly always mentioned the summit day diary. It had apparently reduced many people to tears, just as the summit itself had made me cry.

I sent the piece through to the newsdesk and, while I had the satellite link, sent an email to my twin sister. I thought it was time my family knew the truth about what I'd been doing for the past 10 weeks. The message was brief and to the point. "I didn't lie to you when I told you on March 29 that I wasn't climbing Everest with Ranulph Fiennes. He was on another team. But he didn't make it and I did. Love, Grania."

The first thing Meg did was call my parents. There were tears on both ends of the phone, partly at the release of a worry they didn't even know they had and partly out of joy. It was the first really good news that the family had heard since Joe's death. My brother-in-law Fred, father of Joe, summed it up in an email, sent to me just after I got home. "Right now it's just great to have some real heart-warming, spirit-raising, life-affirming family news."

Joe would have been thrilled if he'd known about it, Fred commented in the email. "He would have been happiest of all to hear the news. Just ecstatic; really loud and ecstatic. Gordon Richards on one side of the family, and Everest-conqueror Grania Willis on the other."

Knowing his and my sister's views on an after-life and anything to do with religion, I felt I couldn't tell him that Joe did know. He'd been with me all the way, so of course he knew.

Over dinner that night, Jez, usually the funny man, made an emotional speech thanking Russ for his efforts and congratulating him on a hugely successful expedition. Thirty-seven on the summit and, with Paul on his way, everyone safely back down. It was a remarkable achievement, even by Russ's exacting standards. Suddenly Jez was choking back tears and, as I turned to congratulate Russ who was sitting next to me, I was amazed to see that he too was crying. The strain of the last few days was all too visible on his face.

We all raised glasses or bottles to toast Russ's success. The chinking of glasses and the shouts of cheers soon brought back the party atmosphere. Along with most of the team, I had decided to have a celebratory beer, but before I'd got halfway through it I felt light-headed. The combination of altitude and almost five months of alcohol-free living made my body react in most uncharacteristic fashion. Even more uncharacteristically, I left the rest of the bottle undrunk.

There was actually double cause for celebration. Late on – it felt like midnight, but was probably only about 8.30 or nine o'clock – Russ got a call on the radio from Dean to say that he and Paul were on their way down the moraine and would be back at camp soon.

We didn't see Russ again that night. He'd gone straight up the moraine to meet Paul and Dean. We knew that Paul was going to be sleeping in the comms tent with Russ and that he was still in a bad way. There was talk of going to visit him, but I thought he would probably prefer to be left alone. He had, quite literally, been fighting for his life over the past 48 hours, and I felt that the last thing he needed was a whole bunch of visitors. I decided to wait till the morning before going to see him.

To my surprise it was Paul who came to see us the next day. We'd just finished breakfast down in the red tent when this gaunt, bearded creature walked in. Were it not for the Aussie accent and the missing right arm I might not have recognised him. He appeared to have lost about three stone in two days.

I leapt out of my chair and rushed over to kiss him. He seemed almost too fragile to hug, but I hugged him anyway. It was such a relief to see him. Even if he did look horrendous, at least he was alive.

We cleared a space for him at the table and he sat down, almost gingerly, as though he was scared he might break. In truth, he looked as though he would break. He ate very little and, although the Hockey sparkle was missing, he was at least able to talk.

He said that he'd already had an Australian television station on the phone to him that morning, asking about his ordeal. The journalist had told him to stay on the line, they were going to go live on air in a couple of minutes. "I just said 'fuck off' and put the phone down", Paul said. "I don't know how they knew about what happened or how they knew where to get hold of me", he continued.

"Well I did mention you in my piece in this morning's *Irish Times* and that would have been on the web too", I said. "Someone must have picked it up, but I don't know how they got the number for here."

There was a lot of good-natured bantering about "bloody journalists", which I countered by reminding them all that I was just a housewife. But obviously the Australian media, hungry for news on their one-armed Everest climber, had picked up my story on the web. It started a media frenzy that went on all day.

It wasn't until later in the afternoon that Paul and I got a chance to talk. The two of us were chatting in his tent, right down at the bottom of the Himex camp. Russ was endlessly traipsing down from the comms tent to yell down to one or other of us that there was a phone-call, more "bloody journalists" wanting to do interviews. Paul's brother was amongst the callers, ringing to say that the press were hounding him for quotes because they couldn't get hold of Paul. In between phone-calls, Paul told me the full details of his nightmare descent.

"Basically I ran out of steam", he told me. "Then I realised I was getting pulmonary oedema and it was getting progressively worse. I always had oxygen, but it wasn't getting into my blood."

He barely remembered getting down the Second Step, he told me, except that it was horrific. But by the time he had negotiated the First Step, the four Sherpas with him were getting concerned about their own safety. "The Sherpas were saying they didn't want to die, so I told them that they should just leave me and get themselves down the mountain. I didn't want them dying because of me."

By then Paul had virtually given up on himself, but the Sherpas had no intention of deserting their charge. As he groped his way along the north-east ridge, he noticed a large crack. "I fantasised about lying down in it for a rest, but I knew that would have been the end of me. I kept thinking of my three kids and that made me keep going." Russ's words reminding Paul of his family had obviously worked. Seeing seven dead bodies on his way down probably kept him going too.

"My goggles were iced up because I didn't put them in my jacket on the summit so I was really worried about snow blindness", he went on. "I had a major migraine type headache because of the problem with my goggles and the oedema. I was just totally done in.

"Anyway, step by painful step, I got back to camp IV. Dean did his best for me, but he thought I was going to die during the night. So did Russ", he said, looking at me with dull eyes that echoed the trauma he'd been through. "I hyperventilated on oxygen for hours, pulling about one breath a second. The average person at rest at sea level pulls about 12 per minute."

He recalled very little of the climb down from camp IV the following day, except when he staggered "more dead than alive into Russell's arms just above ABC". I don't know which of the two was more glad to see the other, but Paul was in no doubt that he owed his life to Russ and to his loyal Sherpa. "Russ's decisions and tactics by telescope and radio and Nima's staying by my side saved my life", he said with emotion. He didn't look at me.

It was eerie listening to Paul talk. We both knew he'd been very lucky, but hearing him speak brought it home to me just how close to death he'd been.

Later in the afternoon I was in the red team mess tent playing cards when Woody came in to tell me there was yet another phone-call. Even though it was not much past four o'clock, the guides had started their traditional afternoon meeting early and I could see why when I ducked in through the flap into the comms tent.

Russ and the guides were all sitting cross-legged on the floor. Most of the chairs had already been packed away ready for the yak caravan that would be arriving in the morning to transport all our gear back to base camp. The lads were well stuck into a bottle of whisky. An empty champagne bottle lay discarded on the floor.

"I thought we weren't having champagne until tomorrow", I said in mock disapproval. "You're not", Russ rejoined, to widespread mirth. I remembered how protective Lachhu had been of the summit champagne, which he kept in a secret stash somewhere in base camp. He wouldn't tell anyone where it was, answering inquiries by saying simply, "For when you come down". I knew I wasn't going to get anywhere remonstrating with the floor-dwellers. I went and did my radio interview on the phone.

Dinner that evening was a very relaxed affair. We all ate in the red tent. The first team of summiteers had gone down to base camp earlier that day so there weren't enough of us to justify two mess tents and two kitchens.

The Italians called over with more supplies of dried meats and local cheeses. Paul, despite losing his lunch, had re-found his appetite and some of his old sparkle. And everyone, particularly the guides after their pre-dinner cocktails, was in great form. Pudding, to the delight of both Paul and Woody, was mango.

Being a member of the yellow team, I didn't get to hear the mango joke until the night we were at interim camp on the way up to ABC for the second and final time. Kevin had lifted the lid off one of the giant saucepans used to bring food from the cook tent. "It's mango", he said. There was quite a bit of laughter and it was only afterwards that I realised it was just the red team members laughing. Jez and I sat there looking bemused. The Japanese sat there looking inscrutable.

It was Woody who explained. Paul, a fluent Japanese speaker, had told the red team that mango sounded incredibly like the bawdy Japanese word for female genitalia. Despite the fact that mango was a regular feature on the pudding menu, the joke never wore thin. That last night in ABC showed that it still hadn't.

Paul and Woody started a surreal discussion about the relative benefits of old and young mango. Both agreed that older mangoes were preferable. "They're more experienced, they know what they want", Woody said with a glint in his eye.

But it was Fujibayashi who trumped the two Antipodeans. Lifting the lid of the saucepan and peering inside, Fujibayashi said – so quietly that I think I was the only one who heard him – "These look like very experienced mangoes". He calmly replaced the lid, his serene features never altering apart from an almost imperceptible crinkling around the eyes.

Chieko and I were last to leave camp the following morning. We soon caught up with Paul and Narly, who were moving pretty slowly. And it wasn't long before we overtook Fujibayashi, who was on his own, and a large group of yaks carrying down our gear. Despite a detour when Chieko decided we could take a short cut down the moraine above interim camp, we were first to reach the stepping stones across the river, which was now swollen with glacial melt-water.

We decided to take a break on the far side, where the flattened terrain and circular piles of yak dung suggested it was a regular stopping place. Sure enough, when the yak men arrived after herding their charges across the river, they sat down on neighbouring rocks and lit cigarettes while the yaks wandered around, their noses ploughing furrows in the dust as they foraged for anything vaguely resembling food.

The yak men were doing their share of foraging too. They approached us, hands outstretched, looking for biscuits. Chieko gave them some digestives. They didn't seem to like the look of my protein bar, so they bypassed me and went over to Fujibayashi, who'd just joined us. He had opened a can of Coke and taken a swig out of it. One of the women, her hair scraped off her face to display filthy cheeks weathered to a taut and ruddy finish, walked up to him and virtually took the can out of his hand. Fujibayashi surrendered his precious drink without a word. I think he was too tired to object.

He stood up shortly afterwards and said he was going to go on. Chieko waited while I finished my bar and then we set off after Fujibayashi, overtaking him on the next incline. But we had plenty more traffic to overtake on the next few kilometres of track, ending up weaving our way in and out of a large group of yaks.

Chieko didn't seem at all comfortable when the yaks came within close range, whimpering on my behalf when I got caught between two of the long-horned creatures in one unsuccessful overtaking manoeuvre. Once we had got passed them all, she confessed that she had had what she termed an "incident" with a yak earlier on in the expedition. She was to have another one later that day.

The ice on the lakes that we had crossed on the way up to ABC was now looking desperately patchy. Russ's advice to us was always to follow the yak dung so that we wouldn't get lost on the route between base camp and ABC. There was no yak dung on the ice. We decided not to risk an unscheduled and freezing dip.

Sticking to the undulating moraine on the left, we waited until we found a safe crossing place to take us back over to the final ascent before the track dropped down past Mallory's camp I site. It was all such familiar territory now, but there was an unfamiliar noise about it this time. Everything had been frozen solid on our last trip up. There was still plenty of ice, but parts of the river had broken free of its wintry chains and was now crashing and boiling down over the mingled debris of rocks and broken ice.

There was still one small band of yaks to overtake, but they were easily dispatched and Chieko and I continued the descent unhampered after that. Coming down the final incline, it was a shock to see that the small flat plain where the Chinese team of surveyors commissioned to measure the mountain had set up camp was now totally deserted. All that was left to mark the spot was a series of small cairns.

What they marked for us was the start of the home stretch, the last never-ending leg before base camp. It was only another 40 minutes or so to our goal, but it seemed like the longest 40 minutes of our lives. Chieko was trailing along silently behind me, although she did occasionally mutter "ascending" whenever she saw any sort of an incline. But at last there were no more ascents in sight and we could see where the shallow gully opened out into the plain that housed base camp.

A group of yaks and their accompanying yak men were coming towards us. They'd obviously dropped their load down at the Himex camp and were heading back up to ABC for a second run the following day. The piercing whistles and high-pitched clicks of the yakpas talking to their beasts carried to us on the still afternoon air.

As they drew level with us, one of the young Tibetans suddenly broke away. He was dressed in trousers of an indeterminate dark colour that were stiff and shiny with dirt and an equally grubby jacket slung over one shoulder. He marched determinedly up to me with his right arm extended, grabbed my hand and shook it vigorously, piercing me with amazing greeny brown eyes. "Hello, how are you?", he said and, without waiting for – or obviously even expecting – an answer, dropped my hand and hurried on to rejoin his companions.

But our next encounter was even more bizarre. Only minutes later we saw another group of yaks heading our way. We were on the lower of two narrow tracks and the yaks were split between the two trails. As I scrambled onto the upper path, I called over my shoulder to Chieko, "Come up here. They'll go onto the bottom path when they get near us."

She scurried up and stood beside me, right in the line of fire if the yaks didn't do as I had predicted. The frontrunner on the top track, obviously the joker in the pack, decided to play chicken. But it was him who chickened out, galumphing down the slope to join his companions at the last minute. But, as he tried to force his way in amongst the yaks on the lower path, his horns got entangled in the rope on the lead yak's load and he was swept along, unable to extricate himself and heading straight for Chieko.

She stood there, rooted to the spot and mewling with something approaching terror. I grabbed her and pushed her behind me just as the Siamese-twinned yaks lumbered past us. I was shaking with laughter. Chieko was just shaking with fear. She did eventually see the funny side of it, however, and even joined in the fun when I regaled the others with the tale – substantially embellished – at base camp.

Ten minutes later we could see an empty plain spreading out before us. Base camp, which had been thronged with tents when we left, was now completely deserted. Not a single tent marred its rocky surface. For a fleeting moment we wondered if the Himex team had gone without us, but after another few metres the familiar cluster of tents revealed itself to us from behind the moraine.

Apart from a single tent pitched in the shadow of the memorial mound just next to the Himex camp, we were the only team left on the mountain. It wasn't until weeks after I'd got home to Dublin that I discovered that the tiny lone tent housed Adventure Peaks leader Di Gilbert and her client Jake Meyer, who – at the age of 21 years and four months - had just become the youngest ever Briton to climb the mountain, deposing Bear Grylls, whose book had played such an important role on my path to Everest.

Flinging our backpacks down outside our own tents, Chieko and I headed straight for the mess tent to get food. I stopped off to book myself a shower as I went past the kitchen tent, before tucking in to a feast of cheese and biscuits, washed down with hot chocolate. It was a peculiar mix, but it tasted divine to me.

Even more divine was the shower when I finally got to it. The body being washed was a long way off divine, I knew, but nearly everyone had lost weight to a greater or lesser degree. Buttocks seemed to have been particularly singled out. It was as though someone had come along with a giant bacon slicer and simply cut away the cheeks.

We decided later, with imaginations fuelled by copious quantities of Lachhu's stashed champagne, that there was a blue barrel somewhere high up on the mountain that had everyone's bums in it. I think my breasts were probably in it too. A sort of bums and boobs barrel. I suggested that we should radio up to the Sherpas and ask them to bring the barrel back down for us. I could visualise them spilling the contents out onto the ground so that we could all rummage through and claim our belongings.

It was late when we got to bed that night. And not just late by mountain standards. I vaguely remember my watch saying 1.30 as I switched off my head torch. It didn't seem to be too much later, and in fact it wasn't, when I heard Peg's cheery voice outside asking me if I wanted to go on a rock collecting expedition. It was daylight, but I knew it was early. I looked blearily at my watch. Five-thirty! "No thanks, Peg, I've only been in bed four hours", I said, asleep again almost before I'd turned over.

After I returned home to Dublin, numerous people asked me if I had bought back a stone from the top of the mountain. I spouted the Tibetan and Nepali eco-creeds back at them. "Take only photographs, leave only footprints", I said sanctimoniously, but in reality I was annoyed with myself that I hadn't brought back something. It was purely because I had forgotten, not because I was being puritanically green.

But, when we arrived in Kathmandu, I discovered that I had – unwittingly – brought back a stone from the mountain. Our blue barrels had all been left in the hotel lobby and most of us spent the final afternoon transferring the highly pungent contents of the barrels into our suitcases in preparation for our departures to the four corners of the earth the following day.

It was only when I had reached the bottom of the barrel and taken out my climbing boots that I realised that the huge rock which I'd put in at ABC to act as ballast against the winds was still in there. Some poor yak had carried it the 22 kilometres from ABC to base camp. Peg suggested that I should take it home, chip it into pieces, varnish the bits and give them to my friends as a souvenir from Everest. "That's really scraping the bottom of the barrel", I told her.

There was no bed tea on our last morning, no sing-song "Good morning" outside our tents, everyone was too busy packing up camp. Russ had told us that we would be leaving at nine, but the first of the trucks arrived before seven, audible a long way off as it crunched and wheezed its way across the rocky, uneven plain. It was the perfect alarm clock.

I leapt out of my sleeping bag, feeling surprisingly good after drinking far more than my share of the champagne. Excitement at the prospect of going home had sluiced away the toxins from the previous night's excesses. Emaciated I may have been, but I felt vibrant and more alive than I had for the past 10 weeks.

I had my duffels packed in record time. As I was dragging the bags across the rocky, dusty ground, Keela, one of the cook boys came over to me. "I take, Willis", he said, grabbing the two duffels from me and throwing them onto his back. Having addressed me as Didi for the entire expedition, he had taken to calling me Willis the night before when I'd asked him to find my barrel for me.

"It has Willis written on it", I'd said. I was Didi no more.

I wanted to leave one of my North Face sleeping bags for Karsang. Both David and Paul had given literally all their climbing gear, right down to their boots, to their Sherpas. At that point neither of them had any intention of climbing another mountain, although they both changed their minds when they got home. But I had plenty more climbing planned and had also pledged to auction off my summit gear at a gala dinner for the two charities.

That meant that my sleeping bag was the only thing I had left to give to Karsang. I knew he probably wouldn't have any use for it, as Russ supplied all the gear for the Sherpas, but at least he'd get a decent sum of money if he decided to sell it.

I gave the bag to Keela and told him that it was for Karsang, but then realised that I hadn't properly thanked him for getting me to the summit and he was already back up the mountain with the other Sherpas collecting oxygen bottles and tents. I needed to write him a note. I borrowed pen and paper and sat down in the mess tent where the others were already breakfasting, but my mind was as blank as the piece of paper in front of me. What could I possibly say to Karsang? What we'd shared together on the mountain couldn't be expressed in words, especially when there was such a huge language barrier. But I wanted to get my gratitude across to him. His and Sissel's timely intervention had probably saved my life.

I asked advice from everyone in the tent, but it wasn't until I had a pile of scrumpled pieces of paper in front of me that someone pointed out that Karsang wouldn't be able to read it anyway.

So I kept it brief, writing simply: "Karsang, thank you for getting me to the summit. I couldn't have done it without you. You saved my life. Grania." I put an x at the bottom. It was unlikely he'd know it was a kiss, but I felt he deserved a paper kiss, even if he would have been mortified at the thought of the real life version.

With nothing left to do and almost an hour before we were due to leave, I took my camera and scrambled up the mound towards the monuments behind the Himex chorten. As I passed Marco Siffredi's memorial, I thought of Slovenian Marko and the other five climbers that had died on the mountain in the past few weeks. Why had these men, all infinitely more experienced than me, been singled out? And why had I been spared? The capricious moods of the mountain were hard to fathom.

I looked up at the vast triangular peak. It seemed inconceivable that only four days earlier I had stood on the summit. I felt humbled and knew I had been blessed to get to the top on my first attempt. Russ had told me it took him four goes before he made it, but it was his experience that had paved the way for my success. After 63 nights under canvas, 37 of the Himex team had reached the summit, almost two-thirds of the 60 that summitted from 400 who had attempted the north side that season. It was an impressive statistic.

I continued on up to the stone plaque that had been erected by the Chinese surveying team, hoping that it would finally and definitively clear up the debate about the height of the mountain. Someone had tied a white prayer scarf round the base of the roughly hewn plaque. A stonemason had engraved both sides with lettering, now highlighted with red paint, but neither the Chinese nor the English versions shed any light on the re-measurement. The figures 8,8 and then two spaces for the new height were exactly as they had been when we had left base camp three weeks earlier.

Disappointed, I took photos anyway and was so engrossed in my task that it was only the sound of engines being started that made me realise I was about to be left behind. Jamming my camera back in its case and stopping only for one last lingering look at the mountain, I raced back down the scree slope to Russ, who was co-ordinating operations in the midst of an apparently chaotic jumble of barrels and gear. Much to his consternation, I flung my arms round his neck and kissed him. Then, after thrusting a wad of notes into his hand for Karsang, I turned and leapt into the back of the jeep.

Our driver shoved the jeep into gear and we were off, bumping uncomfortably over the rocks. I turned to look back at the remnants of our base camp. Russ had already put us out of his mind and was back in command of the packing up operation. In a couple of days time there would be nothing left. It would be as though we'd never been there.

I looked up at the ravishingly beautiful mountain that had been the sole focus of my life for the past 10 weeks and for many months beforehand. Even as it dwindled in size as the twisting, lumpy road carried us away towards Tingri, it was still a massive presence on the horizon. And when it finally vanished from view, obscured by the dusty brown foothills, I knew it would always remain as a massive presence in my life.

The day I had arrived back at ABC, Monica and I had stood looking up at the summit and swore we'd never come back. Now I was leaving and I felt as though my heart was being wrenched from my chest. It was though I was being torn from the arms of my life's only true love, a fickle and dangerous love undoubtedly, but an all-consuming passion that now could never be re-kindled. Even if I came back it would never be the same again.

I was unusually quiet for most of the drive to Xangmu. Even the barrage of text messages that came through on my phone as we neared Tingri cheered me only fleetingly. Seeing Cho Oyu as we left the godforsaken village served only to increase my feeling of loss.

But gradually, as the dessicated brown landscape of the plain was replaced by the verdant lushness of the gorge, I felt my spirits rising. A mad night in the seedy border town of Xangmu started the re-acclimatisation process and two wonderfully relaxing nights in the hectic bustle of Kathmandu sent me home on a wave of exhaustion and euphoria.

Those were two feelings that were to feature for several weeks after my return to Dublin. There was an emotional and gentle reunion with my family at Heathrow airport. We'd all been through so much heartache with the loss of Joe and they were genuinely thrilled to have something to celebrate. But the greeting at Dublin was sheer unadulterated joy as my friends cheered and welcomed me home at close to midnight with banners, flowers and champagne.

There were no press photographers or television cameras, those were to come over the next few days, so I could enjoy the moment with my friends who had given me so much support in the build-up to the expedition. We drank champagne in the airport car-park and then went back to my Dublin north-side home for more bubbly. And chips.

The next few days seemed to be an endless succession of photo-calls, press conferences, radio and television interviews. I'd finally decided that I liked being on the opposite end of the spectrum. I relished being the interviewee instead of the interviewer. And when the media moved on, when I became yesterday's news, I was distraught. I felt like a junkie in need of a fix. Overnight I had become a media whore.

But I found succour in the warmth of friends' congratulations and the outpouring of support from people I'd never even met. Simple words were enough to delight me.

The night I arrived back at Dublin airport, in the thick of the welcomes, Carmel made it very clear that she thought I should I call a halt to my adventure career. I was carrying a copy of American long distance swimmer Lynne Cox's book *Swimming To Antarctica* that I'd been reading on the plane. As soon as she saw the title, Carmel grabbed the book and flung it across the arrivals hall. "Well you're not doing that!", she said in mock rage. She was only half joking.

So many people asked me what was I going to do next. Friends were incensed on my behalf. "Hasn't she done enough?", they'd say beadily, jumping to my defence. But it was Mairin McGrath, who works on *The Irish Times* switchboard, who put it perfectly when she said, very simply, "Enjoy it forever, Grania". And I will.

Glossary

ABC – advanced base camp, sited at 6,400 metres on the north side of Everest.

Abseil – (or rappel) method of descending steep ground or sheer rock or ice by sliding down a rope using a friction device to control speed.

Acclimatisation – the process of physiological adaptation to living and climbing at high altitude in thin air and with less oxygen.

Altitude sickness – also referred to as acute mountain sickness (AMS), altitude sickness is a pathological condition caused by an inability to adapt to high altitude. AMS can occur at altitudes as low as 2,500 metres. Symptoms are headaches, fatigue, shortness of breath, nausea, unsteadiness and dizziness, loss of appetite, insomnia, weakness and possibly seizures and coma. The most serious symptoms of altitude sickness are due to oedema, fluid accumulation in the tissues of the body, either in the lungs (pulmonary oedema) or the brain (cerebral oedema). Both are potentially fatal.

Belay – the act of one climber safeguarding another climber or climbers on a rope. In the event of a fall, the belayer controls the rope using a belay or friction device.

Bivouac – often referred to as a 'bivvy', a bivouac is a temporary overnight stop on a mountain without a proper tent.

Cairn – a small pile of stones usually placed by other climbers or walkers to mark a route.

Col – a dip in a ridge, usually between two peaks. Col is a Welsh word meaning saddle.

Carabiner – oval metal snap links used for, among other things, attaching rope to an anchor and clipping into fixed lines. A carabiner is basically a metal hook with a sprung gate. Those without a locking gate are called snap-links.

Chang – a Tibetan alcoholic drink made of fermented barley.

Chorten – a stone altar or shrine, built by the Sherpas at base camp and ABC and consecrated by holding the puja.

Cornice – an overhanging mass of snow formed by prevailing winds and projecting over the edge of a ridge.

Couloir – an open gully.

Crampons – steel spiked frames that can be fitted to boots to give grip on ice and firm snow slopes. There are usually 10 spikes under the foot, with two at the front

– the front points – which are used for climbing.

Crevasse – a crack in a glacier surface, which can be both wide and very deep. Made by the movement of the glacier over the irregular shapes in the glacial bed or by bends in its course.

Cwm – deep, rounded hollow at the head or side of a valley. The Western Cwm on the south side of Everest is also known as the oven, because of soaring daytime temperatures.

Death Zone – above 8,000 metres, the air is too thin to support human life for extended periods and the body is quite literally dying. The air on the top of Everest contains only a third of the oxygen at sea level.

Diamox – a drug, Acetazolamide (trade name Diamox), which was originally used to treat glaucoma and epilepsy, but was found to speed up acclimatisation and relieve mild cases of altitude sickness. The drug forces the kidneys to excrete bicarbonate, the base form of carbon dioxide, so counteracting the effects of hyperventilation that occurs at altitude. Acetazolamide stimulates the respiratory system to breathe more regularly and can also be taken to treat sleep apnea, which can develop at higher elevations.

Dohedral – the summit tower, the final rocky outcrop at the top of the North Pillar just below the summit ridge. The entire North Face drops away below the narrow traverse here.

Dry tooling – the use of ice climbing equipment, i.e. ice axes and crampons, to climb rock.

Jumar – a climbing tool, similar to a clamp, that can be slid up a rope but locks on the rope to support weight when pulled downwards, allowing a climber to haul himself upwards on the steepest terrain once a fixed rope is in place.

Face – a steep aspect of a mountain or crag.

Fixed rope – also known as fixed lines. The Sherpas fix rope onto anchors on prolonged climbs up steep ground or on exposed areas. The anchors can be manmade, such as pitons or ice screws, or natural, such as rock formations.

Glissade – the usually voluntary act of descending a steep snow slope in a controlled manner, which can be carried out sitting, standing or crouching. Glissading is an alternative to plunge stepping and cuts down on descent time.

Gorak – large Himalayan raven.

Hypoxia – a pathological condition in which the body is deprived of an adequate

214

oxygen supply. Hypoxia is often associated with high altitude. Symptoms of generalised hypoxia include headaches, fatigue, shortness of breath, nausea and unsteadiness. In its most extreme form, hypoxia can cause seizures, coma and death.

Khumbu icefall – the glacier on the Nepalese side of Everest between the western shoulder of Everest itself and Nuptse. The icefall, which drops steeply in a series of seracs and crevasses, is constantly moving and is one of the most dangerous areas of the mountain.

Kora – pilgrimage circuit round the Tibetan monasteries on which the more devout pilgrims prostrate themselves as they walk.

La – Tibetan for mountain pass.

Moraine – accumulation of stones and debris carried down by a glacier.

Naismith's Rule – devised in 1892 by Scottish mountaineer W.W. Naismith as an aid to estimating the length of time it would take to walk a predefined route in the hills, including ascents and descents. Naismith's Rule states that the average speed is five kilometres per hour, with an additional 10 minutes for every 100 metres of ascent.

Puja – a religious blessing ceremony, used in both the Hindu and Buddhist religions. A mountain puja involves the chanting of prayers, offerings to the gods, including food and drink, and the burning of juniper. Gear that will be used on the climb is blessed. The Sherpas are unwilling to set foot on the mountain until a puja has been held. A puja string, usually red, is knotted and blessed by a lama before being given to Sherpas and other climbers as part of the puja ceremony. Tradition dictates that climbers do not take off the puja string once it has been knotted round their neck.

Qomolangma – the Tibetan name for Everest, meaning Goddess Mother of the Universe.

Raksi – pronounced rakshee, this is a distilled version of chang or barley beer. A popular drink in Nepal.

Ri – Tibetan for mountain.

Ridge – the line along which two faces of a mountain meet.

Rock band – a wall of sheer rock.

Sagarmatha – the Nepalese name for Everest, meaning Forehead of the Sky in Sanskrit.

Serac – a pinnacle of ice, usually unstable and dangerous.

Sherpa – a race of hill people originally indigenous to the far eastern region of Tibet, near Everest. Sher means east and pa means people in the Tibetan language. Prior to the early 1900s, these Buddhist people lived a nomadic or semi-nomadic lifestyle. They migrated across the Himalaya more than five centuries ago and now live mainly in the high valleys of the Everest region. In general Sherpas adapt well to extreme altitude and are invaluable for Himalayan expeditions, doing much of the hard work such as fixing lines and setting up camp. Traditionally, the names of Sherpa men reflect the day on which they were born – Sunday – Nima; Monday – Dawa; Tuesday – Mingma; Wednesday – Lhakpa; Thursday – Phurba; Friday – Pasang; Saturday – Pemba.

Sirdar – the head Sherpa, who manages all the other Sherpas in a climbing expedition. The Sirdar is typically the most experienced guide.

Sling – a closed loop of nylon, which can be attached onto the climber's harness so that a carabiner on the opposite end can be clipped onto the fixed line or rope up the mountain as a safety precaution.

Spindrift – loose powder snow carried by the wind.

Traverse – to move horizontally or diagonally across a rock or snow slope. Also the ascent and descent of a mountain by different routes.

Tsampa – roasted barley flour, used to make porridge and cakes. It is also made into tsampa patties, which are fed to the yaks.

White-out – condition of driving snow and mist with a snow background, which makes it virtually impossible to judge distance or distinguish between solid ground and space.

Yak – a long-haired bovine found in Tibet and throughout the Himalayan region of south central Asia. The word yak refers to the male of the species; a female is a dri or nak. Wild yak stand about two meters tall at the shoulder, domestic yak are considerably smaller. Yaks are used as beasts of burden by farmers and for transporting gear for climbing expeditions. They also provide milk and meat. The pack animals are often crossbreeds of the yak and common domestic cattle. These crossbreeds are known in Tibetan as dzo or dzopkyo. Yak handlers are known as yakpas.

Yellow Band – the highly visible thick layer of yellowish sedimentary sandstone close to the top of the mountain. The Yellow Band is above high camp on the north side and below the Geneva Spur on the south.